E-Government and Websites

This volume in the Public Solutions Handbook series focuses on various e-government initiatives from the United States and other nations, and will help guide public service practitioners in their transition to e-government. The book provides important recommendations and suggestions oriented toward practitioners. It also makes a significant contribution to the field of e-government by showcasing successful models and highlighting the lessons learned in the implementation processes.

Chapter coverage includes:

- Online fiscal transparency
- Performance reporting
- Improving citizen participation
- Privacy issues in e-governance
- Internet voting
- E-government at the local level

E-Government and Websites is an invaluable resource and reference for public managers, enhancing their ability to deliver public services as promised—efficiently, effectively, and within the budgets that citizens have entrusted to their municipalities.

About the Editor

Aroon Manoharan is an Assistant Professor of Public Administration at Kent State University. His research focuses on e-governance, performance measurement and reporting, strategic planning, organization theory, and intergovernmental relations. His work has been published in the *American Review of Public Administration*, *State and Local Government Review*, *Public Administration Quarterly*, *International Journal of Public Administration*, *International Journal of Organization Theory and Behavior*, and *International Public Management Review*. He holds an MPA from Kansas State University and a PhD from the School of Public Affairs and Administration, Rutgers University–Newark.

THE PUBLIC SOLUTIONS HANDBOOK SERIES

MARC HOLZER, SERIES EDITOR

MUNICIPAL SHARED SERVICES
A Public Solutions Handbook
Alexander C. Henderson, Editor

E-GOVERNMENT AND WEBSITES
A Public Solutions Handbook
Aroon Manoharan, Editor

THE PUBLIC SOLUTIONS HANDBOOK SERIES

MARC HOLZER, SERIES EDITOR

E-Government and Websites

A PUBLIC SOLUTIONS HANDBOOK

Edited by
Aroon Manoharan

Routledge
Taylor & Francis Group
NEW YORK AND LONDON

First published 2015

by Routledge
711 Third Avenue, New York, NY 10017

and by Routledge
2 Park Square, Milton Park, Abingdon, Oxon, OX14 4RN

Routledge is an imprint of the Taylor & Francis Group, an informa business

Library of Congress Cataloging in Publication Data
E-government and websites : a public solutions handbook / edited by Aroon Manoharan.
pages cm.—(The public solutions handbook series)
Includes bibliographical references and index.
1. Internet in public administration. 2. Electronic government information. 3. Public administration—
Technological innovations. I. Manoharan, Aroon, 1979– editor of compilation.
JF1525.A8E1975 2015
352.3'802854678—dc23
2014026940

ISBN: 978-0-7656-4656-9 (hbk)
ISBN: 978-0-7656-3727-7 (pbk)
ISBN: 978-1-315-71954-2 (ebk)

Contents

Part III Applications

Series Editor's Introduction

The impetus for this series of public management handbooks is simply that public managers must have ready access to the best practices and lessons learned. That knowledge base is surprisingly extensive and rich, including insights from rigorous academic studies, internal government reports and publications, and foundation-supported research. Access to that knowledge, however, is limited by substantial barriers: expensive books and academic journals, "thick" academic language and hard-to-decipher jargon, and just the sheer volume of information available. Our objectives in initiating this series are to identify insights based in practice, to build competencies from that knowledge base, to deliver them at an affordable price point, and to communicate that guidance in clear terms.

GROUNDED INSIGHTS

Each volume in the series will incorporate case-based research. Each will draw helpful insights and guidelines from academe, government, and foundation sources, focusing on an emerging opportunity or issue in the field. The initial volumes will, for example, address shared services for municipalities and counties, e-government and websites, managing generational differences, government counter-corruption strategies, public-sector innovation, and performance measurement and improvement.

COMPETENCIES

We are initiating this Public Solutions Handbook series to help build necessary competencies, empowering dedicated, busy public servants—many of whom have no formal training in the management processes of the public offices and agencies they have been selected to lead—to respond to emerging issues, to deliver services that policymakers have promised to the public, to carry out their missions efficiently and effectively, and to work in partnership with their stakeholders. Enabling practitioners to access and apply evidence-based insights will begin to restore trust in their governments through high-performing public, nonprofit, and contracting organizations.

Just as important, students in graduate-degree programs, many of whom are already working in public and nonprofit organizations, are seeking succinct, pragmatic, grounded guidance that will help them succeed far into the future as they rise to positions of greater responsibility and leadership. This includes students in master of public administration (MPA), master of public policy (MPP), master of nonprofit management (MNPM), and even some master of business administration (MBA) and doctor of law (LLD) programs.

AFFORDABILITY

Handbook prices are often unrealistically high. The marketplace is not serving the full range of public managers who need guidance as to best practices. When faced with the need for creative solutions to cut budgets, educating for ethics, tapping the problem-solving expertise of managers and employees, or reporting progress clearly and transparently, a grasp of such practices is essential. Many handbooks are priced in the hundreds of dollars, beyond the purchasing power of an individual or an agency. Journals are similarly priced out of the reach of practitioners. In contrast, each volume in the Public Solutions Handbook series will be modestly priced.

CLEAR WRITING

Although the practice of public administration and public management should be informed by published research, the books that are now marketed to practitioners and students in the field are often overly abstract and theoretical, failing to distill published research into clear and necessary applications. There is substantial valuable literature in the academic journals, but necessarily to standards that do not easily "connect" with practitioner audiences. Even in instances when practitioners receive peer-reviewed journals as a benefit of association membership, they clearly prefer magazines or newsletters in a straightforward journalistic style. Too often they set the journals aside.

I am proud to announce the second volume in the Public Solutions Handbook series: *E-Government and Websites*, edited by Aroon Manoharan. As governments are transforming to e-government to enhance their delivery of virtually all services, practitioners and administrators are seeking to meet citizens' expectations by identifying and adapting best practices across the world. E-government not only promises to transform the nature of government interactions with both citizens and businesses but also affects the efficiency of internal processes.

In particular, this volume offers a citizen-centric perspective beyond e-government to e-governance. "E-government" refers to the practice of online delivery or facilitation of services by government to citizens, whereas "e-governance" refers to participatory opportunities for citizens to provide opinions and advice as to the efficacy of government websites. Beyond direct services, e-governance enables citizen-users and advocacy groups to interact with and advise their governments, and contributors to this volume underscore this potential. This book is especially useful in that it provides case studies detailing recent applications of e-government and e-governance. Consisting of chapters from authors in the United States and other nations, it will help guide public managers in transforming their governments across the spectrum of e-government to e-governance.

Each chapter contains key suggestions for practitioners and illustrates successful stories and lessons learned in the implementation processes.

This is an important new handbook for public managers who are pursuing the promises of e-government and e-governance. It will necessarily find a permanent niche on the desks of many public managers, empowering them to deliver public services as promised—efficiently, effectively, and within the budgets that citizens have entrusted to their municipalities.

Marc Holzer
Editor-in-Chief, Public Solutions Handbook Series
Dean and Board of Governors Distinguished Professor
of Public Affairs and Administration
Rutgers, The State University of New Jersey–Campus at Newark

Introduction

Aroon Manoharan

Governments have been increasingly transforming to e-government to improve their service delivery, and public administrators are seeking to learn from best practices across the world. E-government holds promise beyond the cost-saving potential of previous reform initiatives; it also provides citizens unique opportunities to participate in the democratic process. Such online interactions were initially very passive and primarily focused on one-way communication and information dissemination. Gradually, online participation included two-way communication that enabled the active participation of citizens, accompanied by greater access to technology and an increase in the use of social media. Such transformation has resulted in a conceptualization of the dual concepts of e-government and e-governance, where "e-government" refers to a one-way dissemination of information from government to citizens, and "e-governance" pertains to a two-way dialogue and interaction between government and its citizens.

This book offers a citizen-centric perspective of these two concepts, with "e-government" referring to the practice of online public reporting by government to citizens and "e-governance" representing the initiatives in which citizens can participate and provide their opinion on government websites. The volume consists of chapters from the United States and around the world, and it aims to help guide governments in their transformation to e-governance. Furthermore, this book contains key suggestions and recommendations for practitioners, illustrating successful stories and lessons learned in the implementation processes.

Part I primarily focuses on the e-government concept, which involves online public reporting by government to citizens and the public relations perspective of e-government. The potential of e-government to improve government public relations is largely unexplored, even though it enables public administrators to fulfill their democratic responsibilities and implement their mission. In Chapter 1, "E-Government and Public Relations: It's the Message, Not the Medium," Mordecai Lee explores the public relations perspective of e-government and websites, and emphasizes the focus on purpose more than the technology itself. According to the author, e-government, websites, platforms, and social media decisions should come only *after* purposes and goals are clearly determined and an informed judgment is made that a new effort is worthwhile because it clearly contributes to a basic and specific agency mission. The chapter provides eight potential purposes of public relations and e-government that help clarify the intention underlying *what* the communication effort is aimed at accomplishing. This chapter also focuses on the transparency aspects of e-government, particularly as the public pushes for more awareness of how its tax dollars are spent. As many researchers have pointed out, e-government will allow for greater government transparency and openness, thus leading to a better-informed citizenry. In Chapter 2, "Understanding and Measuring Online Fiscal Transparency," Jonathan B. Justice, John G. McNutt, and Edward S. Smith Jr. present a conceptual overview of fiscal transparency and the role of information and communication technology (ICT) in transparency. Efforts both to understand the extent and quality of online fiscal transparency and to implement or improve transparency are facilitated by good measures of quantity and quality. The authors synthesize the key elements from literature into a framework for conceptualizing and measuring online fiscal transparency, drawing lessons for continuing efforts to advance the understanding and practice of transparency.

Chapters 3 and 4 continue this discussion on attaining an informed citizenry through e-government by examining the practice of "e-reporting," or electronic reporting, through government websites. Much has been said about the transformation potential of e-government with regard to efficiency and effectiveness, as well as the introduction of a new paradigm in public administration. However, there is less emphasis on the more traditional reporting practices of e-government websites. The practice of reporting and external communication by governments does help develop a well-informed citizenry, which is crucial for a successful democracy. In Chapter 3, "Improving the Effectiveness of E-Reporting in Government with the Concept of Multiple Accountability," Thomas J. Greitens and M. Ernita Joaquin examine the online reporting of administrative and programmatic performance information, which is a constant theme for public managers across the globe. Better performance, more transparency, and heightened accountability to citizens are often touted as the benefits of this type of performance reporting. By examining performance-reporting tools such as organizational report cards, online scorecards, and dashboards, the authors suggest that a careful examination of the multiple accountability pressures surrounding their implementation is needed to determine their effectiveness in e-reporting. In Chapter 4, "Global Trends in E-Performance Reporting," Marc K. Fudge explores the use of performance measurement information reported on government websites in cities around the world. E-performance reporting is a way to provide vital information to a large number of people in a timely and cost-effective manner, as well as a useful tool for public managers to compare and benchmark their municipality's success and failures across jurisdictions.

Part II discusses the e-governance concept, which involves citizen participation through government websites and raises the possibility of full-scale e-democracy. The process of online participation and two-way communication between government and citizens entails the active participation of citizens through the increasing use of computers and social media. These possibilities open up opportunities for governmental agencies to interact with their public on a new level, and the chapters in Part II discuss such trends. In Chapter 5, "A Critical Analysis of the Potential of Information and Communication Technologies for Democracy and Governance," Matthias Finger proposes a new start for e-governance, emphasizing that the potential of ICTs for government is much larger than what we have seen so far. The chapter shows that this potential covers all the main areas in which government is active, namely policymaking, regulation, and service delivery. It focuses particularly on the participatory aspect of e-government, or e-democracy, whereby citizens will be involved not only at times of elections and sometimes referenda but along the entire policy process, ranging from policy formulation to implementation, and at all levels of government. In Chapter 6, "Keys to E-Governance: Technology or Civil Society?" Robert J. Dickey and SeJeong Park demonstrate that the issue of e-governance must be addressed from both technological and social perspectives. This chapter examines e-government projects by four governmental entities in the Republic of Korea: the central (national) government, Seoul Metropolitan City (metropolitan government for the nation's capital), Daegu Metropolitan City, and Gangnam District (a local government within Seoul). Based on their study, several technological innovations have created enhanced opportunities for citizen access; however, the governance process itself has made fewer strides.

Citizens and policymakers have demanded that government be more efficient with its resources, and government use of ICT was a direct response to these demands, also allowing for more channels of communication and public participation. This is encouraging; however, researchers have not thoroughly examined what drives governments to provide their citizens with online channels to participate in the governmental process. Understanding these factors would better allow for the most efficient use of technology in the most appropriate manner. In Chapter 7, "Improving Citizen Participation via E-Government: The Why and How," Yueping Zheng and Yuguo Liao discuss the importance of citizen participation, the impact of e-government on citizen participation, and the factors affecting the development of e-participation. Recent e-government studies have shown that governments tend to place less emphasis on citizen participation, but e-government has tremendous potential in improving this phenomenon. By focusing on the factors that enable online citizen participation, the chapter provides valuable suggestions to governments in their efforts to promote a participatory democracy through websites. The significance of online citizen participation has also been emphasized by the various stage models of e-governance, many of those proposing e-participation as the end-stage goal. As governments gradually adopt the e-government initiatives, the stages will have been implemented to various levels and magnitudes. Accordingly, there must be a way to hold citizens accountable for their participation within a newly developing e-government system. In Chapter 8, "Puzzling Out the Wisdom of E-Crowds in Trustworthy E-Government Practices: From Technological Applications to Networks," Younhee Kim and Seunghwan Myeong discuss practical agendas to implement a trustworthy e-government system that could be a baseline reference to initiate e-government plans on the basis of technological, managerial, and relational dimensions.

Part III examines the applications perspective of e-government and e-governance, with a focus on e-voting, shared services, and e-government development among local governments. With the prevalence of new technologies, the potential of public participation through voting is being revisited, as is its impact on the electoral process. In Chapter 9, "E-Voting: Domestic and International Successes and Failures," Cecilia G. Manrique and Gabriel G. Manrique focus on the impact of electronic voting at the local, state, and national levels in the United States and identify where it is being implemented in other parts of the world. The study also examines successes and failures in the implementation of e-voting; explores why it has succeeded in some places and failed in others; and determines the factors responsible in governments' adoption of e-voting, as well as problems and issues arising as a result of its implementation.

The chapter that follows continues the discussion on factors and determinants of e-government success, with a specific focus on local governments in the United States. Recent studies have shown an increased interest in county governments given their significance in regional development, as well as their provision of state- and municipal-level services. In Chapter 10, "E-Government in U.S. Local Governments: Disparities, Obstacles, and Development Strategies," Hua Xu and Hugo Asencio focus on the development of e-government among small and medium-size local governments in Alabama. While there is a large amount of empirical literature on e-government based on surveys of state governments, large municipalities, and countries, there is a relative dearth of research focusing on small local governments in more rural areas. Through its examination of Alabama county governments, the study identifies the environmental and institutional factors that affect the progress of e-government, and provides recommendations on policy and program strategies that can facilitate the development of e-government for local governments. In Chapter 11, "Relevant Issues of Accountability and Transparency in IT Shared Services," Gautam Nayer explores the phenomenon of shared information technology services, with particular emphasis on transparency and accountability. Shared services represent an important application of e-government, encompassing all variations of community services shared between either several departments of a municipality or between municipalities. The chapter examines the implementation of shared IT services in Australia, the United Kingdom, and the United States, and discusses the critical issues and solutions, as well as its relevance for transparency and accountability.

Overall, this book presents a wide range of chapters on e-government and websites, and it will be of interest to practitioners, researchers, and students. The volume provides key suggestions and important recommendations oriented toward practitioners, and it should serve as a valuable guide to governments in their transformation to e-governance, and in their efforts to enable active citizen participation online.

Part I

E-Government and Public Reporting and Public Relations

1

E-Government and Public Relations

It's the Message, Not the Medium

Mordecai Lee

Right now, somewhere, there's a meeting going on at a government agency. Senior managers are pondering how to be au courant, to demonstrate that the agency is at the cutting edge of e-gov technology. After all, gotta keep up with the Joneses! And some of the newest and youngest employees are using a couple of platforms that none of the grown-ups have ever heard of, let alone understand what they do and what their attraction is to users. Adding insult to injury, a few agencies with similar missions in other regions of the country or other countries are already doing whatever the latest IT or techie fad is. Someone chirps up at the meeting and says, "Hey, let's do all those new things!" Everybody else nods sagaciously, indicating yes, we should show that we are as up-to-date and with-it technologically as the next agency. Committees are formed, platforms are established, and—presto—the agency can now say it, too, is at the cutting edge of e-government.

The purpose of the chapter is to serve as the "Hey, wait a minute" interruption, with the designated role as the agency's annoying spoilsport and party pooper. This focuses on the need to put the horse before the cart. Specifically, there are two killer questions to raise at the meeting to deflate the balloon of doing the Next Big Thing simply because it's there:

- What, specifically, do you want to *accomplish*?
- *Why* does the agency need to do this?

Only after clarifying the answers to these questions should the management meeting proceed to the methods of doing it. E-gov, websites, platforms, and social media decisions should come only *after* purposes and goals are clearly determined and an informed judgment is made that the new effort is worthwhile because it clearly contributes to a basic and specific agency mission. After all, e-gov technology is merely a *means* to a goal, not a goal in and of itself.

Just as important, the specifics of e-gov are changing at a rapid, though incremental, pace (Norris and Reddick 2013). A decade ago, 4G, tablets, pads, smartphones, Twitter, and Foursquare did not exist. A decade from now, they will likely be so passé that they will be considered primitive, anachronistic, and quaint; superseded by better, faster, and smarter online technology and devices. With just about everything networked online, government managers are in a continually changing "new social operating system" (Shoop 2012). In 2014, a Midwestern public university was on Facebook, Twitter, Foursquare, Flickr, YouTube, Pinterest, and Pandora (University of Wisconsin–Milwaukee 2014). In just a few years, this list will be old-fashioned. Given this reality, the intent here is to focus on what you're trying to accomplish, not on using any particular platform, mobile device, or media to get there. In this case, the destination is the only thing that counts, not the journey.

The above two questions about doing e-gov also relate to the difference between business administration and public administration. Some people assert that these two management activities are essentially the same, merely occurring in different sectorial settings. Countering them, Wallace Sayre quipped that public and business administration are "fundamentally alike in all unimportant respects" (Allison 1980, 27). The constraints, context, and democratic environment truly impinge on government management so significantly that the skills of a successful businessperson would not automatically transfer to the public sector. So, just because something is new in IT or digital communication that has been successful in business does not guarantee that it's the same for government. For example, the Obama White House sought advice from top business executives on the use of new technologies, "but the private sector's entrepreneurial zeal may not translate so easily to federal agencies" (Kang 2010). Government *is* different.

It is also important to note one of the impacts of the e-gov transformation now under way. Preceding it, there had been a relatively stable typology of the silos of marketing, customer service, transparency, accountability, citizen participation, performance reporting, public relations, co-production, and branding. However, new technologies, means of communication, and platforms have largely blurred those separate categories. They are no longer mutually exclusive, one-goal-one-activity kinds of undertakings. Rather, in a public administration equivalent of multitasking, different goals and roles are converging and often accomplished through the same effort. The traditional silos of line and staff functions in government are gradually coalescing, overlapping, and becoming interwoven. For example, marketing and e-customer service are increasingly the same. Ditto for citizen participation and co-production. These discrete subject areas increasingly share and use the same e-gov platforms and technologies to accomplish their (somewhat) distinct goals. But, the *goals* of those different activities continue to be relevant and important. In that sense, all the following chapters, while differentiated by varying starting points and topics, need to be seen as pieces of a whole. Different areas of expertise and literatures are largely ending up in the same zone, namely that e-gov and websites are transforming public management. Everything relates to everything else.

The increasingly unified field of e-gov applies to this chapter as well. While using the prism of public relations (PR), note the wide scope that e-gov PR encompasses in the totality of the organization's external communications. In general, the emergence of Web-based and cloud-based government has been to change *qualitatively* the orientation of public-sector bureaucracies. According to Margetts (2012, 456), the revolutionary effect of e-gov is to make government agencies "become externally facing." Hence, by its inherent nature, e-gov orients government agencies outward toward external communication and interaction with the public.

In that context, PR is closely related to such activities as marketing, accountability, and customer service. The key is that the *purposes* of government PR are inherent to public administration and reflect many silos and functions. No matter how much e-gov transforms the public sector, these PR purposes are valuable and important to good government.

OVERVIEW: WHAT ARE YOU TRYING TO ACCOMPLISH?

Back to the two questions of the preceding section: What, specifically, do you want to *accomplish*, and *why* does the agency even need to do this? This reflects a basic approach to governmental external communication in general. In the context of this book, you will see that public relations as an aspect of e-gov is not a collection of media tricks, hot technologies and platforms, and the latest personal devices. Rather, it is a *purpose-oriented* management activity.

First, public relations is a venue for government agencies to engage in the public accountability that they are obligated to in a democracy. Given that an informed public is the sine qua non of democracy, public administration imposes on civil servants the duty to keep the citizenry informed of the general record and stewardship of the agency. In the amorphous way that democracy works, this public reporting activity contributes to the processes of modern democracy. These are required for all government agencies. Second, public relations helps a government agency accomplish its tangible mission by using external communications to implement the agency's raison d'être. In that respect, public relations is a pragmatic tool for doing public administration. There is a third purpose that public relations serves, but one that is politically very sensitive. An effective public relations program can help an agency obtain the support of various public constituencies. In turn, that support can influence the decision making by elected officials about the future of the agency.

The combination of government PR with the new tools of e-gov implements the definition of communication as a two-way and circular activity. The most influential PR theoretician of modern times, James Grunig (1997), has posited that sophisticated and effective government PR (as well as for the business and nongovernmental organization sectors) is two-way symmetrical communication. The tools of e-gov PR are not merely a way for governments to communicate outwardly with its citizens, but, just as importantly, they are a way for people to connect with their governors. For example, citizens are now much less likely to *write* a member of Congress or *call* city hall. Now, citizens have quicker and more convenient ways to initiate communication with government. These trends affect government management as much as the elected side of the public sector. An agency's commitment to e-gov must include facilitating two-way communication, such as the receipt of communication from the public and the proper handling and responsiveness to those incoming messages.

Here is a model of best practices for twenty-first-century government public relations (Lee 2012b). It is based on *purposes*; that is, *what specifically* is the public administrator trying to accomplish? Building on the previous three underlying reasons for external communication (democratic, pragmatic, and political), the model identifies eight potential purposes for government PR:

I. Mandatory activities: Democratic purposes of e-gov PR
- 1. Media relations
- 2. Public reporting
- 3a. Responsiveness to the public: As citizens

II. Optional activities: Pragmatic purposes of e-gov PR relating to program implementation
- 3b. Responsiveness to the public: As customers and clients
  (4–7. Public outreach)
- 4. Increasing the utilization of services and products
- 5. Public service and public education campaigns
- 6. Seeking voluntary compliance with laws and regulations
- 7. The public as the eyes and ears of an agency

III. Dangerous, but powerful activities: Political purposes of e-gov PR
- 8. Increasing public support

In this model, there are eight discernible purposes for PR, e-gov or otherwise. For each of these purposes, there is a clear intention underlying *what* the communication effort is aimed at accomplishing. The first grouping (I) details what a government manager must do, regardless of the mission of the agency. In a democratic form of government, every agency must engage in external communication to be responsive to the news media; to report to the public and other oversight institutions on its record of accomplishment and performance; and to be responsive to the public-at-large as citizens, who are ultimately the sovereign in a democracy.

The second grouping (II) focuses on how PR can help a government manager implement the agency's mission. These are the pragmatic impacts that PR can have. However, they are optional in the sense that the administrator can decide whether to engage in PR to facilitate program management or not. The third (III) is a political tool for enhancing the agency's power. However, it is dangerous in the sense that political oversight institutions can call out the agency for improper propaganda and as violating the norm that a government agency should be a more passive actor in the political realm.

PURPOSE 1: MEDIA RELATIONS

The most routinized of government PR purposes is news media relations. The central denominator of this activity is of government communicating with the public-at-large through an intermediary. With the fracturing of what had been the news business, the boundary between traditional reporters and other news media observers is increasingly fuzzy. Nonetheless, no matter how much technology, platforms, and social media change the public's sources of news and methods of delivery, the traditional duty of public administration to cooperate with intermediating news institutions continues unaffected. The legacy news media will evolve and be replaced by *something*, and then *those* new media will eventually be replaced, too. Several e-gov and media generations from now they might not even be called news media, but successors will continue to be intermediaries. They will be purveyors of news on developments in public affairs to relatively large audiences, no matter how fractured the mass public might become.

Generally, media relations is partly a reactive activity, responding to inquiries and requests from reporters and other intermediaries for information. Also, an agency's media relations can be proactive, giving the organization an opportunity to try to generate media interest in an activity, event, or milestone.

Whether active or reactive, e-gov and websites provide enormous opportunities for agencies to communicate with these news intermediaries. The focus needs to be on how technology can enhance the purpose of media relations, not an endorsement of any particular platform or the latest toys and tricks. For example, the time-honored set piece of a news conference can be extended in so many ways, including live streaming, feeds, remote locations, online, interactive, and multimedia. A news conference can be a global event. Reporters throughout the world can audit it, can submit questions (by text or orally), and can receive handouts. Live updates by agency staff with short summaries of each round of Q&A can be made available nearly in real time. Near-instantaneous transcripts can be posted online for universal access. Promises to find out answers to questions that were not anticipated can be posted later and accessed by all, not just the person who asked the question.

A good example of how much e-gov can improve media relations was a description of the before and after media relations by the U.S. Centers for Disease Control during the swine flu public-health emergencies in 1976 versus 2009. An agency official said that in 1976 "the CDC did not hold news conferences and it took it five days to respond" to news developments. In contrast, during the 2009 swine flu outbreak, the CDC had a multimodal war room and "held news conferences, sometimes even daily, at which reporters from around the world ask questions by phone. They can be seen live on the agency's website . . . as well as a constantly updated Facebook page and Twitter feed" (McNeil 2009). Further, the diminution of highly expert health-beat reporters meant the need to convey information in a way that general assignment reporters would understand. Also, the CDC recognized the need to rebut information placed on the Internet by marginal groups claiming to have scientific knowledge supposedly suppressed or ignored by the CDC. Violating the practice of old-time media relations, the CDC recognized that it needed proactively to reply to rumors, no matter how ludicrous or unscientific. The 2011 movie *Contagion* presented some gripping (fictional, but realistic) scenes of the CDC's ability to have a more active approach to media relations, the influence of the online world, and the close relationship between media relations and actual policy implementation (Lee 2013).

During the U.S. military involvements in Iraq and Afghanistan, the Defense Department assigned some of its in-country public affairs units to *localize* news for U.S. audiences by preparing and submitting information on the activities of reserve and National Guard units from particular states and cities (Krane 2004). Such information was not of interest to the national (and international) news media, but it was welcomed by local outlets. This was an example of how e-gov technologies can permit tailoring domestic news for local audiences and bypassing the traditional news gatekeepers and intermediaries. A few years later, a senior military officer was concerned that efforts to convey to global Muslim audiences news about U.S. policies were nearly at a situation of the tail (of media relations) wagging the dog (of actual policy actions), instead of vice versa (Shanker 2009). Good point and important to keep in mind. That gets back to purposes: *What* are you intending to convey?

In times of crisis, media relations is even more important (Garnett and Kouzmin 2009). Government agencies need to be ready to step into the glare of intense interest and desire for information. In general, the principles of emergency media relations are to get it out, get it all out, and get it out as fast as possible (Lee 2008). The evolution of new technologies and e-gov are perfectly suited to this. When the whole world is watching, the media intermediaries and end audiences want and need the agency to use every possible platform to communicate what it knows. Again, the movie *Contagion* helped convey this (Lee 2013). One typical concern for public officials is the truism that initial reports can sometimes be wrong. In the world of e-gov, better to release a flawed version now and then correct it later rather than refusing to release it because it's not confirmed *enough.* In e-gov, minutes, even seconds, matter. The potential for improving crisis media relations with new instant communication technologies and platforms demonstrates how significantly, quantitatively and qualitatively, e-gov contributes to better public administration.

PURPOSE 2: PUBLIC REPORTING

Public reporting is the most traditional of all external communications activities in modern public administration. It dates back to the 19th century, when agencies published annual reports. The difference between public reporting and media relations is that the former entails direct communication between government and the citizenry, whereas the latter uses an intermediary. The central principle of public reporting is that it provides post hoc information as a kind of "we thought you'd like to know what we did last (year, quarter, etc.)." Given the emphasis on conveying information to the lay public, this is now sometimes called popular reporting (Yusuf et al. 2013). During the twentieth century, reporting often deteriorated into unreadable financial and budgetary compilations. But the original premise of reporting, of accounting to the public-at-large of the agency's record and stewardship of public funds in the near past, remains an important part of public administration in a democracy.

As communication technologies have changed, agency reporting has adapted. In the 1930s, the U.S. Department of Interior experimented with a radio version of its annual report. Congressional conservatives, fearing the power of that new medium, protested and defunded it (Lee 2011, 155–157). In the 1950s, cities and federal agencies experimented with movie versions of their reports (Campbell 1953).

Then came e-reporting (Lee 2005). At first, agencies merely scanned their hard-copy annual reports and placed them on their websites. When the technology got better, they posted hot links within the text that permitted citizens interested in a specific topic to locate quickly the section of the report dealing with it. Social media became a way to flag these reports and link interested audiences to them. Web-enabled, open-source government provided citizen-auditors with as much information as they wanted (Kavanaugh 2006). For example, Neil Barofsky, the inspector general of the bank bailout program (Troubled Asset Relief Program, or TARP), which had begun in 2008 after the market crash, routinely placed his reports on his office's website, a prosaic activity in terms of sophisticated e-gov PR. In 2009, six months into his job, he expected perhaps 50,000 hits by curious taxpayers. It was 12 million. By 2011, it had had 50 million hits. Barofsky (2013, 159–160) concluded that citizens were "deeply interested in the inner workings of TARP." This was neither high tech nor advanced e-government. But such modest approach to reporting, perhaps even primitive in e-gov terms, significantly contributed to democracy.

The sky is no longer the limit. Governments are only slowly exploring the full potential of e-reporting (especially with performance results), but the trend is inevitably bound to accelerate (Schatteman 2010). One writer characterized these developments as "transformational" in that technology has expanded and enhanced government's ability to bypass the media and communicate directly with the public (Cullen 2010, 68).

The methods of delivery of public reports are as infinite as the technologies and platforms that will be invented. But the goal remains simple: government agencies are expected to inform the citizenry about what they did in the recent past and how they stewarded public funds (Tagesson, Klugman, and Ekström 2013). From that point on, the opaque processes of public opinion and democracy take over—and the politically neutral civil service needs to step back and let those dynamics play out without any further overt role or participation (see below Purpose No. 8 on public support).

With the expansion of e-gov technologies, e-reporting is gradually shifting to nearly real-time information. Post hoc reports can morph from annual ones to *daily* or even more frequently if there is a desire for it. For example, travelers can access current information on security wait lines at an airport they're about to depart from (Ensign 2013). The possibility of such real-time reporting puts enormous pressure on government agencies to process and release accurate information as quickly as possible. Easier said than done sometimes. As citizen expectations rise, so do the possibilities of the reporting mechanism failing or crashing. This happened in Baltimore in 2012 when the CitiStat system failed, prompting complaints that timely information was not being provided (Broadwater 2012). Robert Behn (2012) suggested that the next generation of CitiStat-type systems be called PerformanceStat 3.0 or CollaborationStat. These will no doubt grow in usage and popularity.

However, real-time reporting, when for the purpose of "news you can use," is probably no longer e-reporting per se. The key to keep in mind is that the purpose of e-reporting is post hoc information, whereas real-time government information can be more in the nature of "now hoc" data. It is a major contribution to government-to-citizen (G2C) communication, but it no longer has the intended purpose of reporting as a democracy-motivated PR activity.

PURPOSE 3: RESPONSIVENESS TO THE PUBLIC

3a—Responsiveness to the Public: As Citizens

Public administration is *not* politics. A government agency cannot change its mission simply because it might be falling in public popularity. That is the job of elected officials to decide. However, given that government agencies operate in the context of the public, one of the basic functions of public management in a democracy is listening to the public on multiple levels. Active listening then leads to modified agency behavior so that it can do a better job and be more responsive to the citizenry. One way to do this is through citizen participation and advisory functions regarding current agency operations and planning for the future.

The rise of e-gov is transforming the old-fashioned concept of citizen participation and agency responsiveness to the public-at-large. Online tools are proliferating, each facilitating more methods of engagement, access, and transparency (Evans and Campos 2013; Leighninger 2011). As interactive technologies evolve, nearly all the permutations of social media can be utilized to provide new venues of citizen input and public administration responsiveness (Thomas 2012, 190–193; Ben-Yehuda 2012). Some will end up being transformative, others failures, and some might even promote *too* much citizen participation, if such a thing could be. But those conclusions will take some time to reach.

3b—Responsiveness to the Public: As Customers and Clients

Because of the major qualitative differences between the private and public sectors, the business mantra that "the customer is always right" is not necessarily true for government. Sometimes laws and regulations prevent doing something that a private or nonprofit organization might do. Nonetheless, public administration is a people business and agencies seek to serve its clients and customers as well as permitted.

The emergence of new e-gov and communication platforms including social media have added a new dimension to providing quality services to the agency's consumers (Lee and Elser 2010). As e-gov evolves, so do the best practices for quality customer service. In general, the public administrator's goal is to use the benefits of technology to engineer increasingly better client experiences (Carbone 2008). The key is to view the agency from the outside. How would a client or customer experience your agency when trying to get information or services?

For example, the increasingly old-fashioned concept of telephone call centers, such as 211 and 311, are gradually migrating to online websites, usually using improved voice-response and voice-recognition technologies. This not only saves money on training and staffing but also saves users time by getting them the information they want faster, more comprehensively, and with near-zero inaccuracies or conflicting answers (Mosebach 2011; Lohr 2009). Generally, government websites are convenient and welcomed by customers, even welfare applicants (Hetling, Watson, and Horgan 2014; Marks 2012). The use of government websites by the public-at-large is passing the tipping point, with a majority using and preferring that method of access (Sternstein 2010). For example, instead of a conventional FAQ website page, the California Department of Motor Vehicles posted a series of Web videos called the "Answer Man" (Rich 2012). It was a more engaging way of answering common questions. (But what about an Answer Woman?) Another e-gov example of customer service entailed a Snow Belt city government, Milwaukee, Wisconsin, offering text alerts regarding snow emergencies and related parking restrictions (*Milwaukee Journal Sentinel* 2009). Such initiatives lead to increasing usage and then create a virtuous cycle: the more the public welcomes online communication, the more agencies can expand their reliance on them (Marks 2011; Miller 2011; U.S. Social Security Administration 2009b).

PURPOSES 4–7: OUTREACH

Responsiveness to citizens for democratic purposes or to customers for pragmatic purposes, concentrates on the communication of *information*, of reducing the friction inherent in a transparent, digital, and online government. In a sense it is process oriented, not content oriented.

Using this typology of purposes, the shift now is to *transactions*, of conducting substantive business between government and citizens. While categories here are presented as part of the purposes of government PR, one could just as easily classify them as marketing. Much of the growing literature on public-sector marketing and branding is applicable and helpful (Eshuis and Klijn 2012; Kotler and Lee 2007; Zavattaro 2013).

Treating marketing as a subgenus of PR helps perceive these transactions as the result of robust public *outreach* by government. Outreach conveys the effort to use communication technologies to facilitate the provision of goods and services. The initiative is the government's, to migrate as much of its outputs and products to e-transactions. The particular motive may be to save money or increase user convenience. Regardless, note the importance of the action itself, namely of viewing e-gov PR as a pragmatic approach to implement the substantive mission of the agency through the most efficient managerial techniques.

The nearly unlimited potential of e-gov greatly expands the ability of government to reach out to specific and targeted slices of the public and deliver whatever product that demographic is seeking. A 2011 study (Waters and Williams) of government agencies' use of Twitter documented that it was mostly to disseminate helpful information outward. In that case, the potential of social media for two-way and interactive communication between government and the public was only at its initial stages. Future developments and enhancements in that direction are inevitable.

Purpose 4—Outreach: Increasing Utilization

At least for public administration, it is not true that "if you build it, they will come." In fact, it is often the opposite. Citizens who are eligible for a new government service or product need to be *informed* about it before knowing to *apply* for it. In a generic sense, government needs to advertise the availability of a new program and do so in a planful way to reach the demographic that the new service is targeted to help. This purpose for outreach, of taking the initiative to inform a market niche, calls for proactive public administration. The increasing sophistication of e-gov and website technology permits government to advertise its wares, sometimes as free media, sometimes as earned media, but always with the same purpose: to increase the utilization of what it has to offer.

Sometimes outreach is about wholly new programs and services, other times about using e-gov to increase the utilization of existing programs. For the former, the federal Department of Health and Human Services faced a major task of educating the public about the new benefits of the 2010 Obama health-care act. So, for example, it conducted information campaigns about the expansion of Medicare services and a broader "Share the News: Share the Health" effort online and in the legacy media (Lee 2012a, 263). In another case, the Internal Revenue Service (IRS 2009) wanted to publicize the existence of new tax breaks available to citizens as part of the 2009 economic stimulus law. It placed on YouTube and iTunes catchy material explaining in easy-to-understand ways what the new benefits were and how to access them.

Regarding increasing the utilization of an existing program, in 2009 the Social Security Administration faced an imminent problem of the retirement of the baby-boom generation. The old-fashioned method of filling out a print form would overwhelm the agency with paper. So, in a service-based e-gov approach, it created the option of applying online. Then, more to the point of this discussion, it launched a multimedia PR campaign to *inform* those aging boomers of the simplicity and convenience of applying online. Cleverly, the agency picked actress Patty Duke as a spokesperson, because she had been the star of a popular TV program watched nearly universally by boomers when they were growing up (U.S. Social Security Administration 2009a).

Sometimes a PR campaign can seamlessly use legacy media and e-gov to help maximize the potential of reaching the desired segments of the public. For example, in 2012, a state Department of Transportation placed a color ad in the largest circulation newspaper in the state with the tease headline: "Have you heard?" The short text informed readers about a redesignation and numbering of a major highway and then suggested that "for additional details go to" a dedicated website it created on that specific subject (Wisconsin Department of Transportation 2012). In another case, the U.S. Interior Department's Bureau of Land Management (2010) was seeking to reach new audiences to adopt wild horses. Far from the Great Plains, the bureau used color advertising in midwestern newspapers to try to catch the attention of readers who otherwise would not know about the program. In turn, the print ad referred interested applicants to a website for more information and opportunities for adoption.

Purpose 5—Outreach: Public Service and Public Education Campaigns

Generally, citizens expect their government to avoid engaging in propaganda, in the sense of trying to convince the populace of the merits of a particular idea. This is most clear in the case of partisanship. During the administration of a president, for example, it is perfectly all right for government agencies to engage in post hoc public reporting (see Purpose 2) by disseminating information on their work and, as they may see it, their accomplishments. But it is strictly verboten for the agency to go one step further, by saying, "Therefore, reelect the President."

One of the three exemptions to this de facto ban on propaganda in public administration is that agencies are permitted to engage in persuasive campaigns for widely held values. (The other two are presidential communications and wartime [Lee 2012c, 3–5].) So, a multiplatform effort to persuade bike riders to wear a helmet for safety purposes is OK. Other familiar ones promote water conservation, encourage hand-washing during flu season, and the U.S. Forest Service's Smokey Bear campaign to reduce wildfires. These persuasion efforts are sometimes called nudges, when society benefits in situations such as "decisions that are difficult, complex, and infrequent" or circumstances that "have poor feedback and few opportunities for learning" (Thaler and Sunstein 2008, 247).

The emergence of e-gov and websites has expanded the venues for promoting safe and healthy behaviors. For example, several federal agencies had the mission of encouraging workers to begin planning early for their retirement income needs. At first, they issued a hard-copy brochure. Then, in 2008, they moved it to the Web. The *Wall Street Journal* said the move made what had been a moderately useful effort into a "top-notch" retirement calculator. By going online, users could have mathematical calculations done for them and could store their information for later use (Ruffenach 2008).

In another effort, the Security and Exchange Commission (SEC) had routinely conducted public-service campaigns in legacy media with recommendations to consumers on their investment decisions. In 2009, it created the website Investor.gov. The site was "the SEC's first-ever devoted exclusively to investor education." A reporter complimented it for being "loaded with tips on just about any aspect of investing." It also had an easy-to-use link for filing complaints online (Gores 2009).

The U.S. Department of Health and Human Services had a long-term goal of shifting medical records from hard copy to electronic, and a more specific goal of persuading citizens of the importance of having easily accessible and comprehensive family health histories. The potential of e-gov and websites provided a perfect way to promote this. The department created a website for citizens to develop and store their family health tree. This would eliminate multiple serial efforts to fill out forms as emergencies arose, would reduce errors, and would facilitate providers' obtaining relevant and accurate information on a patient quickly (Neergaard 2009).

These examples of administrative agencies indicate how much e-gov and websites can improve the scope, impact, and usefulness of public-service campaigns. These focused on subjects that were not controversial, political, or partisan; rather, government was promoting behaviors that were healthier and safer. (A public-service campaign to promote *support* by public opinion for a new law as a "good thing" is more controversial, but justifiable—at least in principle [Lee 2012a, 267].)

Purpose 6—Outreach: Voluntary Compliance

While government has coercive powers, the interests of democracy as well as administrative efficiency encourage agencies to seek voluntary cooperation and compliance by the citizenry. This relates to laws and regulations the agency is responsible for enforcing. A strictly enforcement-oriented regulatory regime is expensive. Generally, citizens in a democracy want to be law abiding but lead hectic lives. Government agencies can derive significant benefits from an active communications effort to be sure citizens are aware of restrictions and regulations that may affect them. And sometimes an ever-so-slight nudge can have major beneficial effects.

The evolution of e-gov and websites is significantly expanding bureau efforts to promote voluntary cooperation. In London, when a major demonstration was about to occur, the police urged participants to "follow us on Twitter." A spokesperson said the general message was to "keep your phones on" (Associated Press 2011). Similarly, the police department for a state capitol building created a new website and Facebook page "in an effort to increase public awareness of Capitol hours and regulations" (Roller and Stein 2011). In another case, the mere threat of publicity was used to obtain the voluntary compliance by tax cheats. A state taxation department created a website naming taxpayers who were delinquent. Eager to get their names taken down, tax arrearage payments increased substantially (Associated Press 2009).

Using PR for voluntary compliance has also proved useful to transportation departments. For example, in 2012, Los Angeles had to close a major section of its freeway system during a weekend to facilitate repairs. In preparation for the media-dubbed "carmageddon," the department used traditional and e-gov venues to communicate the upcoming disruption and to discourage traffic during that time (Associated Press 2012). It worked. In preparation for a longer-term construction disruption, a state Department of Transportation (DOT) created a dedicated website and Facebook and Twitter pages to help alert drivers to travel times, alternate routes, and ramp closures (Wisconsin DOT 2011). The sites also encouraged signing up for e-mail notifications of urgent alerts and updates.

In 2012, the municipal government of Minneapolis provided a textbook case of a comprehensive effort using multiple platforms to obtain voluntary compliance. The issue was prosaic. In autumn, there were some parking restrictions so that the sanitation department could sweep up piles of fallen leaves that homeowners had raked to their curbs. To vacuum up the leaves, the department needed a clear street, with no parked cars blocking access. Besides temporary "No Parking" signs, the department made automated calls to residents of the block to be swept the next day, placed information on Twitter and Facebook, ran public-service announcements on cable TV, and released on YouTube versions in Spanish, Somali, and Hmong (Harlow 2012). A nice effort. Were there still noncompliers who had to be towed? Sure. But imagine how many more there would have been if the department hadn't done its outreach to maximize voluntary compliance.

These are examples of how information begets citizen compliance and cooperation. It is axiomatic that the information revolution of e-gov will create and invent many new beneficial technologies and platforms to disseminate information. In turn, those new developments will further assist in obtaining voluntary compliance with laws and programs.

Purpose 7—Outreach: The Public as the Agency's Eyes and Ears

Citizens can help in the process whereby government provides services. In the academic literature, this is sometimes called co-production. Before e-gov, when a citizen called 911 to report a fire, that citizen was acting an extension of the fire department. With e-gov, this approach to public administration is increasingly applicable to many functions, not just emergency services. In public works, alert citizens can easily notify the department of abandoned cars, locations of potholes, or traffic signals that are out of commission. In health care, a federal agency has organized Senior Medicare Patrols for citizen-consumers to report fraud and abuse (U.S. Administration on Aging 2012). Two writers concluded that of all the benefits of e-gov, "the greatest power of the Internet lies in drawing citizens into the work of agencies as coproducers of value" (Reeher and Mitchell 2008, 260).

All social media are particularly well suited for expanding the public's role in co-producing government services (Meijer 2012). Involving citizens as the eyes and ears of government continues to be common in law enforcement with e-gov further enhancing that. For example, in 2010 the U.S. Department of Homeland Security (DHS 2012) launched a long-term multimedia campaign to promote its slogan "If you see something, say something." Copying the popularity of the names of Apple devices, police chiefs developed a campaign called iWatch as "the 21st century version of Neighborhood Watch" (Sullivan 2009). Another example is New York City's big data analysis of requests for information received by its 311 system for early identification of trends and of problems experienced and reported by citizens (Feuer 2013).

In the area of natural resources, a state agency routinely used social media to help involve individuals as the eyes and ears of the department. For example, it asked hunters to text violations they observed of hunting laws and regulations, asked naturalists to submit their trail camera photos of wildlife, and sought volunteers to report bear and bobcat sightings for a statewide census (Jones 2010; Milwaukee Journal Sentinel 2011).

New technology also facilitates a kind of reverse co-production, when agencies alert citizens on a *personalized basis* of emergency conditions. For example, in 2011, the Federal Communications Commission (FCC) announced a new Personal Localized Alerting Network in New York City. It allowed citizens with "an enabled mobile device to receive geographically-targeted, text-like messages alerting them of imminent threats to safety in their area" (U.S. FCC 2011). Similarly, a sewerage district created a service to alert targeted residents "via e-mail or mobile phone text message if a burst pipe has cut off water service to their home or will snarl traffic" (Helderman 2008). These examples of use of e-gov for co-production are likely mere glimpses of the potentialities of e-gov PR.

PURPOSE 8: INCREASING PUBLIC SUPPORT

There is a red zone that surrounds one practice of external communications in the public sector. Civil servants should never use PR (e-gov or otherwise) if the explicit or apparent primary purpose is to increase public and political support for the agency. For example, public administrators cannot urge citizens to contact elected legislators to lobby them to increase the agency's annual budget, approve an expansion of a program, or authorize a new agency mission.

But generalized support for an agency, just short of that red line, sometimes happens. A 2012 study of local government showed that e-gov participation opportunities and transparency led to increased trust in government (Kim and Lee 2012). In an example that merges legacy media and e-gov, the Federal Deposit Insurance Corporation (FDIC) paid for full-page ads during the banking collapse in 2008 to assure savers that deposit insurance remained financially strong. It referred readers wanting more information to the agency's website (U.S. FDIC 2008). While possibly justified by jittery savers ready to start a run on a bank, the ad also indirectly promoted citizen approval for, and support of, the agency itself as a "good thing." Similarly, the Army National Guard placed a full-page color ad in the *New York Times* to trumpet its continuing relevance to national defense. That this was a government agency doing the advertising—not a nonprofit "friends of" advocacy group—was apparent because the URL for more information was the ".mil" domain (U.S. Army 2007).

It is also accurate that effective e-gov PR can improve that agency's standing in the eyes of the public. That, in turn, can be interpreted by political institutions as expressions of public support for the agency. Then, as a result of that positive public opinion, elected officials may seek to look good to the voters by making decisions that are friendly to the agency. But this can only be a *by-product* of good PR. Therefore, an active effort by an agency to accomplish the previously stated seven purposes can have the secondary effect of benefiting the agency itself. This should not be pursued directly, but the results redound to the political benefit of the agency.

For example, in 2012, the American Customer Satisfaction Index (ASCI) noted that the IRS was at that time gaining in citizen satisfaction as a result of its emphasis on e-filing rather than paper returns. This meant that e-gov technology not only was facilitating transactions but also was increasing user satisfaction with an agency. Another agency with strong satisfaction ratings was the National Weather Service, which benefited from e-gov technologies, especially on-demand venues for citizens to access geographically tailored and up-to-date weather forecasts. Generally, effective use of social media can lead to increasing citizen satisfaction with government (Kim and Robinson 2012). Inevitably, this could be transmuted into the political perception of public support for the agency.

SUMMARY AND CONCLUSION: ADAPTING TO THE FUTURE

This introductory chapter has emphasized the importance of focusing on the purpose, not the technology, of e-gov PR. Specifically, two central questions: (1) What do you want to accomplish? (2) Why does the agency need to do this? If you follow these guidelines, then the right kinds of communication strategies will present themselves as the obvious and precise solutions. Some may be e-gov related, and others may be legacy media, such as old-fashioned newspapers. No matter.

Rarely, if ever, would a public administration practitioner need to choose any one-best-way method of e-gov PR. There never is. The optimal answer is not to choose just one, but to *do everything.*[1] The impact of good communication comes from repetition and multiple platforms so that you reach every nook and cranny of the audience you're targeting. Some audiences may be at the cutting edge of technology and IT, and others may be late adopters. There may even be slivers of the public you can reach only on the twentieth century side of the digital divide. It is virtually impossible to overcommunicate. For example, in political PR (a subject that must be kept far away from PR in public administration), the conventional wisdom for election advertising is that for a message to have impact, the audience should be exposed to it at least ten times.[2] Even a comprehensive e-gov PR effort, which focuses on any of the specific purposes discussed here, is unlikely to exceed the supposed minimum of ten exposures. Just go forth and communicate!

Finally, the pace of technological development is so fast that inevitably new e-gov methods and platforms will arise in the foreseeable and unforeseeable future. Good—and no matter. Good because they will likely further improve e-democracy and e-public administration. No matter because they are unlikely to affect the basic *purposes* of e-gov PR. *Plus ça change, plus c'est la même chose.* Even if the next stage is, say, paperless PR, the approach suggested here of focusing on the purpose and intent before zeroing in on the method of communication will not change. The key point to keep asking yourself is this: Can this latest new, *new* thing in e-gov help accomplish a specific *purpose?* If so, how?

KEY POINTS

- When using e-government public relations to improve public administration, don't let the tail wag the dog. Before plunging into the specifics of technologies and platforms for a communication effort, there's a need for a "hey, wait a minute" interruption to shift the focus from means to ends. Marshall McLuhan famously observed in the 1960s that "the medium is the message." Not for government PR. The message is more important than the medium.
- The two key questions to answer during the "wait a minute" approach are the following:
  - *What* specifically are you trying to accomplish?
  - *Why* does the agency need to do this?
- Answering those questions leads to better subsequent decisions regarding which e-gov technologies and platforms to use.
- While answering the two "wait a minute" questions, it's usually helpful to determine the general orientation of the planned communication effort. It might be *mandatory* because it is required of public administration in a democracy. It might be *optional* in that it offers pragmatic ideas to managers to help pursue the agency's substantive mission. Finally, it might be *political* because it would help increase the agency's power and influence.
- *Mandatory* public relations deriving from *democracy* tends to be for one (or more) of three specific purposes:
  - media relations
  - public reporting
  - responsiveness to the citizenry
- *Optional* public relations includes many distinct marketing purposes that managers can *pragmatically* use to implement the agency's substantive mission. They include the following:

  - responsiveness to customers
  - outreach to:
    * increase utilization of agency services
    * persuade the public to engage in healthful and safe behaviors
    * obtain voluntary compliance with laws and rules
    * engage citizens in the implementation of the agency's mission
- Government agencies should not engage in public relations for the ostensible and overt purpose of improving the agency's *political* standing. Elected officials don't like being propagandized by the bureaucracy. Instead, doing good e-gov PR—whether for democratic reasons or pragmatic managerial purposes—can redound to the agency's political benefit through increased public satisfaction with the agency.
- It is inevitable that digital and online technology will evolve and improve over time. While those changes will improve the ability of government agencies to communicate, they will *not* affect the basics of e-government PR. As always, there are two questions that should begin the discussion: *What* are you trying to do, and *why* are you trying to do it?

NOTES

1. This slogan was used early in the twentieth century by a U.S. nonprofit trying to promote prohibition on alcohol. Rather than focusing exclusively on passing an amendment to the U.S. Constitution, it instead pursued its goal in many different ways (Okrent 2010, 18).

2. For readers interested political PR, see Strömbäck and Kiousis (2011).

REFERENCES

Allison, G.T., Jr. 1980. Public and private management: Are they fundamentally alike in all unimportant respects? In *Setting public management research agendas*, 27–41. Washington, DC: U.S. Office of Personnel Management.

American Customer Satisfaction Index. 2012. Federal government gains in citizen satisfaction and narrows gap to private sector. News release, January 19. www.theacsi.org/news-and-resources/press-releases/press-releases-2012/press-release-federal-government-2011.

Associated Press. 2009. Tax shame site pulls in dough. *Milwaukee Journal Sentinel* (WI), August 16, 2B.

———. 2011. Bobbies ready to tweet protesters. *Milwaukee Journal Sentinel* (WI), March 23, 11A.

———. 2012. Carmageddon II on track. *Milwaukee Journal Sentinel* (WI), September 30, 10A.

Barofsky, N. 2013. *Bailout: How Washington abandoned main street while rescuing Wall Street.* New York: Free Press.

Behn, R. 2012. *Bob Behn's performance leadership report* 10, 3 (November). www.hks.harvard.edu/thebehnreport/All%20Issues/November2012.pdf.

Ben-Yehuda, G. 2012. Participation in an age of social media. *Business of Government* (Fall–Winter), 55–57.

Broadwater, L. 2012. New CitiStat director pledges improvements, transparency. *Baltimore Sun*, October 9, 4A.

Campbell, O.W. 1953. San Diego's 1951 annual report. *Public Administration Review* 13, 30–32.

Carbone, L. 2008. Engineering experiences that build trust in government. In *The trusted leader: Building the relationships that make government work*, ed. T. Newell, G. Reeher, and P. Ronayne, 267–285. Washington, DC: CQ Press.

Cullen, R. 2010. Defining the transformation of government: E-government or e-governance paradigm? In *E-government: Information, technology, and transformation*, ed. H.J. Scholl, 52–71. Armonk, NY: M.E. Sharpe.
Ensign, R.L. 2013. Plan for bigger travel delays. *Milwaukee* (WI) *Journal Sentinel*, March 31, 4D.
Eshuis, J., and E.-H. Klijn. 2012. *Branding in governance and public management.* New York: Routledge.
Evans, A.M., and A. Campos. 2013. Open government initiatives: Challenges of citizen participation. *Journal of Policy Analysis and Management* 32, 172–203.
Feuer, A. 2013. The mayor's geek squad. *New York Times*, March 24, 22–23.
Garnett, J., and A. Kouzmin. 2009. Crisis communication post Katrina: What are we learning? *Public Organization Review* 9, 385–398.
Gores, P. 2009. Regulator on web. *Milwaukee Journal Sentinel* (WI), October 24, 2A.
Grunig, J.E. 1997. Public relations management in government and business. In *Handbook of administrative communication*, ed. J.L. Garnett and A. Kouzmin, 241–283. New York: Marcel Dekker.
Harlow, T. 2012. Cars ticketed, towed for street sweeping. *Minneapolis* (MN) *Star Tribune*, November 23, B3.
Helderman, R.S. 2008. New alerts will flag water woes. *Washington Post*, November 12, B2.
Hetling, A., S. Watson, and M. Horgan. 2014. "We live in a technological era, whether you like it or not": Client perspectives and online welfare applications. *Administration and Society* 46, 519–547.
Jones, M. 2010. Hunters asked to text violations. *Milwaukee Journal Sentinel* (WI), November 17, 6B.
Kang, C. 2010. White House seeks tech advice from corporate chiefs. *Washington Post*, January 14, A16.
Kavanaugh, E. 2006. Citizen auditors—Web enabled, open-source government. *Public Manager* 35 (Spring), 20–25.
Kim, B.J., and S. Robinson. 2012. Social media and Web 2.0 for rethinking e-government maturity models. In *Public service, governance and Web 2.0 technologies: Future trends in social media*, ed. E. Downey and M. Jones, 250–264. Hershey, PA: Information Science Reference/ICI Global.
Kim, S., and J. Lee. 2012. E-participation, transparency, and trust in local government. *Public Administration Review* 72, 819–828.
Kotler, P., and N.R. Lee. 2007. Marketing in the public sector. *Public Manager* 36 (Spring), 12–17.
Krane, J. 2004. Military plans launch of own news service. *Tulsa World* (OK), February 28, A4.
Lee, M. 2005. E-reporting: Using managing-for-results data to strengthen democratic accountability. In *Managing for results, 2005*, ed. J.M. Kamensky and A. Morales, 141–195. Lanham, MD: Rowman & Littlefield.
———. 2008. Media relations and external communications during a disaster. In *Disaster management handbook*, ed. J. Pinkowski, 387–399. Boca Raton, FL: CRC Press.
———. 2011. *Congress vs. the bureaucracy: Muzzling agency public relations.* Norman: University of Oklahoma Press.
———. 2012a. Do's and don'ts of public relations for government health care administration. *Journal of Health and Human Services Administration* 35, 258–273.
———. 2012b. Government public relations: What is it good for? In *The practice of government public relations*, ed. M. Lee, G. Neeley and K. Stewart, 9–25. Boca Raton, FL: CRC Press.
———. 2012c. *Promoting the war effort: Robert Horton and federal propaganda, 1938–1946.* Baton Rouge: Louisiana State University Press.
———. 2013. Hollywood takes on public service. *PA Times* 36 (April–June), 6S.
Lee, M., and E.L. Elser. 2010. The nine commandments of social media in public administration: A dual-generation perspective. *PA Times* 33 (Summer), 3.
Leighninger, M. 2011. How should citizens and public managers use online tools to improve democracy? *National Civic Review* 100 (Summer), 20–29.
Lohr, S. 2009. To do more with less, governments go digital. *New York Times*, October 11, BU3.

Margetts, H. 2012. Electronic government: A revolution in public administration? In *SAGE handbook of public administration*, 2d ed., ed. B.G. Peters and J. Pierre, 447–462. Los Angeles: Sage.

Marks, J. 2011. Agencies outline technology-based customer service initiatives. *Nextgov.com*, October 27. www.nextgov.com/mobile/2011/10/agencies-outline-technology-based-customer-service-initiatives/50026/.

———. 2012. Satisfaction with government websites inches up to a record high. *Nextgov.com*, July 24. www.nextgov.com/cio-briefing/2012/07/satisfaction-government-websites-inches-record-high/56965/.

McNeil, D.G., Jr. 2009. Swine flu officials' message: Don't blame shots for all ills. *New York Times*, September 28, A14.

Meijer, A. 2012. Co-production in an information age: Individual and community engagement supported by new media. *Voluntas* 23, 1156–1172.

Miller, S.A., II. 2011. Where's my refund? Check the tax app. *Milwaukee* (WI) *Journal Sentinel*, January 25, 2D.

Milwaukee Journal Sentinel. 2009. City offers text alerts for snow emergencies. *Milwaukee* (WI) *Journal Sentinel*, February 18, 2B.

———. 2011. DNR wants reports of bear, bobcat sightings. 2011. *Milwaukee* (WI) *Journal Sentinel*, April 26, 2B.

Mosebach, J. 2011. How local governments benefit from social media. *National Weblog*, American Society for Public Administration, August 23. http://aspanational.wordpress.com/2011/08/23/how-local-governments-benefit-from-social-media/.

Neergaard, L. 2009. Government service puts family health tree online. *Milwaukee* (WI) *Journal Sentinel*, January 13, 4A.

Norris, D.F., and C.G. Reddick. 2013. Local e-government in the United States: Transformation or incremental change? *Public Administration Review* 73, 165–175.

Okrent, D. 2010. *Last call: The rise and fall of prohibition.* New York: Scribner.

Reeher, G., and G. Mitchell. 2008. From e-government to e-governance: Harnessing technology to strengthen democracy. In *The trusted leader: Building the relationships that make government work*, ed. T. Newell, G. Reeher, and P. Ronayne, 240–266. Washington, DC: CQ Press.

Rich, S. 2012. CA DMV launches "Answer Man" web video series. *Govtech.com*, November 28. www.govtech.com/e-government/CA-DMV-Launches-Answer-Man-Web-Video-Series.html.

Roller, E., and J. Stein. 2011. Police launch website, pages. *Milwaukee* (WI) *Journal Sentinel,* June 7, 5B.

Ruffenach, G. 2008. Uncle Sam's top-notch retirement calculator. *Wall Street Journal*, June 8, 2.

Schatteman, A. 2010. Information technology and public performance management: Examining municipal e-reporting. In *Handbook of public information systems*, 3d ed., ed. C.M. Shea and G.D. Garson, 431–442. Boca Raton, FL: CRC Press.

Shanker, T. 2009. Message to Muslim world gets a critique. *New York Times*, August 28, A9.

Shoop, T. 2012. What the "new social operating system" means for government. *Nextgov.com*, December 3. www.nextgov.com/cio-briefing/2012/12/what-new-social-operating-system-means-government/59905/.

Sternstein, A. 2010. Many Americans use web for government info. *NationalJournal.com*, April 27.

Strömbäck, J., and S. Kiousis, eds. 2011. *Political public relations: Principles and applications.* New York: Routledge.

Sullivan, E. 2009. New local watch program backed. *Milwaukee* (WI) *Journal Sentinel*, October 4, 20A.

Tagesson, T., M. Klugman, and M.L. Ekström. 2013. What explains the extent and content of social disclosures in Swedish municipalities' annual reports. *Journal of Management and Governance* 17, 217–235.

Thaler, R.H., and C.R. Sunstein. 2008. *Nudge: Improving decisions about health, wealth, and happiness.* New Haven, CT: Yale University Press.

Thomas, J.C. 2012. *Citizen, customer, partner: Engaging the public in public management.* Armonk, NY: M.E. Sharpe.
University of Wisconsin–Milwaukee. 2014. Get the latest on the web. *UWM Report*, 35 (June), 2.
U.S. Administration on Aging. 2012. Senior Medicare patrol. www.aoa.gov/AoA_programs/Elder_Rights/SMP/index.aspx.
U.S. Army, National Guard Bureau. 2007. The National Guard always goes to the same place. Where it's needed. Advertisement, *New York Times*, January 17, A7.
U.S. Bureau of Land Management. 2010. Wild horse and burro adoption. Advertisement. *Milwaukee* (WI) *Journal Sentinel*, June 23, 6A.
U.S. Department of Homeland Security. 2012. "If you see something, say something" campaign. www.dhs.gov/if-you-see-something-say-something-campaign.
U.S. Federal Communications Commission. 2011. New York City unveils first-in-the-nation public safety system. News release, May 10. http://hraunfoss.fcc.gov/edocs_public/attachmatch/DOC-306417A1.pdf.
U.S. Federal Deposit Insurance Corporation. 2008. For 75 years, the FDIC has been protecting people's money. Advertisement, *Milwaukee* (WI) *Journal Sentinel*, July 28, 5A.
U.S. Internal Revenue Service. 2009. IRS features recovery tax credits on YouTube, iTunes. News release IR-2009–76, August 21. www.irs.gov/uac/IRS-Features-Recovery-Tax-Credits-on-YouTube,-iTunes.
U.S. Social Security Administration. 2009a. The cousins are back and they're filing online for Social Security benefits. News release, January 6. www.ssa.gov/pressoffice/pr/pattyduke-pr-alt.pdf.
———. 2009b. Social Security's online services continue to win accolades. News release, February 12. www.socialsecurity.gov/pressoffice/pr/onlineservices-accolades-pr-alt.pdf.
Waters, R.D., and J.M. Williams. 2011. Squawking, tweeting, cooing, and hooting: Analyzing the communication patterns of government agencies on Twitter. *Journal of Public Affairs* 11, 353–363.
Wisconsin Department of Transportation. 2011. Change how you go. Not where you go. Advertisement. *Milwaukee* (WI) *Journal Sentinel*, February 20, 8A.
———. 2012. Have you heard? Advertisement. *Milwaukee* (WI) *Journal Sentinel*, May 23, 12A.
Yusuf, J.-E., M.M. Jordan, K.A. Neill, and M. Hackbart. 2013. For the people: Popular financial reporting practices of local government. *Public Budgeting and Finance* 33, 95–113.
Zavattaro, S.M. 2013. *Cities for sale: Municipalities as public relations and marketing firms.* Albany: State University of New York Press.

2

Understanding and Measuring Online Fiscal Transparency

Jonathan B. Justice, John G. McNutt, and Edward S. Smith Jr.

The movement toward open government and fiscal transparency is a worldwide effort that promises the possibility of better and stronger democracy (Lathrop and Ruma 2010). Transparency is also presumed to help combat corruption and waste. Greater transparency in government thus has been an important goal of many reformers both outside and within governments over many decades, and contemporary methods of online information dissemination and communication are seen as one important set of tools for fostering transparency. But how do we know transparency when we see it? Efforts both to understand the extent and quality of online fiscal transparency and to implement or improve transparency are facilitated by good measures of quantity and quality. This chapter reviews efforts by academic experts and advocacy organizations to measure and evaluate fiscal transparency in order to draw suggestions for the practice of fiscal transparency.

There have been a number of research efforts to date aimed at evaluating governments' online fiscal transparency. Notable recent efforts include the U.S. Public Interest Research Group's (PIRG) multiyear research efforts (Baxandall and Wohlschlegel 2010; Davis, Baxandall, and Musto 2011; Davis, Baxandall, and Pierannunzi 2012, 2013). Also important are the subscales from the various e-government studies that address aspects of fiscal transparency (West 2005; Holzer et al. 2009). An examination of these research efforts reveals significant progress in conceptualization and measurement toward addressing a number of methodological and epistemological issues that concern researchers in the field. The examination also indicates that measures such as PIRG's and those produced by a number of academic researchers, though still imperfect from an academic perspective, nonetheless can provide useful guidance for practitioners and citizens seeking to understand and improve their jurisdictions' e-fiscal transparency.

This chapter begins with a conceptual overview of fiscal transparency and the role of information and communications technology (ICT) in transparency. Then it turns to a review of relevant conceptual issues of measurement in the area, followed by a review of measures developed by academic researchers and advocacy groups to date. We conclude by synthesizing the key elements we found in the literature into a framework for conceptualizing, measuring, and implementing online fiscal transparency, and by drawing lessons for continuing efforts to advance the understanding and practice of transparency.

FISCAL TRANSPARENCY OVERVIEW

Fiscal transparency, it sometimes seems, is expected to be all things to all people, so that it is expected to contribute to, if not to deliver directly, many of the fundamental promises of public administration: economy, efficiency, effectiveness, and equity. For example, de Renzio and Masud (2011, 608) cite evidence that fiscal transparency can improve governments' fiscal performance, reduce their borrowing costs, reduce corruption, and contribute to a number of other desirable economic and governance outcomes. Fiscal transparency is also looked to as a way to foster democratic accountability and responsiveness, legitimacy, and citizen participation and social capital (e.g., Justice, Melitski, and Smith 2006; Justice and Tarimo 2012; Robinson 2008).

What, then, is fiscal transparency, which promises so much, and why should we expect so many benefits from it? Is more always better, or it possible to have too much of a good thing? How can fiscal transparency be measured in ways that are valid and reliable? This section examines those questions and highlights some key dimensions of fiscal transparency, focusing in particular on the uses and usability of fiscal information, and on the notion of effective fiscal transparency (Heald 2003).

What constitutes *effective* fiscal transparency—meaning that accurate and sufficient information is available and usable for decision making—turns out to be in large part situationally contingent and audience dependent. A corollary is that we transparency enthusiasts may need to curb our enthusiasm: to the degree that information exceeds the quantity required for a specific audience or decision situation, or that it is abundant and accurate but incomplete, irrelevant, and/or not correctly understood, brute transparency may in fact be ineffective or even distortionary. At the same time, a bias toward making information (and even raw data accompanied by adequate metadata, especially if the data are machine readable) accessible can foster useful accountability on the part of officials. This understanding has implications for the design of efforts to increase (the effectiveness and benefits of) fiscal transparency and for efforts to measure it.

Fiscal Transparency Concepts

Definitions of fiscal transparency are as broad and diverse as its hypothesized benefits. One widely cited definition of fiscal transparency with a focus on national governments (Kopits and Craig 1998, 1) describes it in general terms as

> openness toward the public at large about government structure and functions, fiscal policy intentions, public sector accounts, and projections. It involves ready access to reliable, comprehensive, timely, understandable, and internationally comparable information on government activities—whether undertaken inside or outside the government sector—so that the electorate and financial markets can accurately assess the government's financial position and the true costs and benefits of government activities, including their present and future economic and social implications.

Kopits and Craig (1998, 1) identify three broad dimensions of fiscal transparency: (1) information on governments' fiscal policy forecasts and intentions; (2) openness of governments' fiscal operations and budgets, including the publication of complete budget documents; and (3) the "behavioral aspects" of budget implementation, such as "conflict-of-interest rules for elected and appointed officials, freedom-of information requirements, a transparent regulatory framework, open public procurement and employment practices, a code of conduct for tax officials, and published performance audits."

Heald (2003), beginning with Kopits and Craig's definition, parses fiscal transparency in a number of ways and makes it clear that, among other things, *effective* (as opposed to *nominal*) fiscal transparency is an audience- and context-specific construct. While the requisites of ready availability, timeliness, reliability, accuracy, comprehensiveness, comparability, and understandability of information apply to any meaningful idea of decisionally useful transparency, the approaches to selecting and presenting information that will satisfy those requirements may vary according to the interests of specific stakeholders and audiences—municipal-finance analysts versus accountants versus non-specialist citizens, for instance, or budget officers versus part-time legislators—and those stakeholders' abilities to make sense of different presentations of information. Other design- and measurement-relevant dimensions of transparency described by Heald (2006) include the distinction between *event* (inputs, outputs, and outcomes) or *process* (an organization's stipulated policies and procedures and/or its actual practices) transparency, and whether transparency is accomplished through *retrospective* presentation or happens *in real time.*

In the empirical literature on fiscal transparency, three distinct basic categories of fiscal-transparency construct are common, but they are a bit different from Kopits and Craig's (1998) three dimensions. One area of focus is on *ex ante* budgetary transparency—the provision of timely and high-quality information on governments' fiscal forecasts, intentions, and allocations, and the openness of government budget contents and processes (e.g., Alt, Lassen, and Rose 2006). A second is *ex post* compiled governmental financial and performance reporting—the publication of timely, complete, and accurate financial and performance reports and audits, such as comprehensive annual financial reports (CAFRs) compliant with generally accepted accounting principles (GAAP) (e.g., Cheng 1994; Ingram 1984), popular annual financial reports (PAFRs) (e.g., Carpenter and Sharp 1992) and citizen-centric reports (Association of Government Accountants 2013), and performance reports (e.g., Governmental Accounting Standards Board 2003; Smith 2004). A third category includes more specific, transaction-level transparency, such as laws and practices related to freedom of information, conflict-of-interest disclosures, and—most recently, as the technology has become increasingly available and familiar—online "checkbooks" that disclose individual payments made by governments and sometimes contracts entered into and various subsidies and grants as well: broadly, "who receives state money and for what purposes" (Davis, Baxandall, and Musto 2011, 1).

Each of these forms of transparency is somewhat different from the others in terms of its audiences, information requirements, uses, and contributions toward good fiscal governance. Transparency of fiscal forecasts and budget contents and processes is likely to support a focus on questions of social resource allocations and broad fiscal priorities. Transparency in the form of financial and performance reporting can facilitate the holding of officials accountable for their stewardship of public resources and can make it possible to monitor and predict governments' fiscal health and prospects for sustaining a desired level of public services while meeting all their financial obligations over time. Transaction-level transparency can facilitate corruption control and citizens' monitoring of the efficiency, effectiveness, and appropriateness of expenditures by "following the money" at a level that identifies individual recipients, purposes, and transactions.

The Role of Information and Communication Technology

In the spirit of the New York Bureau of Municipal Research's early twentieth-century budget exhibits, contemporary reformers concerned with advancing government transparency in general and fiscal transparency in particular have looked to the most recent developments in mass communications technology as a way of "making government intelligible to the people" (Kahn 1993, 96). At the beginning of the twentieth century the emerging technologies were physical displays of the type pioneered by department stores, world fairs, and museum reformers such as John Cotton Dana. At the beginning of the twenty-first century, those technologies include database tools, the Internet and World Wide Web, and the ever-expanding variety of information and communications technologies (ICT) available for publishing, accessing, manipulating, and presenting data in order to transform it into decision-supporting information.

Even before the development of smartphones and apps, the Web and personal computers brought the potential for decreasing information users' (and to some degree suppliers') costs, and increasing the convenience and power, of accessing and using fiscal information (Justice, Melitski, and Smith 2006). For users, Web access brings the convenience of being able to obtain information at any time, from any place with Internet access. For suppliers of information, once a website exists, the marginal costs of disseminating information can be dramatically less via the Web than through mass printing and mailing, or responding to individual requests. As the International Budget Partnership (IBP 2010) notes, "all governments . . . can improve transparency and accountability quickly and with very little additional cost or effort by publishing online all of the budget information they already produce." Electronic formats additionally offer the potential for making both aggregated and transaction-level information available in searchable, sortable forms either for download or for manipulation via online Web applications. The Government Finance Officers Association (GFOA 2003, 2009, 2010), recognizing these advantages, first recommended in 2002 that governments use their websites for debt-related disclosures and in 2003 that governments post their budgets and financial reports on their websites, and has since then expanded and updated its recommendations for online transparency purposes, content, and formats.

Ongoing rapid developments in Internet, accounting and budgeting, and enterprise database technologies continue to expand the potential for making government budgetary and financial information both available and intelligible to a wide range of users. From early, static applications such as posting PDF files of budgets and financial reports, the range of applications expanded first to include budget-and-finance portals such as Nashville's online Citizen's Guide (Boydston and Aaron 2004), government- and third-party-sponsored interactive budget games that seek to educate as well as entertain (e.g., *New York Times* 2010), and interactive tools for generating visual displays of budgetary information (e.g., City of Los Angeles, CA 2013). The most recent development has been the widespread adoption of government Web portals featuring searchable databases of contracts, grant awards, payments, lobbying activities, and other transactional information—such as the Office of Management and Budget's USAspending.gov, the Recovery Accountability and Transparency Board's Recovery.gov, New York State Attorney General's NYOpenGovernment.com, and online "checkbooks" of the type now implemented by a majority of U.S. states (Davis, Baxandall, and Musto 2011).

This kind of transparency of transaction-level operational expenses is somewhat related to—but also somewhat different from—two of Kopits and Craig's (1998) three dimensions. Transactional transparency is somewhat related to their dimension of budgetary and operational openness in that it illuminates the results of decisions made to implement adopted budgets. It is perhaps more directly related to their "behavioral aspects" in that it provides information that might facilitate detecting (and so, one might hope, preventing) opportunistic behavior by public officials using contracting and payments to serve private rather than purely public purposes.

Transaction-level transparency is also perhaps the form for which recent developments in ICT are of greatest significance, although ICT innovations such as flexible and searchable databases for recording and reporting budgetary allocations and financial transactions, and data-visualization tools, particularly when accessed through user-friendly search and presentation tools made available over the World Wide Web, have potential implications for all four forms of transparency—fiscal, financial, performance, and transactional. For example, the availability of downloadable budget and accounting data can facilitate independent analysis of fiscal forecasts, budgets, and financial reports by allowing users to reorganize and manipulate the underlying components and categories. The ability to search, sort, and download databases of contracts and payments can significantly reduce the time required for outside observers to identify individual vendors' contracts and payments, as well as patterns in procurement and payments. This in turn might promote accountability by facilitating more effective legislative scrutiny, whistle-blowing, and competitive bidding for public contracts (see Halbfinger 2013).

One example is offered by a recent PIRG report (Davis, Baxandall, and Pierannunzi 2012, 11–12):

> [W]hen Minnesota began to require agencies to submit reports on the performance of subsidized projects [to a one-stop online transparency portal], the reports revealed that numerous projects were receiving assistance from two or more funding sources—that is, Minnesota taxpayers were sometimes double- and triple paying for the creation of the same jobs. After the centralized publication of those reports, the double-dipping stopped.

Hopefully, cases like this are comparatively rare. This does reveal the major benefits that can be obtained with active transparency efforts.

Legal and Programmatic Issues of Online Transparency

There are, of course, a number of caveats regarding online transparency. Many of these are by now familiar. Even when it encompasses only information that has long been considered officially public, such as gun-ownership records or real property ownership and valuation records, online disclosure introduces privacy concerns, as the information becomes significantly easier to obtain. Online availability and machine readability also increase the potential for willful misuse or misrepresentation of public records and data by external interests. Further—in spite of our general enthusiasm for the movement toward publishing detailed public data sets—there is the potential to distract from substantive issues and the big picture as we get overwhelmed by details and/or become fixated instead on individual contracts, salaries, or reimbursements. This can be an unintended by-product of excessive disclosure, but it can also be a deliberate tactic by officials: using large volumes of opaque data to obscure, rather than reveal, matters of fiscal importance (Heald 2012, 42).

Less familiar are some other caveats and counterarguments noted by Heald (2003, 2012): the transaction costs and diminishing returns of additional disclosure, the potential for excessive and real-time transparency to interfere with policymaking and administrative processes, the possible distortion of officials' behavior as they react by behaving secretively or defensively or by attempting to manipulate disclosures and their uses, the distortion of decisions through officials' concern about appearances or by providing too much information that attentive special interests and lobbyists can use to gain advantages over less attentive publics and interests, and other complications introduced by premature disclosures or publicity of processes that ought to be conducted in secret. All of these potential downsides apply to transparency in any form but have the potential to be amplified by ICT.

MEASURING (ONLINE) FISCAL TRANSPARENCY

There have been a number of efforts to evaluate online fiscal transparency, both as parts of larger attempts to evaluate e-government efforts as well as those focused on fiscal transparency specifically. Each of these efforts adds to our understanding of the nature of fiscal transparency. In practice, the measurement of fiscal transparency—knowing it when we see it—turns out to be a complex undertaking. While there is no particular controversy over the broad definition of fiscal transparency, it is a very complex, multidimensional construct, to a degree that makes operationalizing and measuring it holistically almost impossible. Further, the distinction between nominal and effective transparency is an important one, and it introduces qualitative nuances beyond simple access to documents and transactional information as well as the challenge of transparency's stakeholder specificity. Still, recent scholarship and advocacy work has generated many good index and scorecard measures at the same time that public officials, public-sector watchdog agencies, and advocacy organizations have experimented with new approaches and refined existing approaches.

Measurement Considerations

One useful consideration to begin with in approaching the matter of how to measure fiscal transparency is Heald's (2012) distinction between (effective) transparency and mere *openness*. Indiscriminate data dumps in particular can constitute a high degree of openness without contributing meaningfully to effective transparency. Indeed, as Heald (2012) and others have noted, publishing large volumes of opaque data can be employed as a barrier to effective transparency, either by making it hard to see the forest for the trees or by offering titillating details involving small sums in order to distract audiences from broader and more consequential taxing and spending actions. (This is not an absolute, however, and in fact under some circumstances, data dumps can have the potential to be transformed into usable and effectively transparent information by intermediaries [see Justice and Dülger 2009; Justice and Tarimo 2012] or sophisticated users, particularly if the data are made available in machine-readable form with adequate metadata.)

The openness-transparency distinction highlights the fundamentally normative nature of the transparency construct and suggests measurement challenges. Quantitative measures might fairly readily be devised for quantifying the amount of data disclosed and the ease of obtaining it, but the usability and relevance criteria that underlie the definition of effective transparency imply that qualitative judgments must be made as well. To what degree and in what ways is fiscal information not just readily available, timely, and comparable but also relevant, subjectively meaningful, accurate, and usable by relevant audiences for the specific judgments and/or decisions to be made or other purposes at hand? Heald (2012, 36) observes that this is one of a number of reasons for skepticism about summary index measures of fiscal transparency: different index creators may have different normative presumptions. Indeed, Heald's preference for retrospective, event-focused forms of transparency, because they foster accountability without interfering in organizational operations, might be taken to reflect a predisposition for a protective rather than developmental model of democracy (for this distinction, see Heald [2006]), favoring accountability and stewardship as the ends of fiscal transparency more than participation and short-term responsiveness.

Heald (2012) also notes that the details of index construction can be tricky and that indexes can rely on unrealistically simplistic assumptions about the relationships among components of the index. While Heald's skepticism is certainly justified, indexes are also indisputably useful for comparing observations over time and in cross section, and as variables for statistical analysis. Careful and well-documented index measures of complex fiscal behaviors and institutions do in fact seem to be attainable, in any event (e.g., Wehner 2006). And for present purposes, even measurements that are less than perfectly successful by academic standards can contribute to our understanding of the elements of effective e-fiscal transparency.

Operationalizing the Dimensions of Fiscal Transparency, Offline and Online

Among the four broad categories of fiscal transparency, the area of *ex post* financial reporting appears to have been the subject of the most extensive prescription in this regard. Summarizing a range of accounting-standards literature from sources including the UK Accounting Standards Board, the Federal Accounting Standards Advisory Board, the Governmental Accounting Standards Board, the International Accounting Standards Board, and the International Public Sector Accounting Standards Board, Prowle, Harradine, and Latham (2012, 33) identify the broad requirements for information content. If they are to meet users' needs and serve their fundamental accountability and stewardship-promoting goals, financial reports must provide information that addresses four questions: (1) Have public funds been used legally? (2) Is the organization financially viable going forward? (3) Have public funds been used as planned? (4) Have public funds been used effectively and efficiently?

In addition to those financial-accounting criteria, we might also add that it is also important, both *ex ante* and *ex post*, to understand the sources of public funds, in order to gain a sense of the net effect of public finances. Other relevant information often neglected by standard financial accounting presentations would include what Heald (2012, 43–44) terms "surrogates" for direct public spending. These include off-budget expenditures (or revenues), tax expenditures, coerced private expenditures such as compulsory insurance, and future commitments that are not recorded as expenditures or liabilities (see, e.g., Gilmour's [2012] account of the Indiana Toll Road lease).

Further, as Prowle, Harradine, and Latham (2012, 37) point out, governments and other public-sector organizations are unlikely to go out of business, so that the areas of priority for understanding their fiscal health might emphasize their long-term ability to provide a desired level of service while meeting financial obligations, within the resource constraint established by the willingness and ability of relevant constituencies to pay the taxes and charges required. This concern with what Groves, Godsey, and Shulman (1981) termed "service-level solvency" introduces elements of political judgment and prediction that likely exceed what we could reasonably expect public organizations to report routinely. And indeed, we might not trust them if they did so. But we might consider one hallmark of transparency to be that governments make available information that would allow outsiders to make well supported estimates of such organizational sustainability.

Reflecting these aspirations for information that is both comprehensive in its coverage and provides purchase for external analysis, Heald (2012, 45–46) offers prescriptions for an ideal condition of fiscal transparency that include accrual-basis statements, inclusion of all entities and fiscal activities, and a hierarchy of documents spanning the range from user-friendly top-level overviews to highly detailed data and technical presentations. Heald also argues that maintaining effective fiscal transparency requires institutional arrangements that facilitate holding fiscal officials accountable: strong and well-resourced legislatures, external analytic organizations (New York City's Independent Budget Office might be a U.S. example), and effective audit requirements and auditors.

In practice, the most widely known qualitative and index measurements of (offline) fiscal transparency at the national level build on normative benchmarks established by the International Monetary Fund (IMF 2007) and the Organisation for Economic Co-operation and Development (OECD 2002). Both are substantially consistent with the conceptions of fiscal transparency of Heald (2003, 2012), Kopits and Craig (1998), and Prowle, Harradine, and Latham (2012). The IMF's (2007) *Code of Good Practices on Fiscal Transparency* establishes 45 normative benchmarks for (national) governments' fiscal transparency in four areas: (1) clarity of roles and responsibilities, (2) open budget processes (including publishing audited financial reports), (3) public availability of usable information, and (4) assurances of integrity. The IMF benchmarks as a group provide a guide to measurement of fiscal transparency that captures essentially all of the categories and dimensions of fiscal transparency noted above, with the exception of complete transaction-level disclosure.[1]

The OECD's (2002) *Best Practices for Budget Transparency* are organized into three parts. The first specifies standards for the content and availability of seven types of budget report, including the budget itself, documents relevant to each stage of the budget cycle (preparation, adoption, implementation, and audit), and periodic special preelection and long-term fiscal reports. The second part identifies specific disclosures that should accompany the budget reports, including information about economic assumptions, tax expenditures, financial and nonfinancial assets and liabilities, employee pension obligations, and contingent liabilities. The third section specifies practices to ensure "integrity, control and accountability": disclosure of accounting policies, maintenance of adequate internal control systems, the conduct of annual audits, and affirmative efforts to facilitate legislative scrutiny and citizens' "understanding of the budget process" (OECD 2002, 14). The OECD practices taken as a whole are consistent with the other specifications cited here but emphasize macro-level fiscal, as opposed to financial or transactional aspects. They make no mention at all of contract- or transaction-level disclosures other than calling for the disclosure of a government's positions in debt-management derivative instruments.

As summarized by Alt, Lassen, and Wehner (2012), the three de facto standards among efforts to compute index measures of (primarily offline and macro-budgetary in focus) fiscal transparency are the national-level Open Budget Index (OBI) (de Renzio and Masud 2011; International Budget Partnership 2009), a national-level index measure based on the IMF's *Reports on the Observance of Standards and Codes,* and the Alt-Lassen index, which has been used at the national level (Alt and Lassen 2006) as well as at the level of U.S. states (Alt, Lassen, and Skilling 2002; Alt, Lassen, and Rose 2006). These indexes reflect generally the same normative presumptions as the IMF *Code* and the OECD *Best Practices*, and they focus on the availability and quality of fiscal documents and information, including some that are designed to be usable by nonspecialist audiences such as legislators and citizens. Bivariate correlations among the three indexes are high, indicating that they are "broadly similar" (Alt, Lassen, and Wehner 2012, 17).

The IMF has assessed the fiscal transparency of more than 90 national governments from 1999 to date, through its Reports on the Observance of Standards and Codes program.

Although the IMF does not compute a summary index measure, other researchers have done so. Significant weaknesses in the underlying data include that the IMF assessments can be performed and published only with the consent of the subject governments, that they rely on data supplied by the subject governments, and that they have not been conducted at the same time for each government. This raises challenges of selection bias, censorship, and noncomparability of data (Wehner and de Renzio 2013).

The Alt-Lassen index has been computed in several variants, for the OECD countries based on responses to a 1999 survey and for the U.S. states in several years using secondary data (Alt and Lassen 2003, 2006; Alt, Lassen, and Rose 2006; Lassen 2010). It is a simple additive index based on 9 to 11 questions that reflect the same normative focus on macro-level fiscal openness as the IMF and OECD standards. The index items are dichotomous. For the most recent version of the Alt-Lassen OECD index (Lassen 2010), they focus on disclosure of fiscally relevant information not traditionally included in adopted budgets, such as contingent liabilities, actuarial projections, long term forecasts, nonfinancial performance measures, and the like (6 points); whether relevant economic assumptions are subject to independent review (1 point); whether financial statements are presented on an accrual basis (1 point); and legal requirements to present justificatory information including *ex post* budget-actual comparisons, projections, and sensitivity analysis (3 points).

A recent version of the Alt-Lassen index for the U.S. states is "based on similar principles" (Alt, Lassen, and Rose 2006, 37) but includes a somewhat different set of nine dichotomous measures that are then normalized as a proportion of the total. One point accrues for each of the following:

1. The budget is reported on a GAAP basis.
2. Multiyear expenditure forecasts are prepared.
3. The budget cycle is annual rather than biennial.
4. Revenue forecasts are binding.
5. The legislature has or shares responsibility for the revenue forecast.
6. All appropriations are included in a single bill.
7. A nonpartisan staff writes appropriations bills.
8. The legislature may not pass open-ended appropriations.
9. The budget requires published performance measures.

The OBI is based on the biennial Open Budget Survey, an effort organized by the International Budget Partnership (IBP), which includes civil society organizations, researchers, and a careful process of peer review and validation (International Budget Partnership 2013; Wehner and de Renzio 2013). The first survey was conducted in 2006 and the most recent in 2012. The survey and index have been revised slightly over time, to reflect lessons learned from implementation, but the IBP and its partners are careful to document those changes and work to maintain year-to-year comparability. Eventually, this should facilitate the construction of a panel data set. Importantly, the Open Budget Survey is answered by researchers not affiliated with the governments being assessed does not require those governments' consent in any way. The survey and index computation are subject to peer review, with editorial decisions publicly explained, and cannot be censored by government officials (Wehner and de Renzio 2013).

The survey's 125 questions are explicitly based on sources that include the IMF and OECD standards for fiscal transparency. The OBI is scored from 0 to 100, based on the answers to 95 questions that focus on the "public availability . . . timeliness and comprehensiveness" of the information in eight "key budget documents" generated throughout the budget cycle, from a prebudget statement to a final audit report (International Budget Partnership 2013). The survey also includes 30 other questions that are not used in calculating the index, most of them focusing on public engagement in the budget process, the strength of the legislature in the budget process, and the strength of the supreme audit institution. Of the 125 questions, none focuses on transaction-level detail. This is consistent with the macro-level, fiscal focus of the IMF and OECD standards. The survey and index are not explicitly concerned with the use of ICT. The words "online" or "Web" appear nowhere in the survey questionnaire. "Internet" appears once, in a question that asks how many different media are used to disseminate a citizens' budget and identifies the Internet as one of the qualifying means of distribution.

Reviewing these state-of-the-art efforts, it is difficult to dismiss completely Heald's (2012) pessimism about the feasibility of devising universally applicable index measures of fiscal transparency. Each of the indexes clearly reflects careful thinking, grounded in the same general body of widely accepted standards of good fiscal practice. Yet even the variants of a single index differ materially from each other in their construction. And anecdotal observations suggest that the reported measures indicate materially greater levels of "transparency" in at least two cases—Delaware as measured by Alt, Lassen, and Rose (2006), and the United Kingdom as measured by the OBI—than is consistent with the judgment of specialists familiar with those cases. Further, all of the indexes are focused primarily on institutional practices and the publication of documents that are unquestionably valuable to experts but not necessarily particularly interesting or intelligible to average citizens or legislators. And except for the single item in the OBI survey, the means of dissemination are not addressed in detail.

Online fiscal transparency then might involve simply using the Web for *distribution* of information—making transparency-related information and resources available online as an additional means of dissemination for documents and transcripts or audio and video of announcements, hearings and meetings; educational materials; and opportunities to question, challenge, or exchange views with officials. Online dissemination in these cases will not transform the information or users' relationships to that information but can make it more widely and inexpensively available. Online transparency might also involve *adding value* through innovative *transformation* of fiscal-transparency information and institutions by taking fuller advantage of ICT to provide content, formats, and tools not available through offline means. Types of online transparency devices already implemented by at least a few governments and intermediaries include games and simulations (e.g., Next 10 2014); interactive presentations, visualizations, and queries (e.g., New York City Comptroller's Office 2014); calculators and tools to compare information across time or jurisdictions (e.g., Radford University 2005), and the publication of detailed data in machine-readable form to facilitate analysis by citizens and intermediaries (e.g., State of Massachusetts 2012).

E-Fiscal Transparency Measurement Attempts to Date

Here, we focus specifically on efforts to construct and compute summary measures of fiscal transparency. These summary measures of e-fiscal transparency include several indexes and a few dichotomous indicators, and they fall broadly into two categories. The first category encompasses measures of budget or financial data presentation as an indicator item or subindex in a larger measure of e-government implementation. A second category comprises measurement efforts focused specifically on the use of ICT to advance one or more dimensions of fiscal transparency. To date, it is possible to discern two groups of measures within the second category. Researchers developed a first generation of relatively basic indicator and index measures, and applied them to government websites as they existed roughly from 2000 to 2004. A second generation of efforts has developed more elaborate and nuanced index measures, perhaps reflecting rapid developments in the scope and sophistication of government websites over the past decade as well as cumulative advances in conceptualizations of e-fiscal transparency. This time period roughly coincides with the transition from Web 1.0 to Web 2.0 in e-government circles, so it represents a transition with multiple points of reference.

Transparency Indicators within More General E-Government Studies

The Rutgers State by State E-Government Study. This study provides a comprehensive examination of state level e-government websites (Holzer et al. 2009). The research rates the states in terms of overall e-government performance. The study also offers a set of subindexes rating individual states on various aspects of the electronic government effort. One of the subindexes deals with content but does not discuss extensively what content is offered, especially in the area of fiscal transparency. Item 46 is budget information, which covers very little of what we are presently dealing with. This study uses methodology that is similar to West's (2005) ongoing studies of e-government performance.

Brown University State E-Government Studies. This series of studies, conducted under the direction of political scientist Darrell West (2000, 2001, 2005) compares state e-government websites on a number of dimensions. Like the previously mentioned study, the methodology uses direct examination of websites by trained evaluators. The study was conducted several times in the period 2000–2007. Again, it evaluates content but not necessarily the content of interest for our work.

United Nations E-Government Studies. The United Nations conducts e-government studies, largely at the comparative national level. These use a survey to collect the data. In 2010, as a response to the worldwide economic crisis and the subsequent pressure on government spending, the studies included items on transparency in government spending and other areas. This was primarily in reaction to the development of special or crisis sites by governments under pressure. They concluded:

> Citizens can recognize transparency—and the lack thereof—when they see it, and providing the public with more and better information on decisions taken and the reasons for them is a major need to be addressed by governments. At least for the moment, many appear to be responding. Some 83 percent of crisis-response websites studied have as a common denominator the use of ICT to increase transparency. (UN 2010, 10)

Unfortunately the resulting data are only for the national level, but they do speak to the rising importance of this type of information. It does suggest that there is increasing interest in including transparency data as a critical component in e-government research.

Organisation for Economic Co-operation and Development (OECD). The E-Government Project of the OECD also conducts a survey of national e-government. Again, owing to the economic and political situations, the organization launched an examination of fiscal transparency. The results were summarized as follows:

> Open, transparent and participative government in the sense of providing free access to (non-sensitive) government information and data collected and managed by government organisations as part of their administrative activities has become a priority for many OECD governments in parallel to chasing efficiency and effectiveness gains. (OECD E-Government Project 2010, 7)

This, again, is useful data only at the national comparative level, but the data do suggest that transparency is an important consideration in e-government research.

Specifically Fiscal E-Transparency Measures

First Generation. The first generation of efforts to measure e-fiscal transparency independent of broader e-government assessments included nominal measures and simple additive indexes. One of the earliest of these (Laswad, Oyelere, and Fisher 2001; Laswad, Fisher, and Oyelere 2005) used a simple dichotomous measure of whether or not New Zealand local authorities with websites reported any financial information at all on those websites. Given that the date of data collection appears to have been around 2000, this was probably about all that small local governments could have been expected to do in practical terms. Groff and Pittman (2004) examined the websites of the 100 largest U.S. cities and assessed whether each site made available any or all of the city's budget, budget summary, comprehensive annual financial report (CAFR), or a CAFR summary including a popular annual financial report (PAFR); and how many pages away from the city's homepage that information was located. Groff and Pittman noted that very few cities published citizen-targeting PAFRs, as opposed to specialist-oriented CAFRs, and that CAFRS were often provided in large—and therefore slow to download, particularly over then-common dial-up connections—and non-searchable files.

Justice, Melitski, and Smith (2006) computed a simple 10-point additive index of online fiscal transparency for a sample of GFOA award-winning U.S. state and local governments based on observations from mid-2004. The index summed 10 dichotomously scored items assessing whether a website included content and features in each of 10 categories: (1) the most recent CAFR; (2) a PAFR; (3) the current budget; (4) a summary of the current budget; (5) any historical data on the jurisdiction's finances; (6) any supplemental financial analyses; (7) the capital budget; (8) material meant to help render the technical information meaningful to nonspecialists, including games, models, or simulations; (9) invitations to participate in budgetary decision making; and (10) contact information for official participants in the budget process. The eighth item in the index in a few cases captured interactive explanatory devices that exploited the distinctive properties of online, as opposed to traditional oral or written, formats for information and communication. The other items primarily evaluated simply whether the Internet was used as an additional means for disseminating information and soliciting citizen input to supplement traditional broadcast, telephone, in-person, and paper-based media for communicating budget and financial information.

Styles and Tennyson (2007) calculated two measures of e-fiscal transparency for each of the 300 largest U.S. cities, perhaps in 2004. Availability of the city's CAFR on its website was measured dichotomously. Accessibility was measured, for those cities making their CAFRs available, by a 10-point, 10-item index. The index included four categories of items, assessing (1) four items evaluating the ease of finding the website and the CAFR within it, (2) three items evaluating the user-friendliness of the CAFR's file size and file format, (3) whether financial data for previous years was also provided, and (4) two other items. Yu (2010) adapted these measures for a study of local governments in China. In another study of the determinants of voluntary government disclosure, Serrano-Cinca, Rueda-Tomás, and Portillo-Tarragona (2009) used a dichotomous measure of whether or not any of five budgetary and four financial-reporting documents was available on a local government's website.

Second Generation. A second generation of indexes includes three developed by researchers examining Spanish local governments. These measures demonstrate more nuanced index construction. They also imply higher standards for the quantity of information provided and capture more of the qualitative dimensions of e-fiscal transparency, possibly reflecting the contemporary ubiquity of government websites and heightened expectations for e-government. While these measures emphasize financial reporting, they also capture to some degree elements of the budgetary dimension of fiscal transparency. They also emphasize the importance of government-stakeholder interaction and what Heald (2012) terms "outwards" transparency: the communication of fiscal information and preferences *to* officials, from citizens and other external stakeholders.

García and García-García (2010) constructed a "reporting index" as the sum of 28 dichotomously scored items that were weighted to allow a maximum potential score of 24.25 points. The items were in three categories: (1) website financial information content—18 items, up to 16.25 points; (2) the number of file formats offered—six formats, up to four points; and (3) items promoting stakeholder-government interaction—4 items, up to 4 points. Pérez, Rodríquez Bolivar and López Hernández (2008) devised an additive "disclosure index" with a maximum score of 18 points comprising 34 items in three equally weighted evaluative categories: (1) "content" or document availability—14 items; (2) quality and usability "characteristics"—10 items; and (3) website "navigability, design and access"—10 items, including items measuring file formats and the provision of interaction-supporting features.

The most complex index computation in this second generation to date appears to be one that generated an overall index from 88 dichotomous items in five subindexes (Gandía and Archidona 2008). The subindexes measure (1) provision of general information—14 items; (2) provision of budgetary information—22 items; (3) provision of financial information—16 items; (4) presentation and navigation—25 items; and (5) "relational Web presence" or interaction-promoting features—11 items. Each subindex is normalized so that potential scores range from 0 to 10, as is the overall index, and the index computation weights each of the 88 items equally in the overall index as well as in the subindexes.

Transparency 2.0. A pioneering effort to evaluate and rank recipient- and transaction-level financial disclosure by U.S. state governments is the U.S. Public Interest Research Group's scorecard measure of "Transparency 2.0" (Baxandall and Wohlschlegel 2010; Davis, Baxandall, and Musto 2011; Davis, Baxandall, and Pierannunzi 2012), and a related measure calculated for large U.S. cities (Davis, Baxandall, and Pierannunzi 2013). Focusing primarily on the expenditure-monitoring dimension of fiscal transparency, but also incorporating some aspects of *ex ante* budgetary transparency, PIRG identified three defining aspects of "Transparency 2.0," a "Web-based spending transparency" that makes effective use of contemporary ICT tools to provide (Baxandall and Wohlschlegel 2010, 8) three defining features:

- a user-friendly Web transparency portal that allows visitors to "search detailed information about government contracts, spending, subsidies [including tax expenditures as well as direct payments], and grants for all governmental entities" including government corporations;
- availability of all expenditure information from a single website—a "one-stop" approach; and
- making searches and data manipulation easy and intuitive for non-specialists, ideally with one or a few simple mouse clicks.

This is contrasted with more traditional "Transparency 1.0," which requires seekers of information to be persistent, patient, and sophisticated enough to know precisely what they are looking for and to navigate the physical (in the case of non-Internet data),

Table 2.1

U.S. PIRG Transparency 2.0 State Scorecard Components (by points)

Scorecard component	2010	2011	2012	Notes
Checkbook-level payment information is provided on a dedicated website (2010) and/or via a linked website (2011 and 2012)	40	35	30	Dichotomous scoring[a]
Searchable by contractor or vendor name	10	10	8	Dichotomous scoring
Searchable by type of product or service	10	10		Dichotomous scoring
Searchable by keyword			8	Dichotomous scoring
Searchable by agency or department			8	Dichotomous scoring
Contract or contract summary available	10	10	10	Scores of 3, 5, 8, or 10 points possible, in various years
Data can be downloaded for further analysis		2	3	Dichotomous scoring in 2011, partial credit in 2012
Previous-year data availability	5	5		Score 3 for 1 year, 5 for multiple years
"Historical expenditures"			5	Score 1 for each prior fiscal year
Information on tax expenditures	10	10	10	Score from 0 to 10 based on ease of access, provision of historical data, explanatory information, and number of tax bases included
Information on economic development grants and incentives	10	10	10	Score from 0 to 10 based on quantity of information and explanation provided
Provision for two-way communication		2	2	Score 1 for contact information, 2 if feedback is invited
Inclusion of quasi-public entities	2	2	2	Dichotomous scoring
Inclusion of link to state ARRA[b] reporting	2	2	2	Dichotomous scoring
Inclusion of local governments' financial data	1	2	2	Dichotomous scoring
Total points	100	100	100	
Subtotals				
Direct vendor payments disclosure	75	72	72	
Other forms of benefit and beneficiary	20	20	20	
Other information	5	8	8	

Notes:
[a]All or no points.
[b]ARRA = American Recovery and Reinvestment Act of 2009.

administrative, and methodological challenges of acquiring, organizing, and making use of data (Davis, Baxandall, and Pierannunzi 2012, 3; 2013, 5).

Beginning in 2010, PIRG has produced three annual reports of its 100-point scorecard measure of Transparency 2.0 for state governments. Although there are enough small changes from year to year in the scoring and index computation to make the assembly of a panel data set challenging, the general approach is the same in every year and reflects the purpose stated by the subtitle, "How the 50 States Rate in Providing Online Access to Government Spending Data." Table 2.1 summarizes the scoring and weighting system used in the three reports to date. The scorecard is heavily weighted toward the provision of detailed, searchable, and analyzable information on individual vendors, contracts, and payments. These elements of disbursement disclosure represent 72 to 75 points out of 100. The identification of other forms of benefit and beneficiary—tax expenditures and individual economic development incentives and grants—makes up 20 points. Other components, representing 5 to 8 points in total, include the provision of information on American Recovery and Reinvestment Act activity, quasi-public entities, and local governments, as well as provisions for two-way communication.

The most recent PIRG project computed a different measure of Transparency 2.0 based on the websites of the 30 largest U.S. cities (Davis, Baxandall, and Pierannunzi 2013). This measure uses broadly the same individual components as the state scorecards but is weighted and detailed in such a way as to capture a broader or more balanced model of fiscal transparency. In contrast to the state scorecard's emphasis on detailed disbursement disclosure, the 12-item cities scorecard assigns roughly equal weights to checkbook-type disclosures, on- and off-budget allocation choices, and (two-way) financial and performance reporting. Checkbook-type disclosures and tools account for 34 of 100 points (5 items); the current budget, 25, and tax expenditures, 10; the current CAFR, 10, and historical budgets and CAFRs, 16 (3 items in all); maintenance of an interactive "service request" portal, 8; and linking most or all of the information to a central transparency website, 7 points.

SYNTHESIS AND LESSONS LEARNED

Synthesizing the conceptual, normative, and empirical literatures reviewed here suggests a tentative approach to delineating major dimensions of the e-fiscal transparency construct, as portrayed in Table 2.2. One of two overarching dimensions encompasses the subject matter of fiscal transparency, for which we have identified in the literature four categories or subdimensions. The subject matter of fiscal transparency includes macro-level budgetary information such as budgets, budget summaries, forecasts, and the like; financial reporting information such as comprehensive and popular annual financial reports and midyear reports; micro-level financial disclosures, including contracts and payments information; and performance information. The evaluative dimension includes assessments of the quantity of data, information, and documentation provided, and of the quality of that information. Quality here encompasses the fundamental characteristics sought in offline as well as online transparency—accuracy, relevance, comprehensiveness, timeliness, and frequency of reporting—as well as several subdimensions specific to the online context. Two further dimensions, implied but not shown in Table 2.2, have to do with audience (e.g., legislators, citizens, creditors) and purpose (e.g., prediction, evaluation, behavioral scrutiny). As the literature reveals, different audiences will have different information content and format needs, at different times, for different purposes.

This is, of course, quite a bit to bite off, and it will likely take significant effort to chew and digest in practice. Although the second generation of measures includes major advances empirically, none of them can really be said to measure fiscal transparency

Table 2.2

Dimensions of Fiscal E-Transparency: Synthesis of the Literature and Checklist for Transparency Design and Evaluation

	Content dimensions			
Evaluative dimensions	Macro-level budgetary transparency	Financial reporting transparency	Micro-level financial disclosure	Performance information transparency
1. Quantity of relevant information				
a. Documents				
b. Data				
2. Quality[a]				
a. Accuracy				
b. Comprehensiveness				
c. Timeliness				
d. Frequency				
e. Ease of access and navigation				
f. Design and presentation				
g. Analysis tools				
Relevance				
Usability				
h. Machine readability of data				
i. Adequacy of metadata				
j. Interactivity and "relational" characteristics				
Online				
Offline				

Note: [a]Measurement of quality is likely to be significantly audience and purpose dependent, as is the matter of how to weight individual topic and evaluation dimensions and subdimensions. Thus, another element in evaluation is to be clear about whether the measurement is intended to be comprehensive or focused on one or more particular topic dimensions and/or specific audiences.

in toto, if our concern is with effective transparency at the user level. A fully comprehensive measurement or system of e-fiscal transparency would likely require many more items and elements than even the Gandía and Archidona (2008) overall e-disclosure index. Still, some of the second-generation academic index measures and the PIRG cities scorecard in particular appear on their faces to capture well the key aspects of whether and how well governments make available key documents and data in usable form. They can therefore be very useful in effect as menus of design choices for implementing e-fiscal transparency.

Further, the audience- and purpose-contingent nature of transparency, which frustrates efforts to devise one best way of being transparent or of measuring transparency, might actually be an advantage in many ways. It is likely to be more feasible to create valid tools and measures of e-fiscal transparency that are specific to particular domains of activity and/or specific audiences and purposes and that meet standard criteria for construct validity. For example, refinements to the 2010–2012 PIRG state scorecards and the underlying state checkbook sites and Web portals might focus the PIRG measure more precisely on what appears to be their primary role or initial inspiration: maximizing the quantity, comprehensiveness, and analyzability by nonspecialists of micro-level financial disclosures and making it straightforward for citizens to act on what they find. Alternatively, checkbook and portal designers and researchers might choose to use only the elements of the PIRG scorecard that focus on individual disbursement disclosure.

There is no question that measuring fiscal transparency in a valid and reliable fashion is worth the effort involved. In terms of practical politics, efforts such as PIRG's can potentially serve as stimulants for citizens to demand and public officials to supply more and better fiscal information. For practitioners, good measurement of the quality and quantity of transparency resulting from their efforts to provide public information makes continuous improvement possible. It also increases the likelihood that high-quality transparency work will gain the recognition it deserves. For researchers, valid and reliable measurement can provide a valuable source of data for research into the quality of governance. As Wehner and de Renzio (2013, 105) observe, "Fiscal transparency is a widely accepted feature of well-run governments, and we can assess its relative presence or absence more objectively than is possible with more abstract catchall notions of 'good governance.'" Repeated measurement, if measures are comparable over time, can generate panel data that will facilitate analysis of the causes and effects of this measure of good governance (e.g., Alt, Lassen, and Rose 2006).

In spite of their limitations, the PIRG measure and the other second-generation standalone indexes of e-fiscal transparency represent significant advances and are important complements to many previous measures. In particular, they capture key dimensions of fiscal transparency—particularly e-transparency and transaction-level transparency—that many other contemporary and previous measures miss. This indicates ongoing progress in developing measures to capture better more aspects of fiscal transparency and e-transparency, in the service of creating scholarly as well as practical and political knowledge.

For practitioners, we think there are three fundamental lessons to be drawn from the efforts of academic as well as advocacy-oriented researchers to define and measure fiscal and e-fiscal transparency (these lessons are also elaborated into our list of seven key points):

- First, the framework this chapter derives from those measurement efforts can serve as a way to structure one's thinking about what aspects of e-fiscal transparency are of the most immediate concern, in order to support the design of goal- and audience-appropriate efforts to implement as well as measure effective e-fiscal transparency.
- Second, the many existing index measures can be seen as toolboxes in which practitioners and researchers can look for the selection of transparency-measurement and transparency-enhancement tools most appropriate for measuring or accomplishing a particular fiscal-transparency task.

- Finally, practitioners as well as researchers should be alert to new opportunities and new developments, as both the practice and the measurement of e-fiscal transparency are rapidly evolving as new tools and technologies are developed.

It is also worth noting a caution: more transparency may not always be better, and greater online disclosure of data might in some instances endanger as well as engender trust in government. A great deal of government and personal information is freely available online. Many people are unaware of how much of their personal life is already readily available to anyone. A recent example is instructive. In the wake of the Newtown Elementary School shootings in Connecticut, a local newspaper plotted gun ownership (Worley 2012) on a Google map, sparking a loud outcry from the gun-owning community (Haughney 2013). This is information that was readily available from public sources (although one county declined the request). Fear of giving information to the government is often palpable.

This dovetails with survey findings about trust and fear of government in general. A very recent study from the Pew Research Center (2013) underscores this point:

> The current survey finds only about quarter (26%) saying they can trust the government always or most of the time, while nearly three-quarters (73%) say that they can trust government only some of the time, or volunteer than they can never trust the government.

While it seems likely that transparency can improve trust in government, it also seems that it can be problematic. MacManus, Caruson, and McPhee (2012), for example, discuss the tense relationship between security, privacy, and transparency in an online environment. While there are always drawbacks and concerns to any innovation, there are many reasons to move ahead. On balance, policymakers will need to carefully negotiate these often dangerous waters in creating new programs.

As we move forward in this exciting policy arena, measurement of results is a key component. In many ways, how we choose to measure an effort defines how that effort will be developed. Like most emerging fields, there is a rich variety of approaches vying for acceptance. The way ahead requires that scholars and practitioners narrow the field and agree on a smaller set of measures where possible. This will facilitate program development and research.

KEY POINTS

1. Know what you mean by fiscal transparency

"Fiscal transparency" encompasses the provision of decision-supporting information about any and all of (1) current budgets and plans for future resource allocations; (2) financial position and results of financial operations (i.e., financial reporting); (3) detailed disclosure of contracts, purchases, and payments (e.g., online checkbooks); and (4) organizational performance.

2. More disclosure is not necessarily better transparency

The quality of fiscal transparency is at least as important as its quantity. Quality has a number of subdimensions but can broadly be understood as a function of the accuracy, sufficiency, and usability for decision-making purposes by public officials, citizens, creditors, and other stakeholders of information disclosure and presentation.

3. Different stakeholders need different information

Different users of information will have different decisional interests and different abilities to make use of information. For many purposes and audiences, better quality of transparency may require limiting the quantity of data provided for initial queries. Balancing parsimony with completeness will usually require making purpose- and audience-specific judgments.

4. Users need help

This includes guidance helping users of all relevant skill levels and substantive concerns to understand the information that is available, what it means, and how to access it. Consider providing access to detailed data as an option for stakeholders who are able to make meaningful use of it rather than as the default view or initial landing page. One contemporary "smart practice" (see Bardach 2012, 109–123) is to establish online transparency portals that link to a variety of presentations of financial and performance information. However, this can be obfuscatory rather than helpful if not accompanied by adequate user guidance, search tools, and metadata. Providing effective instructional materials and the option to get live help will improve usability and satisfaction. Consider working with interested nonpartisan advocacy organizations who can contribute instructional and analytic resources, such as citizen research organizations (for one list of such organizations in the United States, see the website of the Governmental Research Association, at http://www.graonline.org).

5. Technology is not magic

Information and communications technology can enhance the economy, efficiency, and effectiveness of fiscal transparency efforts compared to paper formats, but it is not a panacea. In fact, ICT makes fiscal-transparency design and implementation more challenging, in that it requires making additional design judgments and managing the technological complexities of making the transparency software itself "transparent" to the user (in this context, transparent means that the software becomes largely invisible itself, so that the user is able to focus on the substantive information and decisional tasks of concern rather than on the process of manipulating the technology required to acquire the information).

6. Stand on the shoulders of giants (and ordinary mortals)

The contemporary explosion of interest in technology-enhanced fiscal transparency means that there are many examples of effective as well as ineffective practices available online, and many indexes and other measures of the quality of fiscal transparency. Review existing transparency efforts and evaluations to identify the specific practices and presentation that might be smart for your jurisdiction, stakeholders, and decisional needs.

7. Your needs *are* unique

Details matter, and there is no perfect model of "best" practice that will work for every organization, purpose, and audience. Treat each implementation as an experiment. Design e-fiscal transparency efforts in ways that take account of individual circumstances, needs, and stakeholders. Incorporate into the design ways to obtain user feedback and systematically measure the performance of your transparency techniques. Use expert and stakeholder feedback and criteria to make improvements.

NOTE

1. In terms of transactional disclosure, the IMF benchmarks do include a stipulation that "[c]ontractual arrangements . . . should be clear and publicly accessible" (1.2.4) and that "major transactions" for the "[p]urchase and sale of public assets . . . should be separately identified" (4.2.4).

REFERENCES

Alt, J.E., and D.D. Lassen. 2003. The political economy of institutions and corruption in American states. *Journal of Theoretical Politics* 15 (3), 341–365.

———. 2006. Transparency, political polarization, and political budget cycles in OECD countries. *American Journal of Political Science* 50 (3), 530–550.

Alt, J.E., D.D. Lassen, and S. Rose. 2006. The causes of fiscal transparency: Evidence from the U.S. states. *IMF Staff Papers*, 53, 30–57.

Alt, J.E., D.D. Lassen, and D. Skilling. 2002. Fiscal transparency, gubernatorial approval, and the scale of government: Evidence from the states. *State Politics and Policy Quarterly* 2 (3), 230–250.

Alt, J.E., D.D. Lassen, and J. Wehner. 2012. Moral hazard in an economic union: Politics, economics, and fiscal gimmickry in Europe. Social Science Research Network, July 9. http://papers.ssrn.com/sol3/Delivery.cfm/SSRN_ID2172822_code90796.pdf?abstractid=2102334&mirid=1.

Association of Government Accountants. 2013. *Citizen-centric reporting*. Association of Government Accountants, December 20. www.agacgfm.org/home.aspx.

Bardach, Eugene. 2012. *A practical guide for policy analysis: The eightfold path to more effective problem solving*. 4th ed. Washington, DC: CQ Press.

Baxandall, P., and K. Wohlschlegel. 2010. *Following the money: How the 50 states rate in providing online access to government spending data*. U.S. PIRG, April 13. www.uspirg.org/reports/usp/following-money.

Boydston, R., and W. Aaron. 2004. The citizen's guide to the Nashville budget: Providing better information in better ways. *Government Finance Review* (February), 12–16.

Carpenter, F.H., and F.C. Sharp. 1992. *Popular reporting: Local government financial reports to the citizenry*. Stamford, CT: Governmental Accounting Standards Board.

Cheng, R.H. 1994. A politico-economic model of government accounting policy choice. In *Research in governmental and nonprofit accounting,* ed. James L. Chan, 39–68. Greenwich, CT: JAI Press.

City of Los Angeles, CA. 2013. Annual expenses by departments (graph). https://losangeles.opengov.com/transparency.

Davis, B., P. Baxandall, and J. Musto. 2011. *Following the money 2011: How the 50 states rate in providing online access to government spending data.* U.S. PIRG Education Fund, March. www.uspirg.org/reports/usp/following-money-2011.

Davis, B., P. Baxandall, and R. Pierannunzi. 2012. *Following the money 2012: How the 50 states rate in providing online access to government spending data.* U.S. PIRG Education Fund, March. http://PIRG.org/reports/usp/following-money-2012.

———. 2013. *Transparency in city spending: Rating the availability of online government data in America's largest cities.* Washington, DC: U.S. PIRG Education Fund.

de Renzio, P., and H. Masud. 2011. Measuring and promoting budget transparency: The Open Budget Index as a research and advocacy tool. *Governance* 24 (3), 607–616.

Gandía, J.L., and M.C. Archidona. 2008. Determinants of web site information by Spanish city councils. *Online Information Review* 32 (2), 35–57.

García, Ana Cárcaba, and Jesús García-García. 2010. Determinants of online reporting of accounting information by Spanish local government authorities. *Local Government Studies* 36 (5), 679–695.

Gilmour, John B. 2012. The Indiana Toll Road lease as an intergenerational cash transfer. *Public Administration Review* 72 (6), 856-864. doi: 10.1111/j.1540-6210.2012.02589.x

Government Finance Officers Association. 2003. *Using websites to improve access to budget documents and financial reports.* Government Finance Officers Association. http://gfoa.org/services/rp/caafr/caafr-budgets-to-websites.pdf.

———. 2009. *Best practice: Website presentation of official financial documents.* Government Finance Officers Association. www.gfoa.org/downloads/websitepresentation.pdf.

———. 2010. *Best practice: Using a website for disclosure.* Government Finance Officers Association, October 15, 2010. www.gfoa.org/downloads/debt-using-web.pdf.

Governmental Accounting Standards Board. 2003. *Reporting performance information: Suggested criteria for effective communication.* Norwalk, CT: Governmental Accounting Standards Board.

Groff, James E., and Marshall K. Pitman. 2004. Municipal financial reporting on the World Wide Web: A survey of financial data displayed on the official websites of the 100 largest U.S. municipalities. *Journal of Government Financial Management* 53 (2), 20–30.

Groves, S.M., W.M. Godsey, and M.A. Shulman. 1981. Financial indicators for local government. *Public Budgeting and Finance* 1 (2), 5–19.

Halbfinger, David M. 2013. New site makes it easier to view city spending. *New York Times*, January 22.

Haughney, Christine. 2013. After pinpointing gun owners, paper is a target. *New York Times,* January 6. www.nytimes.com/2013/01/07/nyregion/after-pinpointing-gun-owners-journal-news-is-a-target.html?pagewanted=all.

Heald, David. 2003. Fiscal transparency: Concepts, measurement and UK practice. *Public Administration* 81 (4), 723–759.

———. 2006. Varieties of transparency. In *Transparency: the key to better government?* ed. Christopher Hood and David Heald, 25–43. Oxford: Oxford University Press.

———. 2012. "Why is transparency about public expenditure so elusive?" *International Review of Administrative Sciences* 78 (1), 30–49.

Held, David. 2006. *Models of democracy.* 3d ed. Palo Alto, CA: Stanford University Press.

Holzer, M., A. Manoharan, R. Shick, and G. Stowers. 2009. *U.S. states e-governance report (2008): An assessment of state websites.* Newark, NJ: E-Governance Institute, Rutgers University, Campus at Newark.

Ingram, R.W. 1984. Economic incentives and the choice of state government accounting practices. *Journal of Accounting Research* 22 (1), 126–144.

International Budget Partnership. 2009. *Open budget initiative*. www.openbudgetindex.org.
———. 2010. *Open budget survey.* International Budget Partnership. http://internationalbudget.org/what-we-do/open-budget-survey/.
———. 2013. *Open budget survey methodology.* International Budget Partnership. http://internationalbudget.org/what-we-do/open-budget-survey/research-resources/methodology/.
International Monetary Fund (IMF). Fiscal Affairs Dept. 2007. *Code of good practices on fiscal transparency.* www.imf.org/external/np/pp/2007/eng/051507c.pdf.
Justice, J.B., and C. Dülger. 2009. Fiscal transparency and authentic citizen participation in public budgeting: The role of third-party intermediation. *Journal of Public Budgeting, Accounting and Financial Management* 21 (2), 254–288.
Justice, J.B., J. Melitski, and D.L. Smith. 2006. E-government as an instrument of fiscal accountability and responsiveness: Do the best practitioners employ the best practices? *American Review of Public Administration* 36 (3), 301–322.
Justice, J.B., and F. Tarimo. 2012. NGOs holding governments accountable: Civil-society budget work. *Public Finance and Management* 21 (3), 204–236.
Kahn, Jonathan. 1993. Re-presenting government and representing the people: Budget reform and citizenship in New York City, 1908–1911. *Journal of Urban History* 19 (3), 84–103.
Kopits, George, and Jon Craig. 1998. *Transparency in government operations.* Occasional Paper No. 158, January. Washington, DC: International Monetary Fund. www.imf.org/external/pubs/ft/op/158/op158.pdf.
Lassen, David D. 2010. *Fiscal consolidations in advanced industrialized democracies: Economics, politics, and governance.* Stockholm: Finanspolitiska rådet.
Laswad, Fawzi, Richard Fisher, and Peter Oyelere. 2005. Determinants of voluntary Internet financial reporting by local government authorities. *Journal of Accounting and Public Policy* 24 (2), 101–121.
Laswad, Fawzi, Peter B. Oyelere, and Richard Fisher. 2001. Local authorities and financial reporting on the Internet. *Chartered Accountants Journal of New Zealand* (March), 58–60.
Lathrop, Daniel, and Laurel Ruma, ed. 2010. *Open government: Collaboration, transparency, and participation in practice.* Sevastopol, CA: O'Reilly.
MacManus, Susan, Kiki Caruson, and Brian D. McPhee. 2012. Cybersecurity at the local government level: Balancing demands for transparency and privacy rights. *Journal of Urban Affairs* 35 (4), 451–470.
New York City Comptroller's Office. 2014. Checkbook NYC 2.0. www.checkbooknyc.com/spending_landing/yeartype/B/year/115.
New York Times. 2010. Budget puzzle: You fix the budget. *New York Times*, November 13. www.nytimes.com/interactive/2010/11/13/weekinreview/deficits-graphic.html?_r=0.
Next 10. 2014. What are your priorities for California's budget? www.budgetchallenge.org/pages/home.
Organisation for Economic Co-operation and Development (OECD). 2002. OECD best practices for budget transparency. *OECD Journal on Budgeting* 1 (3), 7–14.
———. 2010. *Towards smarter and more transparent government: E-Government status spring 2010.* Paris: OECD, March 25. www.oecd.org/gov/public-innovation/44934153.pdf.
Pérez, C.C., M.P. Rodríguez Bolivar, and A.M. López Hernández. 2008. E-government process and incentives for online public financial information. *Online Information Review* 32 (3), 379–400.
Pew Research Center. 2013. *Majority says the federal government threatens their personal rights.* Washington, DC: Pew Research Center. www.people-press.org/2013/01/31/majority-says-the-federal-government-threatens-their-personal-rights/.
Prowle, M., D. Harradine, and R. Latham. 2012. Statutory financial accounting in the UK public sector: Relevance and cost? *Journal of Finance and Management in Public Services* 10 (2), 26–39.
Radford University. 2005. Performance measures for Virginia government: A project of Radford University's Governmental and Nonprofit Assistance Center. http://gasb34.asp.radford.edu/perfmeas/.

Robinson, Mark. 2008. Improving transparency and promoting accountability: Civil society budget work in perspective. In *Budgeting for the poor*, ed. Mark Robinson, 1–12. New York: Palgrave Macmillan.

Serrano-Cinca, C., M. Rueda-Tomás, and P. Portillo-Tarragona. 2009. Factors influencing e-disclosure in local public administrations. *Environment and Planning C: Government and Policy* 27 (2), 355–378.

Smith, Kenneth A. 2004. Voluntarily reporting performance measures to the public: A test of accounting reports from U.S. cities. *International Public Management Journal* 7 (1), 19–48.

State of Massachusetts. 2012. Financial data. Massachusetts Open Data Initiative Wiki Space. https://wiki.state.ma.us/confluence/display/data/Financial+Data.

Styles, Alan K., and Mack Tennyson. 2007. The accessibility of financial reporting of U.S. municipalities on the Internet. *Journal of Public Budgeting, Accounting and Financial Management* 19 (1), 56–92.

United Nations. 2010. *United Nations E-Government Survey 2010: Leveraging e-government at a time of financial and economic crisis.* New York: UN Office on Social and Economic Affairs. http://unpan1.un.org/intradoc/groups/public/documents/un-dpadm/unpan038845.pdf.

Wehner, Joachim. 2006. Assessing the power of the purse: An index of legislative budget institutions. *Political Studies* 54 (4), 767–785.

Wehner, Joachim, and Paolo de Renzio. 2013. Citizens, legislators, and executive disclosure: The political determinants of fiscal transparency. *World Development* 41, 96–108.

West, Darrell M. 2000. Assessing e-government: The Internet, democracy and service delivery by state and local government. Brown University, September. www.insidepolitics.org/egovtreport00.html.

———. 2001. E-government and the transformation of public sector service delivery. Presentation at the 2001 Annual Meeting of the American Political Science Association, San Francisco, CA, August 30–September 2.

———. 2005. *Digital government: Technology and public sector performance.* Princeton, NJ: Princeton University Press.

Worley, Dwight R. 2012. The gun owner next door: What you don't know about the weapons in your neighborhood. *Journal News* (New York), December 24. www.lohud.com/article/20121224/NEWS04/312240045/The-gun-owner-next-door-What-you-don-t-know-about-weapons-your-neighborhood.

Yu, He. 2010. On the determinants of Internet-based disclosure of government financial information. Paper read at 2010 International Conference on Management and Service Science (MASS), Wuhan, China, August 24–26.

3

Improving the Effectiveness of E-Reporting in Government with the Concept of Multiple Accountability

Thomas J. Greitens and M. Ernita Joaquin

Online reporting of administrative and programmatic performance information remains a constant theme for public managers across the globe. Better performance, more transparency, and heightened accountability to citizens are often touted as the benefits of this type of performance reporting. Often, public managers use tools such as organizational report cards, online scorecards, and dashboards to achieve this level of online performance reporting. In this chapter, we examine such tools and suggest that a careful examination of the multiple accountability pressures surrounding their implementation is needed to determine their effectiveness in e-reporting.

The public sector now publishes a significant amount of performance data online. Governmental budgets, performance reports, strategic plans, customer satisfaction surveys, and progress on management mandates from policymakers are all now routinely included on e-government websites. Often, this information is quantified on e-government websites with tools such as report cards, scorecards, and dashboards—termed "e-reporting."[1] The often-stated goal of putting such information online and making it a part of the e-government phenomena is to increase transparency and accountability in governmental operations (Justice, Melitski, and Smith 2006; Lee 2004).[2] By increasing transparency and accountability, the hope is that citizens will have additional information at their disposal to help maximize the potential of interactive democracy where citizens use e-government to transform government operations and the society they live in (Fountain 2001; West 2005). Given concerns about the digital divide (Mossberger, Tolbert, and Stansbury 2003), possible negative effects of online information on citizens' attitudes toward government (Grimmelikhuijsen 2010; Putnam 2001), and the propensity of e-government and information technology in general to reinforce existing behaviors rather than transform behaviors (Coleman and Blumler 2009; Hindman 2009), achieving a type of interactive democracy may be too optimistic of an idea. But at the very least, this online performance information provides some basic governmental performance information to citizens who have both the desire and capability to access it. In this way, e-reporting helps to ensure a type of accountability to citizens.

The challenge is that the publishing of online performance information by government lacks any meaningful type of framework or analytical template that governments can follow to determine effectiveness. Previous attempts at frameworks have generally emphasized best practices in terms of displaying performance information or in terms of categorizing performance information in the online environment (Greitens and Roberson 2010; Lee 2004; Schatteman 2010). Such attempts are obviously an important step in ensuring the effectiveness of online performance information. However, such attempts generally do not try to ground their frameworks or best practices in terms of existing theories on accountability, transparency, performance, or citizen engagement. To a certain extent, this makes sense, given the vast diversity of online performance information. Governments are often individualistic in their approach to the collection and publishing of online performance data, because different governments have different rules, mandates, political constraints, information technology systems, and performance concerns.

But this individualistic approach also makes the effective use of online performance information problematic for citizens. For example, observing one type of online performance system in a government, the citizen may expect a similar arrangement in another government. And when that similar arrangement doesn't appear, the citizen may experience disappointment, confusion, or even anger. At best, the citizen could acknowledge that the e-reporting system is for a different government with different types of concerns. At worst, the citizen could speculate that the government is using a different system in an attempt to conceal performance information.

Different online performance systems also prevent effective benchmarking where the citizen can compare similar dimensions of performance across different governments. Admittedly, most citizens are probably not concerned about using e-reporting information in this way. But if e-government is to achieve its promise of governmental and societal transformation (West 2004), then citizens will eventually have to start to use information in this way. The key to such a future is some type of standardization of online performance information that allows citizens to compare one government's performance to another's.

Finally, online performance information is often transitory. As policymakers change, performance mandates on agencies often change. The resulting effect for e-government is that online performance information has been known to disappear as new policymakers implement new policies and performance mandates. For instance, President George W. Bush's Executive Branch Management Scorecard was a type of online performance information that was easily available online during his tenure in office. However, after his tenure ended, this scorecard information transitioned to an archived website and has consequently become just a little harder to find in the online environment.[3] Similarly, the Program Assessment Rating Tool (PART) was another type of online performance information showcased by the Bush administration. Currently, many of its results are still available in the online environment with the entire PART website having been archived at a new URL as of 2013.[4] But, some graphs, performance information, and links to other Web pages have been lost in the archival process, making the archived PART website not exactly the same as the website in use during the years of the Bush administration. The ultimate experience for citizens is confusing. Citizens may view online performance information one day and the next day it is gone, migrated to a different website or, at the very least, inactive.

Perhaps sensing some of these inherent challenges, many governments in the 2010s have started to move from online report cards and scorecards to performance dashboards as a way to more effectively present their performance information. Such a transition is helpful and should make online performance reporting more effective for citizens. However, governments should realize that e-reporting tools are not always optimal. Many times, report cards, scorecards, and dashboards fail in the online environment. We argue in this chapter that such failures can be directly traced back to the inability of governments to analyze the decision to publish online performance data with the concept of multiple dimensions of accountability. Consequently, we provide a basic framework, grounded in the concept of multiple accountabilities that governments may be able to follow when publishing performance data in the online environment. Citizens may also use this basic framework to better understand the online performance information they view and the e-government website they experience.

In the following sections we first examine the different types of online performance reporting, from simplistic agency report cards to performance dashboards. Then we examine the somewhat nebulous concept of accountability in government and distill it into a basic framework used for our analysis. A brief case examination of an online report card and scorecard with the accountability framework follows. In our concluding section, we suggest that e-reporting will dramatically improve if governments consider the concept of multiple accountabilities.

DIFFERENT TYPES OF ONLINE PERFORMANCE REPORTING

In the era of e-government in which we now find ourselves, online performance reporting is important for a variety of reasons. In the interconnected world of the 2010s, citizens especially those in the younger generations, expect such information to be easily available. It also increases the transparency of governmental operations (Welch, Hinnant, and Moon 2005); probably makes governments more democratic (Krueger 2002; Weber, Loumakis, and Bergman 2003); and should help educate citizens to alleviate citizenship deficits, especially among younger generations, among whom the propensity to participate in government is low (Delli Carpini 2000; Latimer and Kendrick 2012; for an explanation of the citizenship deficit, see Nabatchi 2010). All of these reasons suggest that the reporting of online performance information by government has the ability to transform citizens, governmental operations, and society at large. Such reasons confirm the early hype of e-government: that it could eventually transform democracy and governmental operations. Of course, whether online performance reporting, and by extension e-government, can actually achieve such impressive outcomes remains uncertain because of concerns over the digital divide and the uncertain effect of online performance information on citizen perceptions.

To help progress toward this type of e-government, or as some have classified it, e-democracy (Carrizales 2008), online performance reporting has increasingly evolved. In many ways, this evolution has mirrored the change in e-government websites overall from simple advertising vehicles to interactive experiences for citizens, where a multitude of actions are possible. Many scholars have attempted to make sense of this evolution in e-government and develop typologies that could assist in the analysis of governmental websites. For example, seeing it more as an evolution toward e-democracy, Moon (2002) envisioned the evolution in five stages: from basic transactional stages such as (1) disseminating information, (2) enabling two-way communication with citizens, and (3) providing online services and financial transactions, to more transformational stages such as (4) integrating information systems throughout government and (5) enhancing political participating. Viewing it more in terms of website design, the evolution of e-government can also be seen as starting from an initial Web presence that just displays information; to an enhanced Web presence with links and two-way communication such as e-mail; to a limited, interactive portal Web presence with some types of financial transactions available (e.g., paying governmental fines online); to a fully transactional and secure Web presence allowing for all types of transactions; to a full, interactive portal Web experience in which citizens can access multigovernmental responses and records (Garson 2006; Ho 2002; United Nations and American Society for Public Administration 2002). Darrell West (2004, 2005) later simplified this website design approach into a basic classification of e-government websites into (1) billboard stage, (2) partial-service delivery stage, (3) portal stage, and (4) interactive democracy with outreach and performance accountability dimensions.

Using typologies such as these, scholars have discovered that e-government has slowly moved from billboard-style websites that simply publicize information to more interactive, portal-driven systems in which citizens can log in to an enterprise resource planning (ERP) system to access a variety of different services and opportunities (Garson 2006; Ho 2002; West 2005). However, at the same time that e-government becomes more complex in terms of design, the opportunities and services presented to citizens may actually decline (Greitens and Strachan 2011). Additionally, more sophisticated websites can exacerbate the challenges of the digital divide, by which all citizens cannot access e-government equally (Mossberger, Tolbert, and Stansbury 2003; Norris 2001). Consequently, more technologically sophisticated websites may actually end up preventing the goal of interactive democracy from being realized.

In the same way that e-government websites have changed, from relatively simple websites that displayed only information to interactive experiences in which citizens can access more types of information and actual services, e-reporting has also changed. Since the 2000s, online performance reporting has become increasingly more complex, with additional types of information presented. Following the e-government typologies listed already, a similar evolutionary pattern for online performance reporting can be observed: (1) unorganized information, (2) organizational report cards (also called agency report cards), (3) balanced scorecards, (4) performance dashboards, and (5) democratic-impact systems.

The evolution begins with governments presenting unorganized performance information such as budgets, strategic plans, and financial audits in the online environment. The presentation of such information on e-government websites is often not systematic and not easily searchable by citizens. Consequently, transparency is not always ensured. The

Table 3.1

An Example of an Organizational Report Card in the Public Sector

	Overall performance	Activities supporting Mandate 1	Activities supporting Mandate 2
Department I	F	D–	F
Department II	A+	A+	A+
Department III	B–	C+	B
Department IV	F	B-	C
Department V	D–	F	D

Note: If history is a precedent, then both mandates in this example would originate from a politically elected leader.

information can be discovered by citizens, but it is often not easy to interpret. For example, posting several hundred pages of a governmental budget to an e-government website is ultimately a positive development. But it can be hard for citizens to search through those pages and understand the information presented to them. To overcome those concerns, many e-government websites shift toward more systematic approaches, discussed below, that allow for benchmarking and easier access to performance information.

The systematic organization of information begins with organizational (agency) report cards. Organizational report cards are among the oldest types of performance information collected by government and were initially associated with improving service delivery in public-health settings such as hospitals (Gormley and Weimer 1999). With organizational report cards, managers collect performance information on variables of interest and then compare the performance of one unit to another similar unit. At a simplistic level, the final comparison involves the use of letter grades, such as A, C+, and F (for a basic example of an organizational report card for one agency, see Table 3.1).

Organizational report cards share many of the traits of other online performance tools that are discussed later, such as balanced scorecards and performance dashboards. All of these tools try to assess multiple dimensions of performance in some way. In that assessment, it is expected that data will be transformed at some level and that the assessment will be continuous into the future (Gormley 2004). The key differences are that data for organizational report cards are explicitly collected by external assessors and involve specific comparisons between different organizational units (Gormley and Weimer 1999).

At least theoretically, managers and policymakers use report cards as decision aids to help determine funding decisions and managerial actions. Additionally, these report cards allow citizens to make better informed decisions on topics such as choosing a school for their children or choosing a hospital for their care. Many states have even passed statutes mandating that some organizational report cards, especially in regards to school district performance, be made available to citizens (Gormley and Weimer 1999). The concept of organizational report cards becomes confusing, though, since so many media outlets assign their own report card on a variety of governmental topics such as spending, waste,

Table 3.2

An Example of a Balanced Scorecard

	Financial performance	Stakeholder engagement	Internal management processes	Innovation
Department I	Red	Red	Red	Red
Department II	Green	Green	Green	Green
Department III	Yellow	Yellow	Green	Red
Department IV	Red	Green	Yellow	Yellow
Department V	Red	Red	Red	Yellow

and corruption. But official organizational report cards in government are still in use and are a major component of online performance reporting.

Beginning in the 2000s, many governments added balanced scorecards to their complement of online performance reporting.[5] Balanced scorecards originate from the business sector and were specifically suggested in the 1990s as a management-style reform that could improve efficiency and effectiveness in business operations. As originally envisioned, the balanced scorecard collected performance information in four key areas: financial performance, customer engagement, internal management, and innovation (Kaplan and Norton 1992). These four key performance areas maintained a performance balance between the short- and long-term perspectives, financial and nonfinancial concerns, leading and lagging indicators, and external and internal audiences (Kaplan and Norton 1996). Internal assessors collected performance information in these four areas and provided it to managers. In this way, the balanced scorecard was ultimately designed as an internal management device. This made it fundamentally distinct from the concept of an organizational report card, whose intended audience was strictly external. Nonetheless, when government adopted the balanced scorecard approach, it often became one of the most easily accessible online performance reports available to citizens. Part of this is due to the simplicity of balanced scorecards, with their traffic-light pattern of performance information that is both visually striking and simple to understand (see Table 3.2). But part of it is also that balanced scorecards often became adapted as more of a political tool that policymakers publicized as part of their political agenda to transform traditional government (Joaquin 2009).

While the effectiveness of balanced scorecards in government remains in doubt (Jennings 2010; Joaquin and Greitens 2009; Niven 2008), the online presence of scorecards is almost always problematic. They often exist in a Web vacuum and are not linked to actual performance data or to more comprehensive budgetary and programmatic information. Sometimes terminology even becomes a problem as governments erroneously identify report cards as scorecards, scorecards as dashboards, and dashboards as scorecards on Web pages.[6]

But perhaps most troubling, policymakers often use these tools to showcase their political control over agencies and public managers in the online environment, ensuring that the only type of accountability that is certain is a type of political accountability that shows citizens nothing about efficiency or true programmatic effectiveness. Instead, citizens are just shown how quickly a program can achieve a "green" score on some management mandate established by political leaders. Consequently, the current online use of balanced scorecards does not help to increase other types of accountability and transparency to citizens.

Dashboards also originate from the private sector and provide a more comprehensive approach to performance assessment than either report cards or balanced scorecards. They actively monitor processes and activities with metrics of performance and thus provide managers with updated data to analyze problems (Eckerson 2006). In government, one key distinction is that dashboards typically emphasize programmatic outcomes that are tracked and monitored by centralized, database-driven systems (Edwards and Thomas 2005). Thus, while report cards provide information to citizens, and balanced scorecards provide direction to public managers, performance dashboards allow public managers to more effectively manage the day-to-day operations of government (Henderson 2003) (see Figure 3.1 that follows).

Last, there are democratic-impact systems that attempt to quantify basic democratic values such as transparency, individual rights, rule of law, and constitutional integrity (Rosenbloom 2007, see Table 3.3). In this way, these systems move the emphasis for performance reporting from measuring business-like practices such as efficiency and effectiveness to the protection of more basic rights and liberties that public managers should help ensure in a democracy. Such systems help to protect democratic values from being slighted in the constant march to reform government to become more business-like. The use of these systems in government remains small, but when they are used, they are heavily promoted in the online environment (Jaeger and Bertot 2010). Additionally, the usefulness of such systems remains in doubt (Kamensky 2013).

For any of these types of performance reporting tools to be effective, especially in the online environment, accountability has to be considered. Accountability is among the most complex topics of any public administration topic. Scholars have devoted entire books to understanding the notion of accountability and the multifaceted accountability systems of government (Dubnick and Frederickson 2011). In the section that follows, we briefly examine accountability in government and then apply the concept of multiple accountabilities in government for our framework of analysis of e-reporting.

Table 3.3

An Example of a Democratic Impact Scorecard for Department I

	Individual rights	Constitutional authority	Transparency	Rule of law
Financial mandate	Red	Yellow	Yellow	Red
Stakeholder mandate	Green	Green	Green	Green
Internal management mandate	Yellow	Yellow	Green	Green

Note: This table is modeled on David Rosenbloom's (2013) example of a Democratic-Constitutional Scorecard.

Figure 3.1 **An Example of a Dashboard for Department I**

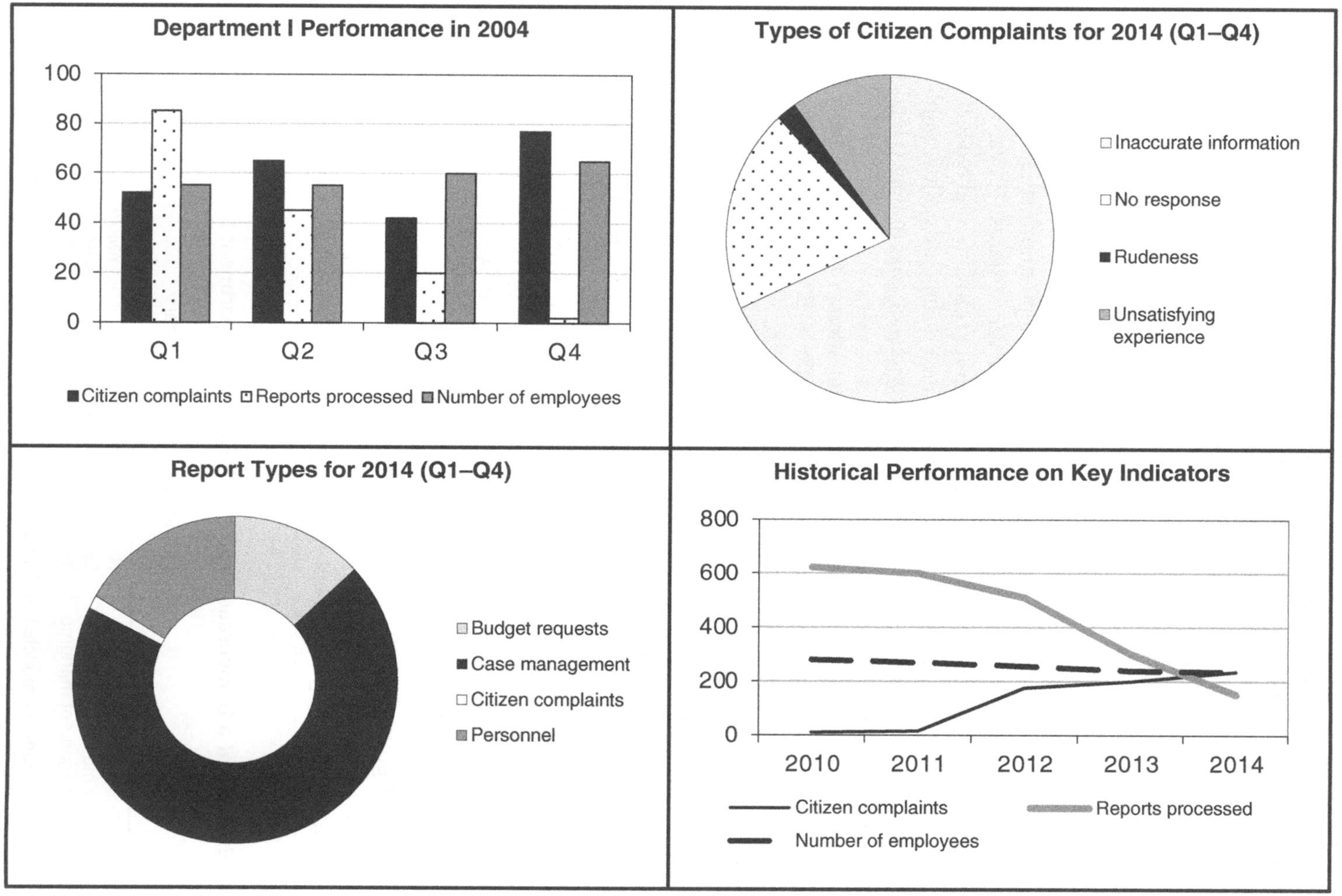

ACCOUNTABILITY IN GOVERNMENT

Making government operations accountable to citizens has always been a major concern of public managers. As far back as 1910, budget exhibits were held that allowed citizens to inspect and view the purchases of their local governments (Kahn 1993; Williams 2008). Around the same time, Progressive reformers suggested an early type of performance-based budgeting and implemented more understandable budgetary line items in an attempt to increase the transparency of government operations and ensure some measure of government accountability to citizens. With the expansion of the administrative state after World War II, policymakers codified such concerns on accountability in the administrative rule-making process with the passage of the federal Administrative Procedures Act in 1946 and various state administrative procedures acts from the 1940s to the 1960s.

Notions of accountability shifted somewhat in the early 1990s after the widespread adoption of governmental reforms based in the ethic of new public management (NPM). During this time, reinventions centered on NPM emphasized business-like reforms to governmental operations such as privatization, outcome-based performance measurement, strategic planning, and "customer-driven" accountability (Osborne and Gaebler 1992). Such reforms arguably added new components to accountability and transparency based on the business-like concept of profit. With NPM and its notions of customer service, programmatic outcomes, and effectiveness, accountability and transparency became heavily connected to cost and the use of performance-driven data. The resulting effect was that new dimensions of transparency, and especially accountability and transparency, centered on performance data became available. Ironically, ensuring this type of NPM accountability made the notion of accountability that much harder to quantify and ensure. After 25 years of implementation, it is clear that not all of the NPM reforms always work as intended (Levy 2010; Meier and O'Toole 2009).

Taken together, these disparate reforms hint at the importance of accountability and transparency to policymakers and citizens since the founding of public administration. They also hint at the different types of accountability in the public sector. Achieving these different dimensions of accountability in government is difficult for a variety of reasons. Perhaps the greatest challenge is that the meaning of accountability is often unclear. At best, the notion of accountability is organization-specific, with different types of organizations having different types of accountability that can be defined by culture and context (Jordan 2011; Koppell 2011; Schillemans and Bovens 2011; Wheeler 2011). And within those organizations, different types of accountability pressures may emerge that eventually create an *accountability dilemma* by which multiple accountability mandates often contradict one another (Dubnick and Frederickson 2011).

These multiple accountability mandates emphasize the institutional context and include bureaucratic accountability (i.e., the supervisor-subordinate context within bureaucracy), legal accountability (i.e., the policymaker controlling the bureaucrat who implements policy), professional accountability (i.e., professional standards guiding the behavior of bureaucrats), and political accountability (i.e., both bureaucrats and policymakers responding to constituent demands) (Romzek and Dubnick 1987). Building on the institutional perspective of how multiple accountabilities shape bureaucratic behavior, other scholars have identified a multidimensional view of accountability that includes liability (i.e., linking performance to actual consequences), transparency (i.e., public access to an organization's activities and processes), controllability (i.e., controlling the bureaucrat or policymaker), responsibility (i.e., controlling the bureaucrat through legal rules and standard operating procedures), and responsiveness (i.e., responding to constituent demands through some sort of action) (Koppell 2005, 2011).

In this study, we use Koppell's (2005, 2011) basic typology of the multiple dimensions of accountability to analyze two different cases of online performance information. Considering that these different, multiple dimensions of accountability are important since they help determine the appropriateness of online performance information, we argue that only those projects that intersect different dimensions of accountability should be heavily promoted by government as e-reporting vehicles. For only when performance projects straddle the accountability dimensions of liability, transparency, controllability, responsibility, and responsiveness can they help contribute to e-government's promise of the transformation of governmental operations and society at large.

Such an approach is admittedly simplistic in terms of research methodology, and perhaps even dangerous, given how the multiple dimensions of accountability are often viewed as barriers to implementation (Dubnick 2005; Joaquin and Greitens 2011). As a result, our approach should be viewed as an illustration of how e-reporting (i.e., the presentation of online performance information) is often ineffective because such presentations of online data often emphasize only one type of accountability, and how the use of multiple accountabilities can be used to determine whether certain types of performance data should really be emphasized in e-reporting projects. Our focus is on the federal government and the online presentation of two of the best-known online performance-information projects of the past 10 years: the Executive Management Scorecard under President Bush and the Program Assessment Rating Tool. Note that both of those projects were not just online performance information projects. Rather, they were whole-scale management reforms and assessments that had an online component. Nonetheless, those online components led to a basic e-reporting system in both projects that was heavily promoted and publicized by the administration. Thus, we believe that both projects are appropriate to analyze in the realm of e-reporting.

CASE ANALYSES

A Balanced Scorecard: The Bush Administration's Executive Management Scorecard

In 2001 the so-called first MBA president, George W. Bush, launched a major executive reform effort, the "President's Management Agenda," or PMA. Bundled into the PMA were the administration's "results-oriented" initiatives in five different areas of federal government management: e-government, competitive sourcing, human capital, financial management, and budget and performance integration. The e-government initiative focused on leveraging information technology to improve the government's ability to provide services in an efficient and secure manner; competitive sourcing was the Bush administration's newly energized implementation of a 1950s-era Circular A-76 to review, for potential outsourcing, performance of federal commercial functions; the human capital initiative focused on strategic actions to meet current government workforce needs; and budget and performance integration focused on strengthening the link between agency performance data and budgeting (Joaquin 2009). With its underlying conservative principles for a lean government that did not crowd out business, yet modeling after business in terms of managerial strategies, the Bush administration through the PMA signaled its determination to control the behavior of the federal bureaucracy.

The PMA directives emanated from the Office of Management and Budget (OMB), which carried out evaluation of the agenda's implementation across the board. Every quarter from 2002 until the close of the Bush administration in 2008, the OMB rated agency performance in each of the five areas. To accomplish this task, the PMA came along with the OMB Scorecard, a performance assessment system embodying a traffic-light style of communicating to the public any agency's achievement (or lack of) in pursuing presidential priorities. Every agency had to communicate with the OMB for its quarterly, annual, and long-term goals in the PMA areas. On the scorecard, green indicated a successful implementation of that agency's quarterly goal for a particular PMA area; yellow indicated mixed results; and red signified unsatisfactory agency performance, from the White House's perspective.

While every agency had to carry out the PMA, the OMB selected only a handful of agencies—26 in all—whose grades were published on the White House website every quarter. How those agencies came to be selected for the list is still unknown. Noticeably, the list comprised a mixture of large cabinet agencies, the U.S. Department of Agriculture and the Department of Defense, for example, and small outfits such as the Smithsonian Institution and the National Science Foundation, all compared on the PMA initiatives, but obviously differing in their organizational capacities to pursue management reforms.

The dynamics behind the design and implementation of the OMB Scorecard during the Bush years illustrated a significant measure of bureaucratic politics and performance assessment politics (Joaquin 2007; Joaquin and Greitens 2009). In both cases, the role of the scorecard as a rating system veered more toward the exercise of political accountability of bureaucracy toward its principal—in the White House more than in Congress—and less toward closing the distance between government and its citizens, spurring innovation, and improving mission performance.

In Joaquin's (2007) study of the Bush administration's implementation of the management agenda and the bureaucratic politics it entailed, some of the tensions and contradictions involving the OMB Scorecard involved the political symbolism of presidential control overriding meaningful measurement of agency performance; the tension between political appointees and career managers regarding the OMB Scorecard; and the bargaining between the OMB and the agencies in getting good scores, and the influence of agency power over the scores eventually obtained.

First, many managers who thought that the White House was imposing a one-size-fits-all performance yardstick in exchange for communicating to the public that it was reforming the bureaucracy did not appreciate the symbolic significance of the scorecard. As they collectively voiced their view of the scorecard as an inadequate performance measure (see Perera 2004), some thought that the real political motivation of the White House was to fill the scorecard with "greens" in the run-up to Bush's reelection campaign (Joaquin 2007). In the agencies' desire to follow the White House's goal of showing as many greens as possible, a column was added to the scorecard, a "milestones" category, to show that even when agencies were not hitting their quarterly promises on the PMA areas (e.g., red), they could still have some greens across their names.

Second, the scorecard displayed the perennial programmatic rift between political appointees, some of whom thought the scorecard was very effective (Perera 2004), and career managers, who perceived it as simplistic and unable to communicate meaningfully the agencies' individual challenges and achievements (Joaquin 2007). Political appointees in agencies, such as the Departments of Interior and Homeland Security and the Small Business Administration, also mimicked the scorecard by creating their own internal scorecards.

Third, because many saw the OMB Scorecard as unrealistic, starting every unit in the "red" column in 2002 as if to show that the entire bureaucracy was low-performing when the Clinton administration had ended, and because managers desired to avoid public embarrassment, behind-the-scenes bargaining became a staple of the quarterly scoring dynamics. Some agencies went to plead their cases to the OMB, some sought their allies in employee unions and Congress to change the scoring mechanism or find some subjectivity in their performance reports to move from red to green (Joaquin and Greitens 2009). Overall, agencies whose leaders bought in to the president's agenda and those that had some "slack" to convey organizational and management reform moved up faster on the scorecard.

Overall, these tensions and contradictions in the OMB Scorecard process were some of the unintended results of the scorecard's design. OMB officials stressed that the scoring mechanism represented accountability: "None of them wants to be seated at the back of the room because they have been red" on the scorecard (Joaquin 2007, 328). Rather than stimulate innovation and reform, however, many agencies viewed the penalizing role of the scorecard more than its encouragement. A former undersecretary of defense explained that agencies' attentiveness to the scores was driven more out of avoiding humiliation, which an OMB deputy director had publicly announced it intended to do with red scorecards (Joaquin 2007; Johnson 2003).

When we use a multiple accountability framework to assess the scorecard, we can quickly determine that it emphasizes the dimension of controllability. Like all balanced scorecards in government, the system is being used to exert policymaker control over the behaviors of bureaucrats. However, liability, transparency, responsibility, and responsiveness were not emphasized in the reform. For example, how some agencies arrived at green scores and other at red scores was unclear. This minimizes concerns over transparency. When the scorecard was published and promoted in the online environment, those absences also occurred, making the online presentation of this scorecard suboptimal. When published online, there was also limited information on the rules governing the process and there was no information on the consequences for the agency of achieving a red score or a green score. Consequently, the scorecard was not an optimal e-reporting that could both transform governmental operations and effectively communicate that transformation to citizens. The scorecard was an internal management device placed on bureaucrats from the elected executive—nothing more, nothing less.

A Type of Organizational Report Card: The Program Assessment Rating Tool

Upon taking office in 2001, the Bush administration announced a series of initiatives to make government more effective and more efficient. One of these initiatives was the Program Assessment Rating Tool, or PART. In this performance assessment, the Office of Management and Budget (OMB) assessed the performance of every federal program on (1) whether the program had a clear programmatic purpose reflected in its design, (2) whether the program had implemented a strategic planning process with appropriate annual and long-term goals, (3) the implementation of effective financial management especially in regard to financial controls and an emphasis on improvement methods, and (4) the program's ability to accurately measure performance.

Assessments were tailored to program type, with specific questions based on specific program services complementing a list of standard questions for every program (OMB 2007; Breul 2007). These assessments were then quantified by OMB into a PART score from 0 to 100 points for each of the four assessment areas mentioned already and published on the Expect More e-government website, where programs were classified as either "performing" or "not performing" on the basis of their PART score.

Whether PART actually improved the management of performance is still unclear. Research indicates that federal managers perceived PART as not increasing the effectiveness of programs (Gilmour 2008). This finding is seemingly reinforced by other research that discovered that PART assessments had a tendency to be subjective. Programs that conservative leaders typically disagreed with, such as regulatory and redistributive programs, received systematically lower PART scores than other types of programs (Greitens and Joaquin 2010). In addition, programs that received low PART scores had often already been targeted for elimination by conservative leaders (Radin 2008). Subjective assessments were also a problem in the PART assessment, as OMB assessors applied inconsistent standards in their interpretation and quantification of results (Government Accountability Office 2004; Radin 2006). Nonetheless, PART assessments were quantified by the OMB, and by the end of 2008 every single federal program was assessed and its results published in an online environment at the website Expect More (www.expectmore.gov).[7]

The online presentation of PART results probably best represents an organizational report card. Such a categorization is by no means perfect. But PART has many of the characteristics of organizational report cards as delineated by Gormley and Weimer (1999). It was developed by assessors external to the program, was used for benchmarking between programs and agencies, and was widely publicized to an external audience through a website that was specifically crafted for citizens. However, it also lacks a feature that routinely defines report cards: regular data collection (Gormley and Weimer 1999).

When we use a multiple accountability framework to assess PART, we can determine that the dimensions of transparency and responsiveness were emphasized. Transparency occurred since there was at least at attempt by the OMB to explain the assessment questions to both public managers, policymakers, and citizens. It could also be argued that responsiveness was emphasized in this reform, since an overriding theme of citizen discourse throughout U.S. history has been to determine whether public sector programs actually work (Radin 2012). However, liability, controllability, and responsibility were minimized in this approach. For liability, it was not clear during PART what would happen to programs with low assessment scores. Would their funding level decrease because programs that do not achieve results do not deserve funding, or would their funding increase since programs that do not achieve results may need more funding to actually achieve something? Similarly, controllability and responsibility became minimized, since it was unclear what sanctions would come from policymakers in regard to low PART assessment scores. As a result, PART was also a suboptimal e-reporting endeavor. It assessed programs and at least tried to show which programs were achieving results, but it lacked the rules necessary to link PART assessment scores with actual changes in organizational programs. At its best, PART was an assessment, probably politicized, of governmental operations without consequences. As a result, it is also a suboptimal e-reporting system.

RECOMMENDATIONS

In this chapter, we suggest that the notion of multiple accountabilities has to be integrated into e-reporting systems by practitioners. For e-reporting systems to be effective, practitioners must use accountability dimensions related to liability, transparency, controllability, responsibility, and responsiveness. Without consideration of those dimensions, e-reporting systems are doomed to be suboptimal and will continue to put more and more data online in more and more complex systems that achieve little. In such a scenario, e-reporting fails to contribute to the promise of e-government to transform governmental operations and society at large.

However, when practitioners consider the dimensions of multiple accountability included in our basic framework, projects with online performance implications can be studied to determine whether they are appropriate for e-reporting. This is not to suggest that balanced scorecards and other performance information should be totally excluded from the online environment. Instead, we suggest that managers use the multiple accountability framework as a decision aid to help determine which online performance information should be a part of an explicit e-reporting system (or at the very least, to help determine which information should be included in publicity to citizens on e-reporting endeavors). In a larger sense, then, the multiple accountability framework can provide a basic categorization of which online information is appropriate to include in an e-reporting system. If the framework discovers suboptimal information, then that information can remain part of the e-governmental website. But it should probably not be included in the online environment as reporting tools that are helping to transform government.

Consequently, our chapter produces three key recommendations to practitioners. First, we recommend that practitioners use the concept of multiple accountabilities to help determine whether their e-reporting system is optimal or suboptimal. As discussed in this chapter, e-reporting systems (and performance management systems in general) often have significant biases and constraints that can be revealed by a basic consideration of multiple accountabilities. Second, we recommend that multiple accountabilities be used as a decision aid to help determine which performance data to publish in the online environment and which data to keep internal to the organization. Such a decision aid should prove valuable to practitioners as the technological ease of publishing online performance information continues to increase in the future.

Our final recommendation concerns the use of balanced scorecards in e-reporting systems. The authors remain extremely doubtful about the appropriateness of publicizing balanced scorecards in the online environment of government and recommend that practitioners be extremely careful in their use of balanced scorecards in e-reporting systems. Because of their striking visuals and simplicity, many citizens may look at balanced scorecards and immediately correlate it with overall government performance. Indeed, it seems as if many policymakers have fallen into similar traps and equate the use of balanced scorecards with genuine reports of government performance (see, e.g., Joaquin 2009). This trap seems especially pernicious in the online environment. Our big fear is that in the future, more and more e-reporting systems will utilize balanced scorecards as their primary reporting mechanism to citizens even though balanced scorecards often fail to incorporate considerations of multiple accountability. Avoiding this type of misuse of online performance data is the theme of this chapter. Hopefully, by considering the concept of multiple accountability, such outcomes can be avoided in the future.

KEY POINTS

- For e-reporting systems to be effective, practitioners must use accountability dimensions related to liability, transparency, controllability, responsibility, and responsiveness.
- Strive for the permanent availability of performance information in e-reporting systems.
- Use the concept of multiple accountabilities when designing and assessing e-reporting systems.
- Use the concept of multiple accountabilities as a decision aid to decide which type of performance data is appropriate to publish for external audiences in the online environment (e.g., on websites).
- Use balanced scorecards as one part of an internal performance monitoring system.
- Realize that publishing balanced scorecards on websites may not be appropriate if other tenets of the e-performance system are not included.

NOTES

1. E-reporting is defined by Lee (2004, p. 11) as "the administrative activity that uses electronic government technology for digital delivery of public reports that are largely based on performance information. E-reporting is a tool of e-democracy that conveys systematically and regularly information about government operations that is valuable to the public at large, in order to promote an informed citizenry in a democracy and accountability to public opinion. E-reports are planned to be citizen friendly, by being understandable and meaningful to the lay public."

2. Note that the Justice, Melitski, and Smith (2006) article emphasizes fiscal performance information.

3. The Bush administration's Executive Branch Management Scorecard is now archived at the website http://georgewbush-whitehouse.archives.gov/results/agenda/scorecard.html.

4. The archived website of the Program Assessment Rating Tool is available at http://georgewbush-whitehouse.archives.gov/omb/expectmore/.

5. We have chosen to identify balanced scorecards and not include a separate designator for scorecards. Generally, governments' use of the term "scorecard" is ambiguous and can refer to what are actually organizational report cards, balanced scorecards, or dashboards (see note 6).

6. A good example of this phenomenon is the state of Michigan's experience with its Economic Vitality Incentives Program. In that program, the state linked additional funding to local governments with the local government's publishing on its website an updated "dashboard" of socioeconomic data related to fiscal stability, economic strength, public safety, and quality of life (Citizen's Research Council of Michigan 2011). Meanwhile, the state of Virginia publishes similar state-level information on its e-government website, but Virginia calls its system a scorecard rather than a dashboard (Council on Virginia's Future 2013).

7. That website is now archived, with some loss of functionality, at http://georgewbush-whitehouse.archives.gov/omb/expectmore/.

REFERENCES

Breul, Jonathan D. 2007. Three Bush administration management reform initiatives: The President's management agenda, freedom to manage legislative proposals, and the program assessment rating tool. *Public Administration Review* 67, 21–26.

Carrizales, Tony. 2008. Functions of e-government: A study of municipal practices. *State and Local Government Review* 40, 12–26.

Citizen's Research Council of Michigan. 2011. *Local government performance dashboards and citizen's guides.* Livonia: Citizen's Research Council of Michigan.

Coleman, Stephen, and Jay G. Blumler. 2009. *The Internet and democratic citizenship: Theory, practice, and policy.* New York: Cambridge University Press.

Council on Virginia's Future. 2013. Scorecard at a glance. http://vaperforms.virginia.gov/Scorecard/ScorecardatGlance.php.

Delli Carpini, Michael X. 2000. Gen.com: Youth, civic engagement, and the new information environment. *Political Communication* 17, 341–349.

Dubnick, Melvin J. 2005. Accountability and the promise of performance: In search of the mechanisms. *Public Performance and Management Review* 28, 376–417.

Dubnick, Melvin J., and H. George Frederickson. 2011. Introduction: The promises of accountability research. In *Accountable governance: Problems and promises*, ed. Melvin J. Dubnick and H. George Frederickson, xiii–xxxii. Armonk, NY: M.E. Sharpe.

Eckerson, Wayne W. 2006. *Performance dashboards: Measuring, monitoring, and managing your business.* Hoboken, NJ: Wiley.

Edwards, David, and John C. Thomas. 2005. Developing a municipal performance measurement system: Reflections on the Atlanta dashboard. *Public Administration Review* 65, 369–376.

Fountain, Jane E. 2001. *Building the virtual state: Information technology and institutional change.* Washington, DC: Brookings Institution Press.

Garson, G. David. 2006. *Public information technology and e-governance: Managing the virtual state.* Sudbury, MA: Jones & Bartlett.

Gilmour, John B. 2008. Implementing OMB's program assessment rating tool: Meeting the challenges of performance-based budgeting. In *Performance management and budgeting: How governments can learn from experience*, ed. F. Stevens Redburn, Robert J. Shea, and Terry F. Buss, 21–48. Armonk, NY: M.E. Sharpe.

Gormley, William T., Jr. 2004. Using organizational report cards. In *Handbook of practical program evaluation*, 2d ed., ed. Joseph S. Wholey, Harry P. Hatry, and Kathryn E. Newcomer, 628–648. San Francisco, CA: Jossey-Bass.

Gormley, William T., Jr., and David L. Weimer. 1999. *Organizational report cards.* Cambridge, MA: Harvard University Press.

Greitens, Thomas J., and M. Ernita Joaquin. 2010. Policy typology and performance measurement: Results from the program assessment rating tool (PART). *Public Performance and Management Review* 33, 555–570.

Greitens, Thomas J., and Lee Roberson. 2010. The challenges of integrating disparate performance data on a governmental website. In *Handbook of public information systems*, 3d ed., ed. Christopher M. Shea and G. David Garson, 443–454. Boca Raton, FL: CRC Press.

Greitens, Thomas J., and J. Cherie Strachan. 2011. E-government and citizen engagement: An overview of state governmental websites. *International Journal of Public Administration* 34, 54–58.

Grimmelikhuijsen, Stephen G. 2010. Transparency of public decision-making: Towards trust in local government? *Policy and Internet* 2, 5–35.

Henderson, Lenneal J. 2003. *The Baltimore CitiStat program: Performance and accountability.* Washington, DC: IBM Endowment for the Business of Government.

Hindman, Matthew. 2009. *The myth of digital democracy.* Princeton, NJ: Princeton University Press.

Ho, Alfred Tat-Kei. 2002. Reinventing local government and the e-government initiative. *Public Administration Review* 62, 434–444.

Jaeger, Paul T., and John C. Bertot. 2010. Transparency and technological change: Ensuring equal and sustained public access to government information. *Government Information Quarterly* 27, 371–376.

Jennings, Edward T., Jr. 2010. Strategic planning and balanced scorecards: Charting the course to policy destinations. *Public Administration Review* 70, S224–S237.

Joaquin, Maria E. 2007. Agency strategy, strength, and adaptation: Implementation of the Bush administration's competitive sourcing strategy. PhD diss., Northern Illinois University.

———. 2009. Bureaucratic adaptation and the politics of multiple principals in policy implementation. *American Review of Public Administration* 39, 246–268.

Joaquin, Maria E., and Thomas J. Greitens. 2009. Presidential policy initiatives and agency compliance: Organizational adaptation to A-76. *Administration and Society* 41, 815–849.

———. 2011. The accountability-performance link: An attempt at distilling some mechanisms in a management reform initiative. *Public Performance and Management Review* 34, 323–349.

Johnson, Clay. 2003. *Ask the White House.* Washington, DC: Office of Management and Budget.

Jordan, Sara R. 2011. Accountability in two non-Western contexts. In *Accountable governance: Problems and promises*, ed. Melvin J. Dubnick and H. George Frederickson, 241–254. Armonk, NY: M.E. Sharpe.

Justice, Jonathan B., James Melitski, and Daniel L. Smith. 2006. E-government as an instrument of fiscal accountability and responsiveness: Do the best practitioners employ the best practices? *American Review of Public Administration* 36, 301–322.

Kahn, Jonathan D. 1993. Representing government and representing the people: Budget publicity and citizenship in New York City, 1908–1911. *Journal of Urban History* 19, 84–103.

Kamensky, John M. 2013. Commentary on David H. Rosenbloom's "Reinventing administrative prescriptions: The case for democratic-constitutional impact statements and scorecards. In *Debating public administration: Management challenges, choices, and opportunities,* ed. Robert F. Durant and Jennifer R.S. Durant,127–130. Boca Raton, FL: CRC Press.

Kaplan, Robert S., and David P. Norton. 1992. The balanced scorecard: Measures that drive performance. *Harvard Business Review* (January–February), 71–79.

———. 1996. *The balanced scorecard: Translating strategy into action.* Boston: Harvard Business School Press.

Koppell, Jonathan G.S. 2005. Pathologies of accountability: ICANN and the challenge of multiple accountabilities disorder. *Public Administration Review* 65, 94–108.

———. 2011. Accountability for global governance organizations. In *Accountable governance: Problems and promises*, ed. Melvin J. Dubnick and H. George Frederickson, 55–78. Armonk, NY: M.E. Sharpe.

Krueger, Brian S. 2002. Assessing the potential of Internet political participation in the United States. *American Politics Research* 30, 476–498.

Latimer, Christopher P., and J. Richard Kendrick Jr. 2012. How young people are using communication technologies as platforms and pathways to engagement: What the research tells us. In *E-governance and civic engagement: Factors and determinants of E-democracy*, ed. Aroon Manoharan and Marc Holzer, 423–446. Hershey, PA: IGI Global.

Lee, Mordecai. 2004. *E-reporting: Strengthening democratic accountability.* Washington, DC: IBM Center for the Business of Government.

Levy, Roger. 2010. New public management: End of an era? *Public Policy and Administration* 25, 234–240.

Meier, Kenneth J., and Laurence J. O'Toole Jr. 2009. The proverbs of new public management: Lessons from an evidence-based research agenda. *American Review of Public Administration* 39, 4–22.

Moon, M. Jae. 2002. The evolution of e-government among municipalities: Rhetoric or reality? *Public Administration Review* 62, 424–433.

Mossberger, Karen, Caroline J. Tolbert, and Mary Stansbury. 2003. *Virtual inequality: Beyond the digital divide.* Washington, DC: Georgetown University Press.

Nabatchi, Tina. 2010. Addressing the citizenship and democratic deficits: The potential of deliberative democracy for public administration. *American Review of Public Administration* 40, 376–399.

Niven, Paul R. 2008. *Balanced scorecard for government and nonprofit agencies.* 2d ed. Hoboken, NJ: Wiley.

Norris, Pippa. 2001. *Digital divide: Civic engagement, information poverty, and the Internet worldwide.* New York: Cambridge University Press.

Office of Management and Budget. 2007. *Program assessment rating tool guidance.* Report No. 2007–02. Washington, DC: Office of Management and Budget.

Osborne, David, and Ted Gaebler. 1992. *Reinventing government: How the entrepreneurial spirit is transforming the public sector.* Reading, MA: Addison-Wesley.

Perera, David. 2004. Feds give low grades to OMB scoring system. FCW.com, July 27. http://fcw.com/articles/2004/07/27/feds-give-low-grades-to-omb-scoring-system.aspx.

Putnam, Robert D. 2001. *Bowling alone: The collapse and revival of American community.* New York: Simon and Schuster.

Radin, Beryl A. 2006. *Challenging the performance movement: Accountability, complexity, and democratic values.* Washington, DC: Georgetown University Press.

———. 2008. The legacy of federal management change: PART repeats familiar problems. In *Performance management and budgeting: How governments can learn from experience,* ed. F. Stevens Redburn, Robert J. Shea, and Terry F. Buss, 114–134. Armonk, NY: M.E. Sharpe.

———. 2012. *Federal management reform in a world of contradictions.* Washington, DC: Georgetown University Press.

Romzek, Barbara S., and Melvin J. Dubnick. 1987. Accountability in the public sector: Lessons from the Challenger tragedy. *Public Administration Review* 47, 227–238.

Rosenbloom, David H. 2007. Reinventing administrative prescriptions: The case for democratic-constitutional impact statements and scorecards. *Public Administration Review* 67, 28–39.

Schatteman, Alicia. 2010. Information technology and public performance management: Examining municipal e-reporting. In *Handbook of public information systems*, 3d ed., ed. Christopher M. Shea and G. David Garson, 431–442. Boca Raton, FL: CRC Press.

Schillemans, Thomas, and Mark Bovens. 2011. The challenges of multiple accountability: Does redundancy lead to Overload? In *Accountable governance: Problems and promises*, ed. Melvin J. Dubnick and H. George Frederickson, 3–21. Armonk, NY: M.E. Sharpe.

United Nations and American Society for Public Administration. 2002. *Benchmarking e- government: A global perspective assessing the UN member states.* Washington, DC: American Society for Public Administration and the United Nations.

U.S. Government Accountability Office. 2004. *Performance budgeting: Observations on the use of OMB's program assessment rating tool for fiscal year 2004.* Report No. GAO-04–174. Washington, DC: U.S. Government Accountability Office.

Weber, Lori M., Alysha L. Loumakis, and James Bergman. 2003. Who participates and why? An analysis of citizens on the Internet and the mass public. *Social Science Computer Review* 21, 26–42.

Welch, Eric W., Charles C. Hinnant, and M. Jae Moon. 2005. Linking citizen satisfaction with e-government and trust in government. *Journal of Public Administration Research and Theory* 15, 371–391.

West, Darrel. 2004. E-government and the transformation of service delivery and citizen attitudes. *Public Administration Review* 64, 15–27.

———. 2005. *Digital government: Technology and public sector performance.* Princeton, NJ: Princeton University Press.

Wheeler, Sally. 2011. Watching the watchers. In *Accountable governance: Problems and promises*, ed. Melvin J. Dubnick and H. George Frederickson, 213–224. Armonk, NY: M.E. Sharpe.

Williams, Daniel W., and Mordecai Lee. 2008. Déjà vu all over again: Contemporary traces of the budget exhibit. *American Review of Public Administration* 38, 203–224.

4
Global Trends in E-Performance Reporting

Marc K. Fudge

As the field of e-government has grown, an increased emphasis by scholars and practitioners has been placed on using information communication technologies (ICTs) to enhance service delivery to citizens (Berman 2008; Anthopoulos, Siozos, and Tsoukalas 2007; Kelly and Swindell 2002). Examples of the public sector using ICTs to transform service delivery include the advent of 311 systems, e-procurement, and geospatial information systems (GIS). Additionally, many cities are using ICTs to promote democratic functions of government through e-town-hall meetings, citizen satisfaction surveys, and most notably, social media. In 2009 President Barack Obama promoted an open government initiative that encouraged federal government departments and agencies to enhance their websites by developing features that facilitated transparency, participation, and collaboration (Office of Management and Budget 2009). Recent studies have found that citizens believe government is more responsive, open, and effective if it utilizes ICTs in a way that promotes service delivery and transparency (Bekkers and Homburg 2007).

When government places its primary concern on the emphasis of service delivery, citizens began to be viewed as consumers of products and not passive users of information. One of the primary concerns public administration must be mindful of as it attempts to utilize ICTs to improve effectiveness and efficiency, however, is maintaining a user-centric focus (Layne and Lee 2001). A balance between providing administrative information pertaining to services and offering channels that increase citizen engagement must be carefully constructed. Citizen focus in government management, according to Layne and Lee (2001), refers to the structure of government and suggests that the organization will change both internally and externally as a result of technology. Internally, power struggles and territorial skirmishes will become less pervasive as public managers acknowledge the importance of cooperation and communication, facilitated by ICTs, to improve performance. Externally, government processes will be designed for the convenience of citizens instead of the convenience of government. "As systems are becoming more and more integrated, citizen review boards may be established in order to review and observe how system integration occurs and its impacts" (Layne and Lee 2001, 135). Review boards and other "watchdog"-type organizations may not be necessary for those local governments that implement e-performance reports.

Converging simultaneously with an emphasis on using ICTs to improve citizen engagement, yet continuing to offer content related to administrative services, is the growing reliance on performance measurement information. As public managers and citizens increasingly rely on performance measurement information to assess effectiveness and efficiency, expectations of its availability subsequently increase (Meijer 2007). Publishing performance measurement data online can assist the public in determining how responsive their government is at delivering services and addressing their needs (Epstein 1984). E-performance reporting may also encourage citizens to utilize channels of communication, if they have been made available on the government website.

This study aims to explore the use of performance measurement information published on government websites, which is referred to as e-performance reporting. The research examines the use, growth, and trends in e-performance reporting among cities around the world between 2007 and 2011. Utilizing results from the 2007, 2009, and 2011 Global E-Governance Performance Surveys, this study provides longitudinal data of e-performance reporting changes and trends from an international perspective. In particular, this research investigates whether performance measurement information is published on the municipal government website and to what extent the information is made available. For example, can performance results be obtained in a searchable database online, or does the site offer contact information to obtain the results of performance measurement?

Findings demonstrate which global cities have developed e-performance reporting initiatives since 2007, the extent of their development efforts, and examples of best practices that others may emulate.

BACKGROUND

E-performance reporting may be viewed as the next logical step in the progression of using performance measurement information. Once a municipality chooses to develop a performance measurement initiative, it should then determine whether data will solely be used as a function to improve management, whether the information will be published for public consumption, or a combination of both. It is possible that e-performance reporting could be viewed as an attempt by government to ensure citizens are provided with access to information in a manner that is easily retrievable, accurate, and timely. Before reporting performance online, however, an effective performance system must be implemented. The development and management of valuable performance measurement data is often difficult and cannot be achieved strictly by mimicking what another city does. In fact, when considering the implementation of a performance measurement system, public managers should ask the following:

- Why are we developing performance measures?
- Precisely which measures do we want to track?
- How will we manage the information?
- What do we ultimately wish to achieve?

Julnes (2007) proposes the use of evidence-information to improve governance, thus resulting in performance improvement. His model suggests that public sector managers begin by assessing the needs of their organization and placing those needs in the proper context.

Stressing the importance of knowing what the results of the improvement measures will yield, Halachmi (2005) says that there are two purposes for performance measurement: enhancing productivity and accountability. Hatry (2007 says that reporting performance measures to external stakeholders allows citizens, elected officials, and interests groups to see what government is doing for them with the resources it is allocated. Essentially, performance reporting serves as an accountability mechanism for stakeholders to hold government to. The Public Performance Measurement and Reporting Network (PPMRN 2008) defines performance reporting as summarizing "information on an organization's performance results in comparison to the organization's previously stated targets. This information may be provided in comparison to previous year's performance, specific standards, or may be benchmarked across other performance efforts. Performance reports should be accessible to the reader and include key information such as the function of the organization, accomplishment in reaching targets, input and output measures, and helpful explanatory information." The Governmental Accounting Standards Board (GASB) proposes suggestions for the use of financial information by governments. According to GASB Concepts Statement No. 1, *Objectives of Financial Accounting*, "financial reporting should provide information to assist users in assessing the service efforts, costs, and accomplishments of the governmental entity" (GASB 1987).

THE VALUE OF E-PERFORMANCE REPORTING

The importance of e-performance reporting to some citizens may be negligible. How often citizens visit government websites and how likely they are to be interested in performance data are two legitimate questions that public managers must consider. Is the expense of creating a performance measurement system and then reporting information to the public a priority? If the public were made aware, however, of the benefits e-performance reporting potentially offers, then their perception of its worth likely would change. In light of fiscal crises many cities face, along with concerns over poor service delivery, e-performance reporting has the possibility of presenting the public with valuable information that will assist them in assessing how effective their government is. Ammons (1985) notes that as the service delivery responsibilities of local government continue to grow, so does the public's insistence that services be provided effectively and efficiently, and that local government programs produce the desired results that citizens seek. The use of ICT increases the expectations citizens have for the public sector while simultaneously providing a mechanism for government to actually improve performance. Government websites that allow citizens only to pay tickets or bills and obtain licenses are viewed as archaic. E-performance reporting, therefore, may serve as one way to improve performance for local governments (Hatry 2007). Further, e-performance reporting is a way to provide vital information to a large number of people in a timely and cost-effective manner.

Additionally, as the terms "transparency" and "accountability" continue to be used in great abundance by public administrators and elected officials, e-performance reporting affords them the opportunity to place substance behind those concepts. A city may use several key indicators to determine the overall success of their Department of Human Services that include workforce and employment programs, day care, adult services, foster care, and adoption. In this case, each indicator relies on several performance measures to determine effectiveness. The measures used to assess workforce and employment programs may include number of referrals, number of people trained, and number of job placements. Another value of e-performance reporting is its ability to allow public managers to compare and benchmark their municipality's success and failures across jurisdictions. Accordingly, Berman (2008, 8) states:

> Government performance has no single criterion of success. While private sector organizations must find out if they are meeting their customers' needs and expectations in order to survive, grow, maintain or increase their market share, there is not a comparable, compelling survival requirement for local governments to consult their constituents.

Without such measures it becomes difficult to assess the performance of government. We simply do not know the results, and more important, we are unsure of whether the strategies implemented are actually achieving the desired results.

INFORMING THE PUBLIC WITH ACCURATE DATA

Citizen trust in government continues to decline for numerous reasons, including undisciplined allocation of resources and the perception of government disinterest in the needs of citizens (Holzer and Yang 2004). The interests of various external and internal stakeholders have also been cited as a reason government organizations have a difficult time building trust with citizens. Kim (2005) suggests that as some organizations attempt to remain responsible to political and legal stakeholders, it causes tensions within the organization. This tension can then lead to hierarchal pressures, thus resulting in decreased employee morale and a decrease in services provided to clients (Kim 2005).

In the provision of service delivery, citizens are often cast as passive recipients who possess homogeneous beliefs and attitudes. Generalizing citizens according to this perspective often results in standardized services on a highly routinized basis. According to Baldersheim and Ogard (2008), ICTs enable customer-oriented approaches to services and afford citizens greater choices because they are more informed. This can occur only once management makes a conscious effort to proceed in this direction (Baldersheim and Ogard 2008).

Even when citizens are asked their opinions on various issues, their responses can be misleading. In a survey conducted by Van de Walle, Kampen, and Bouckaert (2005), asking citizens about their attitudes toward government performance yielded mixed results. They found that citizens may have a positive response to a specific service but a negative opinion of government in general, and vice versa. Publishing performance data online can help citizens determine how responsive their government is at delivering services and addressing their needs (Epstein 1984).

Finally, e-performance reports are likely to have a positive effect on the decisions made by public managers because performance measurement is geared to the production of knowledge that can be used by an organization's stakeholders. These decisions affect an organization's allocation of resources and monitoring of results, and they provide information to citizens and elected officials (De Lancer Julnes 2006). Once government takes the approach that measures are in place to assist government, then performance measurement and e-performance reporting are likely to be more widely accepted.

RESEARCH METHODS

In "Measuring E-Government Impact: Existing Practices and Shortcomings," Peters and colleagues (2004) suggest that one of the aims of a well-funded theory on measuring ICTs is to allow comparison or benchmarking. They go on to state that there may be a valuable mechanism to measure the effectiveness that we are ignoring. It should help to identify how effectively public money is spent and provide a relationship between results and resources used. The aim of this study is to examine the existence and extent of e-performance reporting among cities around the world. Benchmarking the existence and extent of e-performance reporting provides a platform to assess its growth. Furthermore, conducting this study over a period of several years offers insight into trends that may have occurred, along with theories that may clarify those developments.

The methods used to conduct this research began with data gathered from the E-Governance Institute within the School of Public Affairs and Administration at Rutgers University, Newark, New Jersey. The E-Governance Institute conducts the biennial E-Governance Performance Survey of government websites from cities around the world. They began conducting surveys of international cities in 2003, and the information used in this research is based upon data collected from the 2007, 2009, and 2011 surveys. The 2007 and 2009 E-Governance Performance Surveys used a total of 98 measures, and the 2011 survey expanded the number of measures to 104. The measures assess features of e-governance across five broad categories: security and privacy, usability, content, service delivery, and citizen engagement. In 2011, citizen engagement was renamed "citizen and social engagement," to capture features associated with the growth of social networks and media on government websites, thus increasing the number of measures from 98 to 104. For the purposes of this study, the research focused on three measures of e-performance reporting. First, are performance measures, standards, or benchmarks published on the website? Second, does the site have a performance measurement system published online? Third, are the results of performance measurement published on the website? The three measures remained the same and did not change from the 2007, 2009, and 2011 surveys.

On the basis of data from the International Telecommunications Union, the top 100 nations in population and the number of individuals using the Internet were identified. The largest city in each of the 100 nations was then identified to serve as a proxy for each of the cities in that particular nation. The reason population was used as an indicator is because previous research has shown a strong relationship between population and e-governance capacity at the local level of government (Schwester 2009; Holzer and Kim 2003; Moon 2002; Musso, Weare,

Table 4.1

The 71 Cities Included in the Survey

1. Almaty	25. Jakarta	49. Riyadh
2. Amman	26. Jerusalem	50. Rome
3. Amsterdam	27. Karachi	51. San Juan
4. Athens	28. Kiev	52. San Salvador
5. Auckland	29. Kuala Lumpur	53. Santiago
6. Bangkok	30. Kuwait	54. São Paulo
7. Belgrade	31. Lagos	55. Seoul
8. Berlin	32. Lima	56. Shanghai
9. Bratislava	33. Lisbon	57. Singapore
10. Brussels	34. Ljubljana	58. Sofia
11. Bucharest	35. London	59. Stockholm
12. Buenos Aires	36. Madrid	60. Sydney
13. Caracas	37. Mexico City	61. Tallinn
14. Casablanca	38. Minsk	62. Tashkent
15. Chişinău	39. Montevideo	63. Tehran
16. Copenhagen	40. Moscow	64. Tokyo
17. Dubai	41. Mumbai	65. Toronto
18. Dublin	42. Nairobi	66. Tunis
19. Guatemala City	43. New York	67. Vienna
20. Guayaquil	44. Oslo	68. Vilnius
21. Helsinki	45. Paris	69. Warsaw
22. Ho Chi Minh	46. Prague	70. Zagreb
23. Hong Kong	47. Quezon City	71. Zurich
24. Istanbul	48. Riga	

and Hale 2000; Weare, Musso, and Hale 1999). Of the 100 nations identified, 86 cities had an official government website in 2007. In 2009, 87 cities had an official government website, and 92 cities did in 2011. To determine whether a city had an official government website, the city's homepage was defined as the website where administrative and online services were provided by the city (Holzer, You, and Manoharan 2009).

As the number of cities included in the survey grew, it was discovered that some cities did not meet the criteria of population and number of online users each year. To ensure reliability, only the 71 cities that were each identified in 2007, 2009, and 2011 were included in this study; these cities can be found in Table 4.1.

To determine whether a municipal government provided performance measurement information on its website, the survey asked, "Are performance measures, standards or benchmarks published on the website?" Performance measures were defined as "output, efficiency, effectiveness, outcome indicators or an index set by the state to achieve administrative goals." Evaluators could answer the question by indicating one of the following responses: "No," "Performance measures, standards or benchmarks are listed on the website in html (as a webpage)," "Performance measures, standards, or benchmarks can be downloaded from the website," or "Performance measures, standards, or benchmarks are available in a searchable database." To assess the extent to which performance measurement data were made available on the government website, the survey asked, "Does the site have a performance measurement system published online?" This question is designed to probe more deeply, to examine the difference between simply providing some performance data on its website as opposed to publishing an entire performance measurement system online. Evaluators could answer the question by indicating "No" or "The site has a government-wide performance measurement system across all departments." The final question used from the survey examines if a citywide performance measurement system is available online, and whether the results of the performance data are reported on the website. The survey asks, "Are the results of performance measurement published on the website?" The evaluators could answer the question by indicating one of the following responses: "No," "The site offers contact information for obtaining results of performance measurement," "Performance measurement results can be downloaded from the website," or "Performance measurement results are in a searchable database online."

FINDINGS

The results of the research clearly demonstrate a trend in the use of e-performance reporting within cities across the globe between 2007 and 2011. In 2007, 35 percent of cities published performance measures, standards, or benchmarks on their websites. The number of cities reporting performance data online decreased to 24 percent in 2009 and subsequently increased to 31 percent in 2011. The percentage of cities that list performance measures as a webpage has decreased each year since 2007. In terms of allowing users the capability to download performance data, the results of the research is again mixed (as shown in Table 4.2). Of all municipalities surveyed, 18 percent provided this feature in 2007, yet this figure decreased to only 10 percent in 2009. In 2011, the number of cities that provided this feature increased by 5 percent from 2009. The percentage of cities who afford users the opportunity to conduct "searches" to obtain performance measures has increased each year since 2007.

The results displayed in Table 4.3 indicate that 14 percent of cities had developed a government-wide performance system in 2007 and that number decreased to only 7 percent in 2009. In 2011, the number of cities that had a government-wide performance system was again 14 percent.

The results displayed in Table 4.4 show a fluctuation in publishing performance information online. In 2007, 79 percent of cities did not provide e-performance reports. This number increased to 89 percent in 2009, before decreasing to 82 percent in 2011. In terms

Table 4.2

Are Performance Measures, Standards, or Benchmarks Published on the Website?

Year	No	Listed on the website in HTML (as a webpage)	Can be downloaded from the website (e.g., .doc, .pdf)	Are available in a "searchable" database
2007	65%	14%	18%	3%
2009	76%	8%	10%	6%
2011	69%	4%	15%	11%

Table 4.3

Does the Site Have a Performance Measurement System Published Online?

Year	No	It has a government-wide performance measurement system across all departments
2007	86%	14%
2009	93%	7%
2011	86%	14%

Table 4.4

Are the Results of Performance Measurement Published on the Website?

Year	No	The site offers contact information for obtaining results of performance measurement	Performance measurement results can be downloaded from the website	Performance measurement results are in an online, searchable database
2007	79%	4%	11%	6%
2009	89%	0%	10%	1%
2011	82%	4%	10%	4%

of providing contact information to obtain the results of performance information, 2009 was the only year that no city surveyed afforded users this option. In both 2007 and 2011, 4 percent of cities allowed users the ability to contact government to obtain performance data. The results from Table 4.4 show overall consistency in terms of allowing users the ability to download the results of performance information. Only 6 percent of cities allowed users to obtain performance results from a searchable database in 2007. This figure decreased to 1 percent in 2009, before increasing to a modest 4 percent in 2011.

CONCLUSION

The results of this study demonstrate that the majority of municipalities do not engage in e-performance reporting. Furthermore, they generally do not make any performance information available online, nor are users afforded the ability to attain performance data by conducting a website search. Obviously there are significant differences between countries around the world and the cities within each country. Various political, social, and economic policies have varying levels of effect on the country and city in which they exist. These differences are difficult to account for in a study such as this. What conclusions can then be drawn? As a result of this research, it has become apparent that overall, more cities engaged in some level of e-performance reporting in 2007 as opposed to 2009. The number of government-wide performance systems was also greater in 2007 than it was in 2009. Further, while modest, 4 percent of cities allowed users the ability to contact government to obtain performance information in 2007, yet no city provided this option in 2009. Interestingly, as e-performance and the extent of e-performance declined from 2007 to 2009, it generally returned to previous figures by 2011. Although a change in political leadership is constantly occurring, it is unlikely that this significantly influenced the results of this study. It is also less likely that the majority of citizens across the globe grew disinterested in obtaining performance data online and suddenly increased a few years later. What seems to have been a likely predictor of the fluctuation in e-performance reporting and the extent of e-performance reporting is global fiscal crises. During this period, many local governments were forced to reassess their priorities, placing greater emphasis on delivering basic services to the public. A decreased emphasis was placed on maintaining and managing performance measurement systems. While this is unfortunate, it is understandable. There are two perspectives, however, when determining how to deal with fiscal crises. Some public managers believe in a cutback management approach, by which a certain percentage of resources are reduced across all departments (Bland 2007). Another approach is to identify specific departments or programs that seem unnecessary (Bland 2007). The development of performance measurement systems and the subsequent evolvement of e-performance reporting may indeed be viewed as one such unnecessary expense during a fiscal crisis. Another approach that views performance measurement and e-performance reporting more favorable suggests that without collecting data to assess performance, it is more difficult to determine where waste actually exists (Lu 2007). E-performance reporting can have an impact on the performance of an organization if measures are implemented that show how activities can be linked to the budget process. Serritzlew (2006) suggests linking budgets to activities and says that this process increases competition, enhances efficiency, and facilitates control in times of reduced demand. The benefit, he says, is to strengthen the link between activities and resource allocation. The belief in strengthening the link between activities and the budget is based on the premise that the public will view government and public managers as a necessary and important component of society (Miller, Robbins, and Keum 2007). When viewed and applied in this manner, e-performance reporting provides a mechanism to effectively monitor resource allocation through online budget information. This can increase government trust if employees and citizens are able to view data and most importantly, understand resource allocation to support valuable departments and programs. Furthermore, e-performance reporting can help government agencies save funds while providing additional services where most needed.

Indeed, there may be other factors adversely impacting the use of e-performance reporting in cities around the world. Ammons (1985) says that perverse awards systems, fragmentation of local government, lack of political appeal, and the absence of cost-accounting systems negatively affect improvement efforts in government. Cost of implementation and management is another likely factor negatively affecting increased use of e-performance reporting. Finally, conquering public-sector barriers to improvement, in part, requires a commitment from organizational leaders and management while collaborating with front-line employees.

One of the challenges to conducting a study where generalizations are made across various continents and countries is accounting for different political ideologies, public policies, and social values and norms. Another similar limitation to this research is identifying appropriate variables that can be applied with equal weight in the various cities across the globe. Despite these limitations, this exploratory study provides an initial assessment of the existence of e-performance reporting in a global context. Furthermore, it captures a three-year time frame to examine trends and the growth of this valuable component of public administration. Future studies should focus on identifying additional factors that are likely to predict whether or not a city chooses to provide e-performance reports for its citizens.

Ultimately, this study has revealed that e-performance reporting is continuing to gain in popularity and use—even in the brief period during which e-performance reporting showed a slight decline. The public is increasingly interested in knowing what government is doing for them with the resources it has. It is now up to public managers to ensure that valuable information is presented to residents of a community in a clear and coherent manner. Furthermore, demonstrating the inherent value performance measures provide the public and the agency or department using them needs to be clearly articulated. Once there is sufficient buy-in by both public administrators and the public, then the utility of e-performance measures will continue to increase.

KEY POINTS

The following section provides several recommendations public managers should consider as they evaluate implementing an e-performance initiative or modifying a current one already in existence.

E-Performance Reporting

It is suggested that e-performance reporting be used as a continued phase or a next step from performance measurement. The rationale for this approach is to ensure that the collection, analysis, and assessment of performance measures are provided either internally to staff, externally to the public, or both internally and externally. This also creates an environment in which those employees responsible for managing the performance measures understand that their work is important and worthwhile.

Tempering Enthusiasm

Another important consideration for public managers is tempering enthusiasm. While the organization may be excited about the prospect of e-performance reporting and wish to track and report as many measures as possible, we must remember that the e-performance reporting initiative will require a great deal of work. This endeavor will require additional staff hours and potentially take them away from other responsibilities. Also, too much information may have an overall negative effect on those who read the e-performance reports. It is suggested that the most salient measures are those that are reported to the public.

Reporting Performance Measures

Overall, many citizens are less interested in visiting a government website to gain information. It becomes important, therefore, for the public manager to develop clear and coherent reportable measures that are of the most interest to the public. Some ways to increase public interest in e-performance reports are for departments and agencies to highlight their value. Particular emphasis should be placed on the following:

- Cost savings
- Transparency
- Information sharing
- Citizen participation
- Accountability

Public managers who choose to report performance measures online should develop a plan for implementation. The plan should include a list of organizational, technological, and external (e.g., citizens, media, and legislature) barriers and how the organization plans to address each one. Some barriers, such as a lack of technical expertise, may require training and/or hiring new employees. Other barriers, however, such as staff resistance, may be minimized by a particular strategy. For example, if several employees demonstrate disinterest in the initiative, it is recommended that managers identify supporters of e-performance reporting who may act as "champions" to the initiative, thus assisting in encouraging those who have shown a lack of interest.

Contact Information

Many local governments do not provide "contact information" to allow users of e-performance reports to communicate with public managers. Failing to include contact information sends a negative message to the public. The perception of government and the information provided in the reports can be improved simply by allowing the public the ability to discuss the results of the report with a public administrator or manager.

REFERENCES

Ammons, D. 1985. Common barriers to productivity improvement in local government. *Public Productivity Review* 9, 293–310.

Anthopoulos, L., P. Siozos, and I. Tsoukalas. 2007. Applying participatory design and collaboration in digital public services for discovering and re-designing e-government services. *Government Information Quarterly* 24, 353–376.

Baldersheim, H., and M. Ogard. 2008. Innovation in e-government: Analysis of municipal web pages in the Nordic countries. *Information Polity* 13, 125–137.

Bekkers, V., and V. Homburg. 2007. The myths of e-government: Looking behind the assumptions of a new and better government. *Information Society* 23 (5), 373–382.

Berman, B. 2008. Involving the public in measuring and reporting local government performance. *National Civic Review* (Spring), 3–10.

Bland, R. 2007. *Budgeting—A budgeting guide for local government.* Washington, DC: ICMA Press.

de Lancer Julnes, P. 2006. The utilization of performance measurement information. In *Public productivity handbook*, ed. M. Holzer and S. Lee, 285–296. New York: Marcel Dekker.

Epstein, P. 1984. *Using performance measurement in local government.* New York: Van Nostrand Reinhold.

Governmental Accounting Standards Board (GASB). 1987. GASB Concepts Statement No. 1 Summary. www.gasb.org/st/concepts/gconsum1.html.

Halachmi, A. 2005. Performance measurement: Test the water before you dive in. *International Review of Administrative Sciences* 7, 255–266.

Hatry, H. 2007. *Performance measurement—Getting results.* Washington, DC: Urban Institute Press.

Holzer, M., and S.Y. Kim. 2003. *Digital governance in municipalities worldwide: An assessment of municipal web sites throughout the world.* Newark, NJ: National Center for Public Productivity.

Holzer, M. and K. Yang. 2004. Performance measurement and improvement: An assessment of the state of the art. *International Review of Administrative Sciences* 70, 15–31.

Holzer, M., B.Y. You, and A. Manoharan. 2009. *Digital governance in municipalities worldwide: A longitudinal assessment of municipal web sites throughout the world.* Newark, NJ: National Center for Public Productivity.

Julnes, G. 2007. Promoting evidenced-informed governance—Lessons from evaluation. *Public Performance Management Review* 30, 550–573.

Kelly, J., and D. Swindell. 2002. A multiple-indicator approach to municipal service evaluation: Correlating performance measurement and citizen satisfaction across jurisdictions. *Public Administration Review* 62, 610–621.

Kim, S. 2005. Balancing competing accountability requirements: Challenges in performance improvement of the nonprofit human services agency. *Public Performance Management Review* 29, 145–163.

Layne, K., and J. Lee. 2001. Developing fully functional e-government—A four stage model. *Government Information Quarterly* 18, 118–136.

Lu, Y. 2007. Performance budgeting: The perspective of state agencies. *Public Budgeting and Finance* (Winter), 1–17.

Meijer, A. 2007. Publishing public performance results on the Internet—Do stakeholders use the Internet to hold Dutch public service organizations to account? *Government Information Quarterly* 24, 165–185.

Miller, G.J., D. Robbins, and J. Keum. 2007. Incentives, certification and targets in performance budgeting. *Public Performance and Management Review* 30, 469–495.

Moon, M.J. 2002. The evolution of e-government among municipalities: Rhetoric or reality? *Public Administration Review* 62, 424–433.

Musso, J., C. Weare, and M. Hale. 2000. Designing web technologies for local governance reform: Good management or good democracy. *Political Communication* 17, 1–19.

Office of Management and Budget. 2009. *Open government directive* (M-10–06). Washington, DC: U.S. Government Printing Office.

Peters, R., M. Janssen, and T. Engers. 2004. Measuring e-government impact: Existing practices and shortcomings. In *Proceedings of the Sixth International Conference on Electronic Commerce* (ICEC'04) ed. M. Janssen, H. G. Sol, and R. W. Wagenaar, vol. 60, 480–489, ACM, New York, NY.

Public Performance Measurement and Reporting Network (PPMRN). 2008. Key terms. www.ppmrn.net/about/key-terms/keyterms.

Schwester, R. 2009. Examining the barriers to e-government adoption. *Electronic Journal of E-Government* 7, 113–122.

Serritzlew, S. 2006. Linking budgets to activity. *Public Budgeting and Finance* 2, 101–121.

Van de Walle, S., J. Kampen, and G. Bouckaert. 2005. Deep impact for high impact agencies? *Public Performance Management Review* 28, 532–549.

Weare, C., J.A. Musso, and M.L. Hale. 1999. Electronic democracy and the diffusion of municipal web pages in California. *Administration and Society* 31, 3–27.

Part II

E-Governance and Citizen Participation

5

A Critical Analysis of the Potential of Information and Communication Technologies for Democracy and Governance

Matthias Finger

The information and communication technologies (ICTs) have been used so far in a rather conservative way in government. Indeed, ICTs have mainly been applied to digitizing existing services and processes. The idea was to make government more efficient and more effective, without, however, changing its very nature. When it comes to democracy, the main approach was to digitize the voting process. All in all, the practice of e-government has been disappointing, as are the main texts and conferences about e-government. In short, ICTs have been used to enhance the processes of the old government, with no novel approach.

This criticism is especially valid when applied to the question of e-democracy. Although much has been written about e-democracy, e-voting, and e-participation, we still lack a serious and systematic analysis of what ICTs have done for citizen participation in the political process at local, regional, state, and even international levels. There is no real novelty or systematic evaluation of what e-democracy has been so far or of what it could bring in the future.

In short, ICTs in government have not delivered on their promises. Worse, they have actually cemented the status quo of government and prevented much-needed change. Will this be the end of e-government? This chapter argues in favor of a new start for e-governance and strives to demonstrate that the potential of the ICTs for government is much larger than what we have seen so far. This is a normative claim, which will be argued in a normative manner. In particular, the chapter will show that this potential covers all the main areas in which government is active, namely policymaking, regulation, and service delivery. It focuses particularly on the participatory aspect of e-government or e-democracy, whereby citizens are involved not just at times of elections and punctual referenda, but rather along the entire policy process, ranging from policy formulation to implementation; whereby citizens are involved not only at the nation-state level but also at other policy levels (e.g., local and regional politics; supranational politics, such as Europe); whereby citizens are involved not only as individuals but also as citizen groups, grassroots organizations, and so on; and whereby one will see the development of new forms of political participation, in particular political self-organization, enhanced participation, and more. In other words, this chapter is both a balance sheet of e-government and e-governance, as well as an appeal for a new stage in e-governance practice.

Figure 5.1 **Key Concepts**

- *Governance:* Collective problem solving involving both state and nonstate (business, nongovernmental organizations) actors
- *E-governance:* Use of ICTs and the Internet to solve collective problems at the local, regional, national, and global levels, involving government, business, and the third sector in the process, as well as services (e-government), regulation (e-regulation), and policymaking (e-democracy)
- *E-government:* Use of ICTs and the Internet in improving delivery of public services, focusing both on the quality of services and the process of service production
- *E-regulation:* Use of ICTs and the Internet to regulate liberalized services
- *E-democracy:* Use of ICTs and the Internet in involving citizens in the process of public policymaking at local, regional, national, and global levels

To do this, the chapter proceeds along the following lines: first, the balance sheet of e-governance practice, research, and thinking with a special focus on e-democracy is established. This balance sheet is highly critical, especially of the e-government literature, which has failed to see the very potential of ICTs for government transformation. This is, in my judgment, mainly because "e-gov" has been appropriated by public administration specialists.[1]

Second, the conceptual framework is developed, which will allow for greater potential of ICTs in politics. This conceptual framework has two coevolving elements, namely the transformation of government and, more generally, the nation-state, and technological changes, especially in the areas of ICTs. It is these two elements combined that will define the level of potential. This leads to a somewhat normative claim about the role of the ICTs in government transformation, detailed in the three relevant areas: service delivery (the traditional area of e-government), regulation, and policymaking.

Finally, I focus this conceptual framework on the question of policymaking in the network society, that is, on "e-democracy," especially the potential of the ICTs but also the institutional conditions for the technological potential for democracy. It is obvious that none of the forces currently in place—least of all, the governments—has an interest in promoting such an e-governance agenda, given that such an agenda will ultimately change power structures.

A CRITICAL ASSESSMENT OF THE "E-GOV" LITERATURE

The literature on e-government and e-governance has become substantial. It is not necessary to discuss all that literature, as much of it is redundant. For an overview, refer to Anttiroikko's (2007) e-government anthology, but also to many other recent publications on the topic (Huang, Siau, and Kee Wei 2004; Margetts 1999; Mayer-Schönberger and Lazer 2007; Obi 2010; Tubtimhin and Pipe 2009). Also, most of the literature is descriptive and generally anecdotal, characterized by success stories of digitizing one or the other service or administrative process. There is a serious lack of theoretical considerations, let alone theory. This section looks critically at the literature so far. It is structured into two parts: it first discusses the mainstream e-government literature, covering everything that does not pertain to participation and democracy. Here, I briefly summarize what this literature is about and critically appreciate it. The same is then done, in the second part, for the e-democracy literature.

E-Government

This section offers an understanding of the very nature of e-government (or even e-governance). This is above all a philosophical, not a technical, discussion. Yet it is important to have this discussion if one wants to understand the potential and limitations of e-government. Indeed, even participation and democracy follow from this paradigm. Two quotes can serve to locate e-government within the context in which it belongs: government reform. For example, according to the Organisation for Economic Co-operation and Development (OECD 2005, 11), "E-government is the use of the information and communication technologies, and particularly the internet, as a tool to achieve better government." Or further on: "e-government is now widely regarded as being fundamental to reform, modernization and improvement of government" (OECD 2005, 98). In other words, e-government is part of the movement to improve government; that is, it is part and parcel of public-sector reform. Moreover, ICTs are the tools to do precisely that.

More precisely, "e-government is the use of technology to enhance the access to and delivery of government services to benefit citizens, business partners and employees. It has the power to create a new mode of public service where all public organizations deliver a modernized, integrated and seamless service for their citizens" (Silcook 2001, 88). This quote asserts the idea of services to the citizen thanks to the ICTs, which is one of the key elements of public-sector reform.

It is thus important to unambiguously locate e-government within the public-sector reform movement of the 1980s, which is further discussed in the next section. To recall, the core ideas of the public-sector reform movement are transparency, customer orientation, service, and efficiency. These elements constitute a concise summary of what public-sector reform was and still is all about (for the United States, see Osborne and Gaebler 1992; for Europe, see Pollitt and Bouckaert 2000).

E-government follows these same objectives and values, as can be seen from the numerous statements of its main proponents (see Fountain 2001; Mayer-Schönberger and Lazer 2007). Sometimes the word "e-governance" is even used synonymously with public-sector reform objectives (see Riley 2001). On the one hand, ICTs are seen as useful tools to make the public administration more efficient, and by doing so, they help reengineer the administration, also known as "electronic production" or "production networks of administrative actions." In other words, "digital government" or "e-government" is simply the next step in "reengineering government" (see, e.g., Atkinson 2001). However, the idea of reengineering government precedes e-government (Hammer 1996). On the other hand, ICTs and the Internet will help the administration serve their customers better, in terms of both quality and service process transparency, also known as "electronic (public) services." It is important to remember that the idea of a government one-stop shop where citizens are treated as customers again preceded e-government (see Hagen and Kubicek 2000).

Most of what has been written about e-government, and sometimes e-governance, falls within this "reengineering and one-stop-shop paradigm" of public-sector reform. This is not to belittle all the work that has been done by both academics and practitioners of public reform and e-government. This work has been important and continues to be so, as there is a real need to make the public administration more transparent, to improve services and relationships with the citizens (and other stakeholders) as customers, and to become more efficient in the process. It is not to say either that e-government has not contributed to public-sector reform. As a matter of fact, and thanks to ICTs and the Internet, public services were not only improved and better coordinated but also new services were developed. Furthermore, traditional processes were reengineered, and thanks to ICTs, such reengineering took qualitatively new steps, even though ICTs have not managed to restructure the administration. Finally, while public-sector reform, at least in some aspects, concerns involving and delegating more to the private sector, ICTs and the Internet have enabled the creation of (now electronic) production networks, whereby the public and private sectors are better integrated into the production of public services.

In short, e-government has been and continues to be a useful contribution to public-sector reform: it advances the key ideas of transparency, better services (in terms of quality as well as a customer orientation of the services and the public administration more generally), and efficiency, even though this latter point is less obvious. Its contribution is mainly practical, whereby there are concrete ICT- and Internet-based services developed, processes improved, and collaborations inside and outside the enhanced administration.

But here lies precisely the problem with this "reengineering and one-stop-shop paradigm": e-government (or even e-governance for that matter) does not add anything new to public-sector reform, at least not philosophically and theoretically. There is no e-government philosophy or theory of its own, most probably because the initial idea was that technology is a simple tool to do the same things better, with more efficiency and transparency. This is unfortunate because the potential contributions of ICTs to government transformation are actually missed. I return to this point in the next section, when mentioning the much broader potential of ICTs and the Internet to transform the nation-state.

Here, the problem is not only that e-government has been framed from the very beginning as being part of the public-sector reform paradigm, thus stifling the potential of ICTs in general and reducing the contribution of ICTs to improving government services exclusively. E-government is basically "tinkering at the edges" or "digitizing the existent." Rather, and more seriously, the problem is that the public-sector reform movement or paradigm has basically failed to live up to its promises (see Wollmann 2003).

This failure has several implications for e-government: first, it means that e-government practitioners and academics are running after something that no longer exists, or worse, they believe they can continue to perpetuate the public-sector reform movement by technology alone. In other words, "reengineering government by way of the ICTs" has replaced "reengineering government" (without ICTs), even though such reengineering has actually already failed. Or still by way of explanation, e-government has given a second lease on life for a public-sector reform movement that has ceased to exist. Second, this also means that the use of ICTs and the Internet in government is definitely in need of a theory or a philosophy or a paradigm. But of course, such a theory cannot come from technology alone.

E-Democracy

E-democracy is the other main area of e-governance. As with e-government, we will try to understand its theoretical underpinnings, however, the situation is more complex. If e-government is clearly located within the public-sector reform movement and the reengineering paradigm, then e-democracy is more difficult to locate theoretically. Four theoretical groundings of e-democracy are identified here, each of which leads to a different vocabulary and a diverse meaning of e-government.

To start with, there is indeed a theoretical strand that grounds e-democracy in the above-mentioned public sector reform movement. It can be labeled e-voting. The purpose here is not to improve democracy as such but to improve the democratic process by making use of ICTs. Authors are addressing the online presence of the state and its political actors, such as parliaments, political parties, and even politicians (Filzmaier 2001). The ICTs help these political actors to be more present and the political system to be more transparent. As a result, citizens have a better choice of options, also known as "digital citizenship" (Mossberger, Tolbert, and McNeal 2008). A similar idea of improving the political (democratic) process along the public sector reform paradigm can be found in e-voting. Indeed, the voting process becomes more efficient, meaning that voting is made easier; thus, in principle, voter turnout increases. The same idea can be applied to referenda and initiatives in countries where semidirect democracy exists. However, research shows that e-voting has hardly any effect on voter turnout or on citizens' interest in political matters (Feick 2007). This is even the case if one goes beyond the traditional voting process and includes so-called online consultations.

The logical consequence of this kind of research is then an interest in "political social capital" and even digital divide, that is, an interest in the question, for which kind of citizens does Internet voting indeed enhance participation and political interest? Nevertheless, the approach along the public-sector reform philosophy is conservative and not very innovative: one starts out with the existing possibilities of political participation—generally elections and rarely referenda—and asks how these processes can be made more efficient and more user-friendly, so as to optimize the existing democratic system. Not surprisingly, the authors then generally come to the conclusion that the contribution of ICTs and the Internet to democracy are nil or at best enhance the already-existing cleavages between the political haves and have-nots: the ones who already participate in the political system will be able to take advantage of ICTs, whereas the other ones remain unaffected by the "democratic" potential of ICTs.

A second theoretical orientation of e-democracy is grounded in the theories of U.S. communalism: "e-participation" (Chadwick 2006). The U.S. tradition of e-participation comes from so-called communalism (e.g., Etzioni 1993). The focus here is on electronic deliberation, electronic local communities or virtual (political) communities (Hood 1997), and community networks (Gross 2002) or civic networks (Tsagarousianou, Tambini, and Bryan 1998). This approach inspires authors who work on e-governance of cities (van den Berg et al. 2006). Overall, the focus is on the local or the "virtual local," as well as on social interaction, deliberations, and participatory decision making. ICTs and the Internet are seen as an additional opportunity for involving citizens in creating communities thanks to new, technological means of participation.

A third orientation is grounded in (European) theories of social movements, especially (social movement) resources mobilization (McCarthy and Zald 1977), with a focus on mobilizing citizens to influence the state. This is labeled "e-mobilization" (Moulitsas Zúñiga 2008). The focus here is on the mobilization potential of ICTs, generally for activism purposes (Norris 2007). In the same perspective, one may also mention the use of ICTs and the Internet for purposes of campaigning (e-campaigning), lobbying (e-lobbying), and activism more generally (e-activism) (Davis, Elin, and Reeher 2002). The aim is to make use of ICTs and the Internet for social change at national and global levels, whereby the technology offers new opportunities for activism and increases the effectiveness of such activism.

If the three orientations of e-democracy are always illustrated by way of empirical examples and cases, the fourth orientation is mainly philosophical in nature. While the application examples are the foregoing ones, the underlying theoretical discourse is different. Indeed, authors here are grounded in philosophical considerations of deliberative democracy (e.g., Habermas 1981) or strong democracy (e.g., Barber 1984), considerations that again predate ICTs and the Internet. However, on the basis of such philosophical considerations in favor of deliberative and participatory democracy, authors like Lévy (2002) have argued that ICTs enhance the potential for such democracy, which Lévy calls "cyberdemocracy." It is on the basis of such philosophical considerations that ICTs are defined as democracy enhancing, as they are said to favor democratic discussions across boundaries and cleavages.

E-gov is not a well-defined paradigm with a solid theoretical grounding and a generally accepted vocabulary. While it stands mainly for the continuation of the public reform movement thanks to ICTs and the Internet, "e-democracy" is much more eclectic, grounded as it is in public-sector reform theory, U.S. communalism, European social movement theory, and philosophical considerations on strong democracy. No clear and solid theoretical grounding of e-gov currently exists, at least not a theoretical grounding that would integrate and consider ICTs and the Internet differently than simply as an enhancement of already-existing theories. In other words, ICTs and the Internet will further public-sector reform, enhance democracy at a philosophical level, help mobilize activists for social change, strengthen participation, and more. Technology is thus basically seen as a tool that strengthens preexisting social forces or actors. This can, at best, constitute a confirmation of these existing theories, but it can certainly not constitute a solid theory of e-gov.

ICTS AND TRANSFORMATION

There is therefore a need for a theoretically more solid foundation of e-government and especially of e-governance, the more encompassing term. This is a rather ambitious task, as such a theoretical foundation does not exist currently. Within the scope of this section, the two following points are considered: first, the contribution of Manuel Castells is discussed, as he seems to be the only author to have taken on the task of trying to lay a theoretical foundation for the information society. Second, I recall my own contributions in this matter—and highlight their shortcomings.

Broadly speaking, what is needed is an approach that links the evolution of technology with the evolution of society. This is, in essence, a historical approach that relates the evolution of society to the evolution of technology, insisting in particular on the mutual shaping of both, an approach pioneered by Lewis Mumford (1934). More precisely, what is needed is a particular focus within this evolution at the latest stage of the combined technological and societal evolution, namely the information and communication technologies, which go hand in hand with the emergence of the "information society" (e.g., Freeman and Louçã 2002). It is obvious that a solid understanding and theory of e-governance needs to be located within such a framework. A first attempt in this direction has been made by Manuel Castells. In this section, I complement Castell's framework with my own conceptualization of the transformation from government to governance and finally apply both conceptualizations to the evolution of public-service delivery in the network society.

The Contribution of Manuel Castells

Even though Manuel Castells does not focus on a fully developed theory of e-governance, his contributions are the most relevant ones for such a theory. Castells is indeed the only author who has attempted to determine the coevolution between information and communication technologies on the one hand and society on the other. He has done this mostly in his trilogy on the information age (Castells 1996, 1997, 1998; see also Stalder 2006). It is not possible to present here the complexity of Castells's theory, but I focus only on the main relevant aspects for a theory of e-governance, and this in four steps.

At the most general level, Castells's theory is grounded in Marxism, yet he adds a significant element to the Marxists' simplistic analysis of technology. Indeed, Castells distinguishes traditional Marxist modes of production (characterized by traditional Marxist power relationships, such as capitalism) and modes of development, reflecting the technological arrangements of any given time. These technological arrangements do have some autonomy from the capitalist modes of production. The relationship between the two is a dialectic one: modes of production do, but only to a certain extent, shape technology, and technological modes of development, in turn, partially influence modes of production, especially inasmuch as they are taken up by the economy.

A second foundational element of his theory pertains to social change. In the Marxist tradition, yet this time via Alain Touraine (2000), Castells sees social change as stemming mainly from social movements. Social movements create identity, and identity building is the motor of social change. Such identity building takes place against the backdrop of the previously mentioned dialectic relationship of modes of production (currently characterized by global capitalism) and modes of development (currently characterized by pervasive ICTs). In the tradition of Touraine, Castells distinguishes legitimizing identities (those promoted by the forces that currently take advantage of the capitalist mode of production), resistance identities (produced by these actors who are disenfranchised by this mode of production), and project identities (as produced by the actors striving for positive social change). This second part of Castells's theory is quite normative.

These two elements together lead to Castells's analysis of the "network society." The network society reflects the capitalist and now global mode of production, as shaped by the pervasive ICTs, as well as the Internet. For Castells, ICTs and the Internet (i.e., the convergence of telecommunications and computing) constitute a new "informational mode of development," different from the previous modes of development. The novelty of this mode stems from the fact that the technologies act on information, that is, on social transactions. Within a capitalist mode of production, such technological change affecting information leads to competitiveness (and innovation for that matter) and is dependent on the management of information. Similarly, the creation of identity and social change (through social movements) is equally affected by such networked and global information exchange and management.

Finally, the nation-state, according to Castells, is also profoundly affected by these new modes of production (global capitalist networks) and development (timeless and placeless management of information, thanks to ICTs and the Internet), leading to the network society. Indeed, in the network society the state has a serious problem, according to Castells, as it can no longer create identity by integrating its constituency on the basis of its welfare instruments. While the state still has influence, it no longer has the legitimacy of its peoples, that is, power. If traditionally the social movements were creating identity by opposing the nation-state, in the network society they now have to create identity differently, namely by bypassing the nation-state. The state, in turn, has to position itself within this new global network society, which will lead it to further disengage itself from its own constituents.

In short, Castells's theory does indeed constitute a powerful conceptual framework for simultaneously thinking about social and technological change. While it is not a theory on e-governance, it nevertheless constitutes a broad framework within which one can place both the transformation of the nation-state (within a network society) and the role of ICTs and the Internet in this transformation (informational mode of development).

From Government to Governance

Castells does not have a full-fledged theory of e-governance, as this is not his focus. However, he does provide a framework for the bits and pieces of a theory we developed earlier on, a theory that describes in particular the evolution from (e-)government to (e-) governance (Finger and Pécoud 2003; Finger 2006; Finger and Langenberg 2006; Finger and Shahin 2009).

One may agree with Castells when he says that since the globalization of the 1980s, the nation-state is coming under serious pressure, forcing it to adapt and to transform itself. This pressure has structural financial dimensions (e.g., pressure on public finances), legitimacy dimensions (the state needs to legitimize itself in light of other emerging actors vis-à-vis its citizens), as well as pressures to become more competitive. A consequence of these various pressures on the nation-state is that the three functions the state has traditionally assumed, but has not always clearly distinguished, now need to be separated: the functions of policymaking, regulation, and service delivery. Some of them will even have to be abandoned, or at least outsourced.

Traditional policymaking at the nation-state level is being challenged by globalization in two ways: first, as problems become increasingly transboundary in nature, policymaking is moving gradually to supranational levels. Furthermore, new, increasingly global actors emerge—such as transnational corporations and nongovernmental organizations—with whom the policymaking function now needs to be shared. As a result, nation-states increasingly lose control over this function, which in turn exacerbates their problems of legitimation. This increasingly shared nature of policymaking as a result of globalization has been qualified as an evolution from government to governance (Finger and Shahin 2009).

The regulatory function was assumed in the traditional nation-state by the courts. However, in the context of liberalization and globalization, regulatory functions are significantly being developed and extended in particular to arbitrating competition in imperfect markets. The creation of (such imperfect) markets in all areas—including in areas where public monopolies prevailed previously—is the direct result of liberalization and globalization. Consequently, regulation of imperfect markets becomes *the* new form of state intervention. More precisely, regulation is an alternative form of state intervention, replacing public ownership and public provision of services. This evolution has been labeled the emergence of the "regulatory state" (Majone 1997). This consideration is identical to Castells's observation that the state loses power yet still has influence. The only influence (or power) that will be left for the state in the globalized economy will be a type of regulatory activity.

This is also true of the service-delivery function of the nation-state, which is—at least in the case of infrastructure services—being privatized or otherwise outsourced. Over the past 30 years, significant institutional changes have taken place in the areas of telecommunications, postal services, transport, and energy. The provision of those corresponding services has been deregulated, privatized, or otherwise exposed to competition. Services that were previously provided by public enterprises or even public administrative entities are now provided by private operators or by public operators competing with private operators. Yet, as shown already, such deregulation and privatization was compensated for by increased regulatory intervention by the nation-state. Abandoning the provision of infrastructure services, the state has thus evolved into a regulator of corresponding service provision, with subsequent problems of legitimacy (as is shown in the following section).

Service Delivery in the Network Society

It is important to note that this transformation of the state in general, but in particular the privatization of its services, was the result of institutional changes made possible because of profound technological changes (in Castells's terms, because of a profound change in the mode of development). The developments of ICTs (i.e., the informational mode of development) must be mentioned here. In the case of infrastructures, for example, these technological changes allowed for so-called unbundling, or the decoupling of infrastructures from the services provided on the basis of such infrastructures. Furthermore, these technological changes allowed for much more decentralized production of infrastructure services (e.g., decentralized energy production), as decentralized systems can now be better coordinated thanks to ICTs. Finally, liberalization and emerging competition triggered technological innovations in most infrastructures, thus adding to their increasingly dynamic nature (Finger and Künneke 2007).

The question is whether this privatization and outsourcing of public services will be stopped by so-called e-government, or whether, as I think, it is actually made possible by the very application of ICTs to these services (e.g., e-government)? If neoliberal theory is correct, a market "solution" to (e-)government would lead to more efficient, better quality, and ultimately more innovative government services than if these services were exclusively provided by government itself, for instance: comparable markets of infrastructure services, such as electricity markets, higher education markets, health-care markets, and more. If such markets exist, so will competitors, product (or service) development, and innovation, along with consolidation among service providers and market failures. It is also conceivable that some aspects of this market would have to be regulated by government, as is already the case with the electricity market. Similarly, there may be elements—perhaps even key elements—of such an "e-government services market" that would have to be provided by government itself, either because the market would not offer these services or because they constitute a key (public) infrastructure, analogous to a railway infrastructure or an electricity grid (e.g., digital identities or digital signatures). The answers to these questions and considerations will ultimately determine the role of government in e-government. But in any case, the role of government will be reduced, namely to a regulatory role (of government).

While the evolution of the nation-state can easily be placed within the conceptual framework of Castells, this section has made this evolution a little more precise by identifying the three functions—policymaking, regulation, and service delivery—and by analyzing their evolution separately. The focus has been, in particular, on the evolution of the service-delivery function (public services) of the nation-state, showing that the current informational mode of development (to speak in Castells's terms) does not stop before this function. Rather, public-service delivery, as shown elsewhere (Finger 2010), will be permeated by ICTs and the Internet, that is, by the new informational mode of development. However, within the current context of a globalized and capitalistic mode of production, so-called e-government (i.e., the electronic provision of the governments' services) will merely constitute an intermediary step toward their privatization and marketization at a global level. What will be left for the state will be some sort of regulatory function for some of these services the state no longer produces itself.

THE POTENTIAL OF ICTS FOR DEMOCRACY

In the previous section we looked at the service-delivery function of a government and how it is affected by the informational mode of production in particular, and by the network society in general. This function, it was argued, will be outsourced to private actors, and state intervention will at best pertain to the regulation of e-service delivery. In this section, I discuss what happens to the policymaking function in the network society. This discussion builds on Castell's conceptualization, on the one hand, and on my conceptualization of the transformation of the state (e.g., from government to governance), on the other hand. Indeed, if the service-delivery function is so radically affected by combined liberalization (state transformation) and technological development (ICTs), as seen already, it cannot be that the policymaking function remains unaffected. Considering ICTs and the Internet as a simple tool to enhance the voting and election processes is too limited, particularly in light of the conceptual frameworks presented in the previous section. But unfortunately, Castells has not really developed a theory of what happens to democracy in the network society. I develop the considerations here in two steps, first by defining my own approach, which is only loosely related to technological change, and second by placing that approach within Castells's framework.

Policymaking: From Government to Governance

Much has been written about the evolution from government to governance (e.g., Bellamy and Palumbo 2010; Heere 2004; Rosenau and Czempiel 1992; Young 1999). This is not the place to summarize these writings but simply to extract the implications of this very evolution for policymaking. There is, indeed, a generally accepted idea that, with globalization (which is a combined result of societal and technological change; or along Castells's idea, the result of the interaction between the capitalistic mode of production and the informational mode of development), the centers of political decision making move away from the nation-state. One generally considers that political decision making moves to supranational levels (e.g., European Union, United Nations, World Bank). What is considered less often is that some political decision making also moves to the infranational level, that is, to regions and especially to cities. As a matter of fact, it is the cities that are already facing, and increasingly will be faced with, most of the problems of an economic (e.g., competitiveness), ecological, and social nature and therefore will have to come up with solutions to those problems (e.g., Heinelt, Sweeting, and Panagiotis 2005; Sassen 1991).

This displacement of political decision making above and below the nation-state goes in hand with a multiplication of the actors involved in such decision making. This is generally what is labeled "the evolution from government to governance," in which no actor alone is powerful enough to decide. Above the nation-state level, (global) governance implies co–decision making among three types of actors, namely transnational corporations, international nongovernmental organizations, and states, thus underscoring Castells's idea that states still have influence even though they have less power. Similarly, below the state level, corporations, nongovernmental organizations, and nation-states jointly participate in political decision making along with other, more decentralized actors.

This multiplication of levels of political decision making and actors creates problems of legitimacy, as Castells (1996, 1997, 1998) and many others before him have observed (e.g., Habermas 1973). This first of all creates problems of legitimacy for nation-states, which must explain to their citizens why they are still relevant and why the citizens should, therefore, legitimize them. But this is less important here. Rather, the main problem is that none of the other newly emerging centers of political decision making, nor most other actors involved in such political decision making, have the required legitimacy. At best, they can gain what political scientists call "output legitimacy," meaning that they are appreciated by the concerned stakeholders for what they do once they have done it rather than for the initial trust invested in them.

The question is, however, a much more fundamental one: Where, in the network society, are political decisions taken? By which actors? And how are these policy decisions made? This is the real question of the future of e-democracy.

Castells and the Transformation of Policymaking

Castells does not really answer these questions, as his preoccupation is a more general one: he is basically interested in social change in the information age, given his focus on social movements. Where will such social change come from? How does it relate to the network society in general and to the informational mode of development in particular? In regard to our analysis, two of his considerations are particularly relevant here.

First, it is clear that the nation-state is no longer the relevant actor that can make legitimate decisions. Says Castells (1998, 347): "As politics becomes a theater, and political institutions are bargaining agencies rather than sites of power, citizens around the world react defensively, voting to prevent harm from the State in place of entrusting it with their will." This has serious consequences for what has been labeled "e-democracy" at the nation-state level: it certainly explains why ICTs and the Internet are not significant factors in shaping traditional politics. In other words, e-democracy as defined in the e-gov literature is falling short of understanding the changes that have already taken place in the network society.

What, then, are citizens mobilizing for? Here, Castells comes back to this interest in social movements as actors of social change. But we are talking about a new type of social movement: "social movement of the information age." It is these new social movements, and no longer nation-states, that can create what he calls "legitimizing identities" or "cultural codes." Says Castells (1997, 427): "The main agency . . . is a networking, decentered form of organization and intervention, characteristic of new social movements, mirroring, and counteracting, the networking logic of domination in the information society. . . . They [social movements] are the actual producers, and distributors, of cultural codes." Or, more precisely: "Thus, social movements emerging from communal resistance to globalization, capitalist restructuring, organizational networking, uncontrolled informationalism, and patriarchism—that is, for the time being, ecologists, feminists, religious fundamentalists, nationalists, localists, and the vast democratic movement that emerges as the coalition for global justice against capitalist globalization—are the potential subjects of the information age" (Castells 1997, 426).

While one can agree with Castells's appreciation of the growing irrelevance of nation-state politics—and corresponding e-democracy, for that matter—in the information age and the network society, one must be more skeptical about new social movements as the new "subjects" and the new "agency" of the information age. We do appreciate Castells's affirmation that social movements are indeed the producers of cultural codes and ultimately of identity in the information age, but this does not make them automatically the new "agency."

CONCLUSION: E-DEMOCRACY AT WHAT LEVEL?

If indeed social movements are the potential subjects of the information age, one will still need concrete institutional (and ultimately physically located) embodiments of "identity" and "identity politics." These will have to be institutional and physically located embodiments that have some sort of legitimacy in the eyes of constituent citizens (who may or may not be part of social movements). The main relevant embodiments that currently come to mind are cities, or rather megalopolises. There is a significant literature that shows how cities are becoming important actors of—simultaneously global and physically based—identity building (Low 2003). Consequently, these "global cities" may well become the new relevant entities of political decision making. Indeed, "global cities"—rather than new social movements—may constitute the link between the quest for identity in the (global) information society and the new locus of networked (political and cultural) decision making.

KEY POINTS

- Governments need to realize the potential of information and communication technologies (ICTs), far greater potential than in current practice, and take steps to digitize the existing administrative processes.
- Governments need to understand the potential of ICTs to enable two-way, complex and innovative interactions between the citizens and government.

- Governments need to educate the citizens and stakeholders on the potential of ICTs for two-way communication.
- In the case of electronic voting, governments should explore new and innovative ways of consulting and engaging with citizens.

NOTE

1. The term "e-gov" is used in this chapter to cover both "e-government" and "e-governance."

REFERENCES

Anttiroikko, A.-V., ed. 2007. *Electronic government: concepts, methodologies, tools and applications.* Hershey, PA: IGI Global.

Atkinson, R.D. 2001. Digital government: The next step in reengineering the federal government. Washington, DC: Congressional Internet Caucus Advisory Committee. www.netcaucus.org/books/egov2001/pdf/digigov.pdf.

Barber, B. 1984. *Strong democracy: Participatory politics for a new age.* Berkeley: University of California Press.

Bellamy, R., and A. Palumbo, eds. 2010. *From government to governance.* London: Ashgate.

Castells, M. 1996. *The rise of the network society, the information age: Economy, society and culture.* Vol. 1. Cambridge, UK: Blackwell.

———. 1997. *The power of identity, the information age: Economy, society and culture.* Vol. 2. Cambridge, UK: Blackwell.

———. 1998. *The end of the millennium, the information age: economy, society and culture.* Vol. 3. Cambridge, UK: Blackwell.

Chadwick, A. 2006. *Internet politics: States, citizens, and new communication technologies.* Oxford: Oxford University Press.

Davis, S., L. Elin, and G. Reeher. 2002. *Click on democracy: The Internet's power to change political apathy into civic action.* Cambridge, MA: Westview.

Etzioni, A. 1993. *The spirit of community: Rights, responsibilities, and the communitarian agenda.* New York: Crown Publishing.

Feick, J. 2007. Demokratische Partizipation im Zeitalter des Internet. In *Gesellschaft und die macht der technik: Sozioökonomischer und institutioneller wandel durch technisierung,* ed. U. Dolata and R. Werle, 221–240. Frankfurt: Campus Verlag.

Filzmaier, P., ed. 2001. *Internet und demokratie: The state of online politics.* Vienna: Studien Verlag.

Finger, M. 2006. Du gouvernement électronique à la gouvernance électronique: Le rôle des technologies de l'information et de la communication dans la réforme du secteur public. In *Contributions à l'action publique*, ed. J.-L. Chappelet, 89–102. Berne: Haupt; Lausanne: Presses Universitaires Romandes.

———. 2010. What role for government in e-government? *Journal of E-Governance* 33 (4), 199–204.

Finger, M., and R. Künneke. 2007. Technology matters: the cases of the liberalization of electricity and railways. *Competition and Regulation in Network Industries*, Volume 8, No. 3, pp. 301–333.

Finger, M., and T. Langenberg. 2006. Electronic governance. In *Encyclopedia of digital government,* ed. A.-V. Anttiroikko and M. Mälkiä, 2: 629–633. Hershey, PA: Idea Group Reference.

Finger, M., and G. Pécoud. 2003. From e-government to e-governance? Towards a model of e-governance. *Electronic Journal of E-Government* 1 (1), 1–10.

Finger, M., and J. Shahin. 2009. The history of a European information society: Shifts from governments

to governance. In *Global e-governance: Advancing governance through innovation and leadership*, ed. J. Tubtimhin and R. Pipe, 62–83. Amsterdam: IOS Press.
Fountain, J. 2001. *Building the virtual State: information technology and institutional change*. Washington: Brookings Institution Press.
Freeman, C., and F. Louçã. 2002. *As times goes by: From the industrial revolutions to the information revolution*. Oxford: Oxford University Press.
Gross, T. 2002. E-democracy and community networks: Political visions, technological opportunities and social reality. In *Electronic government: Design, applications, and management*, ed. A. Grönlund, 249–267. London: Idea Group Publishing.
Habermas, J. 1973. *Legitimationsprobleme im Spätkapitalismus*. Frankfurt: Suhrkamp.
———. 1981. *Theorie des kommunikativen Handelns*. 2 vols. Frankfurt: Suhrkamp.
Hagen, M., and H. Kubicek. 2000. *One-stop-government in Europe: Results of 11 surveys*. Bremen, Germany: University of Bremen.
Hammer, M. 1996. *Beyond reengineering: How the process-centered organization is changing our work and our lives*. New York: HarperCollins.
Heere, W., ed. 2004. *From government to governance: The growing impact of non-state actors on the international and European legal system*. The Hague: Asser Press.
Heinelt, H., D. Sweeting, and G. Panagiotis, eds. 2005. *Legitimacy and urban governance*. London: Routledge.
Hood, C. 1997. *Virtual politics: Identity and community in cyberspace*. London: Sage.
Huang, W., K. Siau, and K. Kee Wei. 2004. *Electronic government strategies and implementation*. Hershey, PA: IGI Global.
Lévy, P. 2002. *Cyberdémocratie*. Paris: Éditions Odile Jacob.
Low, S. 2003. *The anthropology of space and place: Locating culture*. Oxford, UK: Blackwell.
Majone, G. 1997. From the positive to the regulatory state: Causes and consequences of changes in the mode of governance. *Journal of Public Policy* 17, 139–167.
Margetts, H. 1999. *Information technology in government: Britain and America*. London: Routledge.
Mayer-Schönberger, V., and D. Lazer, eds. 2007. *Governance and information technology: From electronic government to information government*. Cambridge, MA: MIT Press.
McCarthy, J., and M. Zald. 1977. Resource mobilization and social movements: A partial theory. *American Journal of Sociology* 82 (6), 1212–1242.
Mossberger, K., C.J. Tolbert, and R.S. McNeal. 2008. *Digital citizenship: The Internet, society and participation*. Cambridge, MA: MIT Press.
Moulitsas Zúñiga, M. 2008. *Taking on the system: Rules for radical change in a digital era*. London: Penguin.
Mumford, L. 1934. *Technics and civilization*. New York: Harcourt, Brace, and World.
Norris, P. 2007. The impact of the Internet on political activism: Evidence from Europe. In *Current issues and trends in e-government research*, ed. D. Norris, 22–43. London: Cybertech Publishing.
Obi, T., ed. 2010. *The innovative CIO and e-participation in e-governance initiatives*. Amsterdam: IOS Press.
Organisation for Economic Co-operation and Development (OECD). 2005. *E-government for better government*. Paris: OECD.
Osborne, D., and T. Gaebler. 1992. *Reinventing government. How the entrepreneurial spirit is transforming the public sector*. New York: Penguin.
Pollitt, C., and G. Bouckaert. 2000. *Public management reform. A comparative analysis: new public management, governance and the neo-Weberian State*. Oxford: Oxford University Press.
Riley, T. 2001. *Electronic governance and electronic democracy: living and working in the wired world*. London: Commonwealth Secretariat Publishing.
Rosenau, J., and E.-O. Czempiel. 1992. *Governance without government: Order and change in world politics*. Cambridge: Cambridge University Press.

Sassen, S. 1991. *The global city: New York, London, Tokyo.* Princeton, NJ: Princeton University Press.
Silcook, R. 2001. What is e-government? *Parliamentary Affairs* 54, 88–101.
Stalder, F. 2006. *Manuel Castells.* Cambridge, UK: Polity Press.
Touraine, A. 2000. *Sociologie de l'action.* Paris: LGF—Livre de Poche.
Tsagarousianou, R., D. Tambini, and C. Bryan, eds. 1998. *Cyberdemocracy: Technology, cities, and civic networks.* London: Routledge.
Tubtimhin, J., and R. Pipe, eds. 2009. *Global e-governance: Advancing governance through innovation and leadership.* Amsterdam: IOS Press.
van den Berg, L., A. van den Meer, W. van Winden, and P. Woets. 2006. *E-governance in European and South African cities.* Aldershot, UK: Ashgate.
Wollmann, H., ed. 2003. *Evaluation in public sector reform: Concepts and practice in international perspective.* Cheltenham, UK: Edward Elgar.
Young, O. 1999. *Governance in world affairs.* Ithaca, NY: Cornell University Press.

6

Keys to E-Governance

Technology or Civil Society?

Robert J. Dickey and SeJeong Park

Cities showcase their websites as a symbol of modern government. Technology has often been promoted as a tool to improve management and governance. Various studies have suggested, however, that this may not always be the case (see Jho 2005; Lim and Tang 2008); even that 80 percent to 90 percent of information technology (IT) investments fail to meet all objectives (Champ 2001). It appears that in some cases technology becomes an "end" rather than a "means." Objectives may even be determined on the basis of technology, which Kolsaker and Lee-Kelley (2006, 129) have termed a "techno-centric" model, a model that has raised the ire of civil society (Jho 2005) and perhaps reinforces the strengths of insiders (Rethemeyer 2007; Welch and Pandey 2007). We might question whom the website serves: government, citizens, or technophiles.

Another way of looking at the question is whether a website dictates a government's e-governance practices or a vision for e-governance dictates website design. Experiences in South Korea provide many examples of each. But more of the former.

Our concern here is less about government (the institutions) and more about governance (the approach). Governance lacks a common definition: competing definitions may include concerns for distribution of power, inclusion of the private sector, problem solving, and (lack of) hierarchy (Eun 2009). Civil society is often identified as a core ingredient in governance, yet it too suffers from inconsistency in definition (Seligman 1992). Considering the challenges in defining e-governance, it is not surprising that a website may be used as a substitute for the thorny issue of what a government is doing—or attempting to do—through technology.

Here we argue that a vision of governance should dictate governments' Web strategies. A popular depiction of the distinctions between government and governance has been that of rowing versus steering (Osborne and Gaebler 1992). Though an important reminder in the 1990s of the need for government to rethink the service-delivery model, the steering model of contracting out services lacks specific inclusion of civil society as part of the *decision-making* process, and therefore fails to incorporate 21st-century expectations for governance. Today we would call for more hands on the wheel. It is therefore important to ask how websites are enabling participation in decision making rather than simply transferring data. For example, is crowdsourcing a possibility for ordinary governmental activities?

Sailing, instead, is our preferred metaphor for governance. Sailing demands the collaboration of numerous actors (crew) to coordinate the forces of wind, currents, tides, waves, drag, and inertia, in order to attain a mutually desired outcome more or less on schedule. Perhaps even with a bit of rowing on occasion. Neither the helmsman nor pilot-tactician can claim exclusive right to steer. Navigation and propulsion are imperfect. Roles frequently adapt to changing circumstances. In governance, we would be coordinating finance, civil society (including nongovernmental organizations, commercial interests, and individual citizens), political interests, the legal system, and bureaucracy. Good sailors spend years getting wet, know every task, and have learned to respect the roles of all on board. Communication among all hands is critical. E-governance adds technology to the communicative sailboat.

The "e" in these discussions faces similar lack of clarity. In the earliest days of computer networking, "e" often referred to "Ethernet." Today many regard the "e" as shorthand for "Internet-based" (the "e" in the Microsoft Internet Explorer® logo has certainly supported that image); others have included cellular phone technology or cable TV as "e" (electronic) systems. The use of "i" (Internet based) is likewise common. "M-government" (mobile, typically cellular phone-based) is yet another label (see, e.g., Lee, Tan, and Trimi 2006; Emmanouilidou and Kreps 2010). "U-government," which allows for "multi-level interfaces, wireless devices, and nanotechnologies" (Belanger, Carter, and Schaupp 2005, 426) is clearly gaining currency. In this chapter, "e" refers to all types of electronic communications technologies, although the focus is on digital technologies. A touch-tone (analog) phone, therefore, can be included, as it can provide input into a computer-based system through both dial-pad tones and voice-recognition software. We include these various technologies as a reminder that a basic 1990s-era website (sometimes referred to as "Web 1.0") met only the "Ethernet" description, but enhanced modern websites can facilitate multiple technologies. We must also recognize that governments may maintain a presence on numerous commercial systems (e.g., Facebook) as a means of initiating contact and directing traffic to the principal website. We therefore need to consider the Web presence as something more than a website.

Similarly, there is no standard definition of e-government (Yildiz 2007). Pascual (2003, 5) observes that the definition can range from "the use of information technology to free movement of information" as well as "the use of technology to enhance the access to and delivery of government services." He also suggests that technology should aim to change government with new styles of leadership and new ways of deciding, transacting business, listening to citizens and communities, and organizing and delivering information. Considering that most organizations prefer to work with minimal outside interference, Yun and Opheim's (2010, 72) remark that governments "have been slow to incorporate technologies that enhance on-line participation" is hardly surprising.

E-governance, of course, will be dependent on both the definition of governance and the range of technologies deployed. Nyirenda and Cropf (2010, 25) suggest that e-governance "encompasses the participatory aspects of democracies," that is to

Figure 6.1 **Overlapping Domains of E-Governance**

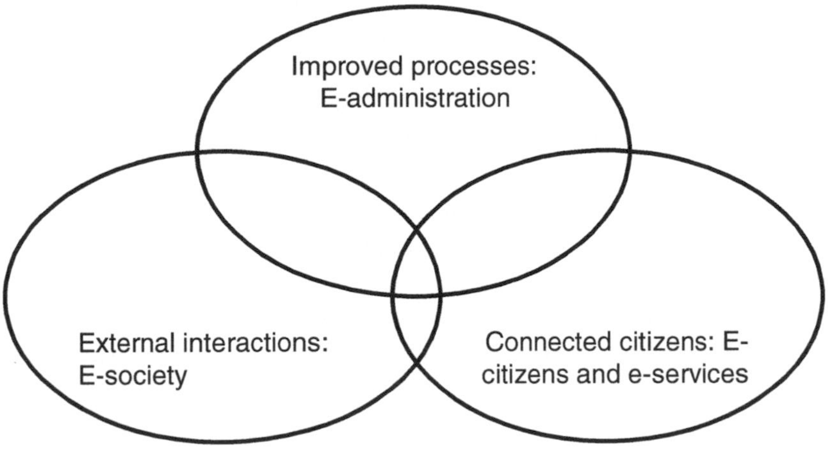

say, something beyond basic e-administration. Kolsaker (2006, 348) suggests that e-government may require a fundamental reconceptualization into an "open systems mode of governance," whereas Spirakis, Spiraki, and Nikolopoulos (2009) distinguish e-democracy from e-government. Heeks (2001) identifies three types of e-governance and displays how they overlap (see Figure 6.1). Yildiz (2007, 650) reports that another preferred term from a decade past was "digital government," a label that lacks any hint of citizen orientation. This lack of clarity, of agreed terminology, threatens to undermine meaningful discussions on the subject.

Here we offer the shorthand term "e-gov" to accommodate the variety of definitions, misunderstandings, and the deliberate blurring of lines between "e-government" and "e-governance" and any other conceptualizations that may arise between or within these fields.

This chapter examines e-gov projects by four governmental entities within the Republic of Korea: the central (national) government, Seoul Metropolitan City (metropolitan government for the nation's capital), Daegu Metropolitan City, and Gangnam District (a local government within Seoul). A variety of technologies have been utilized, and a veritable "alphabet soup" of labels deployed. A number of technological innovations have created enhanced opportunities for citizen access, but the governance process itself has made fewer strides.

SETTING

Until the twenty-first century, Korea was perhaps best known as a battleground. Still the last remaining Cold War conflict zone, the southern half of the peninsula has risen from absolute poverty to become one of the Asian industrial "tigers." The Republic of Korea (South Korea) boasts the world's thirteenth-largest economy, and Korean technology has become a global household name, led by the Samsung, Hyundai, and LG brands.

The Republic of Korea is a unitary state, reflecting a 3,000-year history of centralized government, with "state-centered approaches to public problem solving" leading to "distrust" between government and civil society and an "expectation" that central government undertakes "decisive and sometimes heavy-handed approaches to public problem solving" (Jung, Mazmanian, and Tang 2009, 5). Local government is typically described as consisting of two levels: the upper level includes provinces and metropolitan cities; the lower includes the smaller cities and counties within provinces, and the districts (wards or boroughs) within metropolitan cities that feature locally elected officials and services roughly equivalent to that of a smaller incorporated city or unincorporated county government. Local government authority flows from the central government, as does most of the financing for local government. The nation is frequently described as a neo-Confucian society, in which respect for elders and those in positions of authority is a basic precept.

One of the results of strong central management has been the development of a world-class communications infrastructure throughout the nation of 50 million people. The high population density has assisted in the connectivity of society through information and communication technologies (ICTs): nearly every household across the land is hooked to cable TV and broadband Internet. There are as many cell phones as citizens, and 90 percent of those are smartphones. Instant messaging, such as SMS (cell phone texts) and Internet-based services (e.g., KakaoTalk®) are used more than the telephone itself. Wireless Internet and 4G (LTE) telephone and Internet access is available across all urban and suburban areas, and 3G can be accessed nationwide. Data can be accessed from anywhere, but what data are available?

Annual reports by Transparency International and similar studies have provided the impetus for increasing procedural transparency, particularly in civil applications, where there is a long tradition of corruption. Much of the effort during the period 1995–2005 was focused on governmental efficiency and transparency through the computerization of government data and administration, and citizen access to information. The Internet aspects of this drive have clearly been a success, as evidenced by Korea's top ranking in both the E-Government Development Index and the E–Participation Index within the *United Nations E-Government Survey 2010* (United Nations 2010). Choi and Wright (2004) also recognize that civic groups have become a force to be reckoned with at both the local and the national levels. Governance is taking hold in Korea, slowly but surely.

Still, there has been little collaborative governance in Korea, that is, the "joint provision of services by public, for-profit and nonprofit organizations" (Jung, Mazmanian, and Tang 2009, 3), and much of what exists is of the "government-leading" variety, in which efficiency is prized, and trust between government and other players is low (Park and Park 2009, 95). The three criteria outlined by Carson and Hartz-Karp (2005) for a fully democratic deliberation process—influence on policy and decision making, inclusion of representative population (diversity), and the deliberation process—have been noticeably absent in Korea. In a recent example, the merger of three midsize cities did not incorporate a citizen vote on the matter because of "administrative inconvenience" (Oh 2009).

TECHNOLOGICAL APPROACHES TO E-GOV IN KOREA

There have been a number of technological innovations in Korea's drive to e-governance, some of which were abandoned when the national government chose a different direction. Financial support largely is based on national incentives; therefore, even bottom-up growth is cultivated from the top down. However, pilot projects are encouraged, where a national model can be selected from competing prototypes.

G4C and Other National Government Portals

The South Korean central government established the civil services portal site www.egov.go.kr (now www.minwon.go.kr) in November 2002 under the project name Government for Citizens (G4C) as part of an effort to provide a one-stop, full-service online site for national government services. The Electronic Government Act of 2001 provided the impetus for this multiple-ministries single-window focus (Song 2002), which was built over five years, integrating 11 e-government initiatives (Choi 2003). Whitmore and Choi (2010) praise the portal for being "honest," such as communicating its purpose, history, and future objectives, as well as for its basic function of connecting the user to other governmental sites. The label alone merits consideration: G4C (Government *for* Citizens) rather than the more common G2C (*to* citizens), indicating, as Song (2002, 49) notes, that it is more than simply a conduit from government to the public, but instead

> the most complex stage [of Internet activity] with the highest expected values by developing whole life cycle of the service, providing two-way interactions, and Internet-based transactions, which includes electronic payment.

Consistent with the underlying theme of this chapter (is technology driving the bus?), the Ministry of Information and Communication (MIC) expected control over e-government projects in Korea and competed with various functional ministries to manage the project. Ultimately, the Ministry of Government and Home Affairs (MOGHA, now the Ministry of Public Administration and Safety) was given primacy, with a supplementary role to MIC in terms of developing G4C and the other 10 initiatives: the program includes G2B (business), G2G (governmental internal processes), and infrastructure. Ultimately, the Special Commission on E-Government Korea (EGK) was formed to oversee the various conflicts that arose since, as Choi (2003) observes, leading decision makers in Korea tend to give great importance to input from experts. While he laments the lack of input from civil society at the planning and development stages, which led to significant social strife over issues such as including student data online, Song (2002) notes that it was expected that these social issues would be addressed once service began. Viewed another way, this was a case of "technology first, then citizens."

Citizens have not been left out. At last count, citizens could get detailed information on more than 5,300 services available through various ministries and could request 720 civil services online without visiting administrative offices, including receiving official documents by regular postal services. Citizens could also self-issue 28 civil affairs documents online (Choi 2010).

Numerous other Web-based portals exist for other governmental services. The E-People online petition and discussion portal (www.epeople.go.kr) integrates petitions, proposals, and policy discussion services operated by 303 governmental organizations, including central administrative organizations, local autonomous bodies, and public institutions. Other portals include the Electronic Customs Clearance Service, the Comprehensive Tax Service, and the Single Window for Business Support Services (G4B), as well as various systems designed to facilitate government services, such as document sharing, so applicants need not submit previously processed documents to other governmental bodies.

OPEN and U-Seoul

The "U" in U-Seoul stands for "ubiquitous," an ever-popular and not-inappropriate term relating to wireless communication technologies in Korea. Cell phones and wireless Internet are indeed ubiquitous, but "ubiquitous" also refers to an idealized infrastructure that allows for these and other ICT devices to connect with all other devices, databases, and webpages. Seoul Metropolitan City, and Korea in general, is certainly a world leader in the ubiquitous ICT city movement (for a deeper discussion, see Lee et al. 2008).

In 1998 a growing municipal bureaucracy became cause for concern because of a perceived increase in corruption. The mayor of Seoul declared a "war on corruption," determined to increase transparency through adoption in 1999 of what has become known as OPEN, the Online Procedures Enhancement for Civil Applications (Cho and Choi 2004). The OPEN system continues to score top marks in a variety of e-gov assessments (e.g., Holzer and Kim 2003, 2006, 2008) and is but part of a major thrust by Korean governments to increase use of digital media with citizens (Choi 2003).

According to the Seoul Metropolitan Government website (n.d.):

> E-Government means "A service-oriented government that provides always-accessible and convenient online services for citizens."
>
> The concept of E-Government can be compared with "online administrative service" such as ATMs which were installed in business areas (shopping malls, department stores, etc.) in 1993 when the Clinton administration implemented its Information Superhighway Project.

The OPEN process allowed access to 190 types of administrative systems by 2002, yet it still fell short of citizen expectations as "services remained governmental agency-centered instead of citizen-centered" (Seoul Metropolitan Government, n.d.). The Seoul E-government Development Model (Figure 6.2) indicates the city's march toward e-governance.

The OPEN system provides information on civil applications 24 hours a day via the Internet, and it was designated by the central government of Korea as an advanced tool to foster innovative management in the public sector in November 1999. Within a year,

Figure 6.2 **Seoul E-Government Development Model**

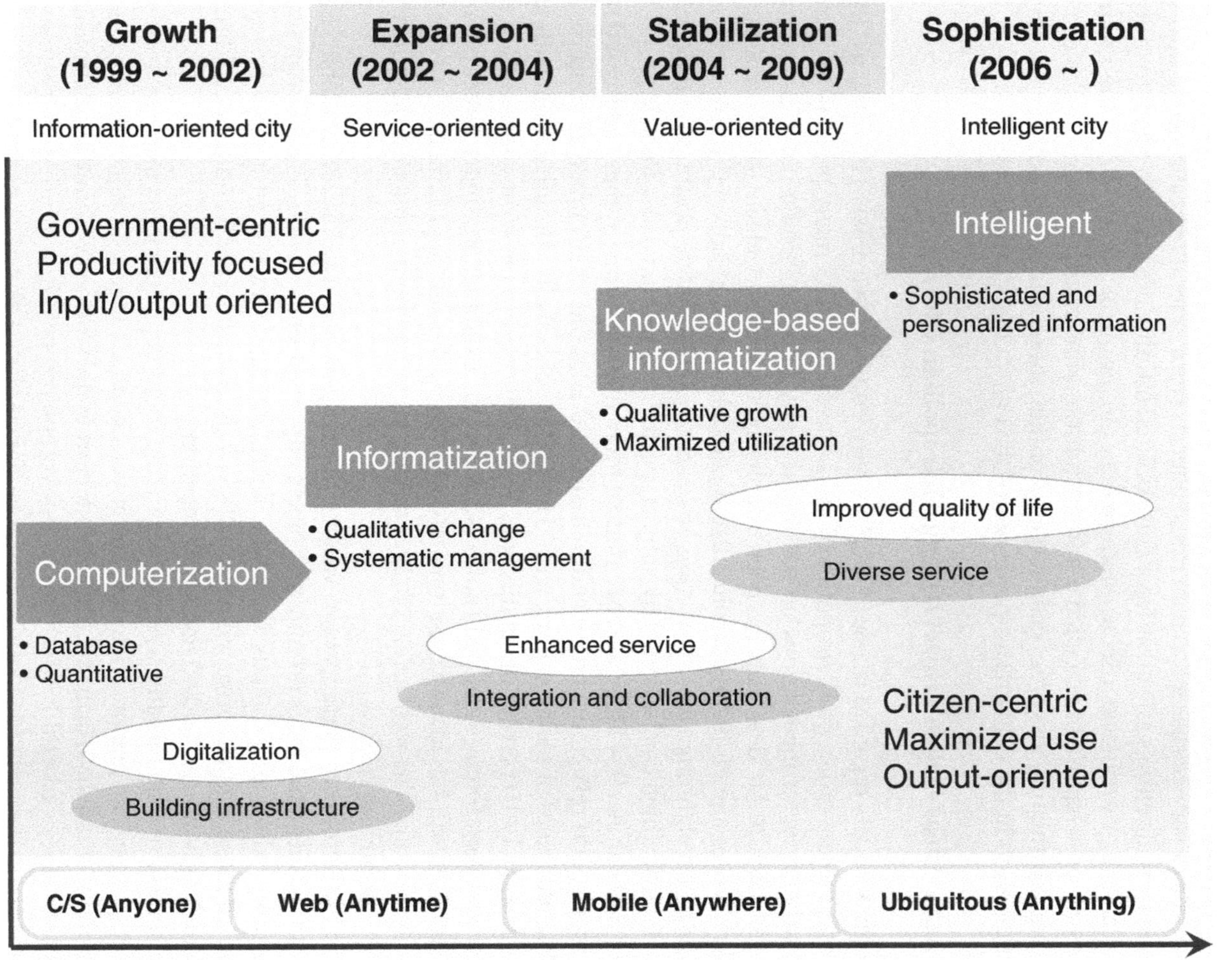

Source: Seoul Metropolitan Government, n.d.

all local governments had adopted the system, and many national organizations have deployed similar programs (Im 2003). OPEN grew into a portal named "One-Click Civil Service" or "e-Seoul," which included links to various national services as well as city services at both the metropolitan and the district level.

As the city's online services have continued to evolve, Seoul City's progress with e-government services has led to numerous requests from cities overseas to share information in formal settings as well as frequently offered training programs in Seoul to officials of overseas governments (Seoul Metropolitan Government 2009). While the program is strong on what might be called e-administration, particularly in terms of citizens obtaining information and processing requests online, there is little opportunity for citizen participation in the deliberative processes of the city in the U-Seoul system.

Citizens' Ideas Online Project (Daegu Metropolitan City)

Daegu is widely regarded as one of Korea's most conservative areas. The Citizens' Ideas Online Project of Daegu Metropolitan City is one the mayor's many projects to encourage private-sector input into what has traditionally been an "inside-only" government administration. An Ideas page has been established on the city website (http://idea.daegu.go.kr), where input is received from citizens and public servants alike. Citizens can watch as ideas travel through the city vetting processes via staff update postings on the discussion board, which can be sorted by subject, poster's name, and date of posting.

In 2009 alone, 914 ideas were submitted; more than one-third of these addressed traffic issues, 200 related to culture and tourism, 170 attacked environmental concerns, 80 addressed issues of social welfare, and 60 looked at general city administration. Although approximately 10 percent of submissions were addressed to the wrong level of government and therefore disqualified (police services, for example, are under direct national administration), 113 ideas were ultimately adopted by the city, approximately 14 percent of submissions. The website encourages citizen input into both efficiency and effectiveness in public service.

To entice citizen participation, various promotions and awards are available. Each month the city announces prominently on the city's website a new Ideas campaign focus, and submissions are promptly reviewed. There are public awards with small prizes for adopted ideas: 7 grand prize winners in 2009, 7 gold medals, 8 silver medals, 27 bronze medals, 24 honorees, and 40 honorable mentions.

Submissions are initially screened within the Ideas department to ensure they are relevant (e.g., not an inappropriate level of government, a suggestion rather than a general complaint or inquiry), then sent to a cross-departmental working committee (section-head level) to assess general feasibility. Upon favorable review, it is referred to the relevant municipal department for consideration of technical aspects as well as research on whether such activities have been attempted elsewhere. Those with positive results are sent to the Ideas Standing Committee, headed by the deputy mayor (the senior-most permanent official of the city) for final review and adoption.

Adopted ideas from civil society have included installing larger street-side litterbins, developing bicycle paths and bicycle storage parks, displaying historical photos of the city, adding urban park commentary signage, and providing for paper-recycling collection in subway areas. Contributions have also included critiques of city operations and staff, which were not eligible ideas for adoption but nonetheless were treated as important insights. Examples include "city staff are too stiff, not kind when asking for identification at the Citizens' One-Stop General Service Center." Other contributions have deep managerial or legal issues attached, such as including citizen participation in the monitoring of citizen–public servant telephone conversations. Additional functions and operational designs to facilitate communication between government and civil society via the city homepage have also been suggested.

Public servants contributed 140 ideas in 2009, processed in a similar manner as those from the public, with 11 ideas adopted. Submissions were classified as follows: 23 in traffic, 19 for culture and tourism, 35 in environment, 10 on social welfare, 30 concerning general administration, and 23 others.

"There's no going back, citizens expect this now," say city staff. The mayor of Daegu was reelected in 2010 on the basis of a platform that relied heavily on his administrative innovations, such as the Citizens' Ideas Project. City staff recognize that this online project, along with other public-private activities, such as the Mayor's Commission on City Government Reform, have provided valuable "outsider" perspectives to city administrators unaccustomed to input from beyond the direct hierarchy. Public suggestions and reports are clearly a step up from the formerly closed network, but the deliberative and analytic processes of government are still firmly enclosed within city hall.

Further improvements are possible. The inclusion of "wikis" or follow-up comments on the tracking page to encourage comments and refinements from other citizens might provide important input before and even during staff analysis. Preliminary staff assessments, if posted in these wikis, could allow for further insights from the community in designated online discussion forums. The current discussion board technology can allow for continuing content, but the overall design is rather archaic and does not indicate that discussions on concepts would be welcomed or considered.

The Daegu Citizens' Ideas Online Project often faces financial issues, specifically for ideas that are too costly to implement, regardless of efficiency factors.

E-Democracy and T-Gov (Gangnam District of Seoul City)

Gangnam is one of 25 autonomous districts within the nation's capital city of Seoul: Gangnam is the financial hub of Korea, the home of most of the nation's major business conglomerates as well as approximately 550,000 residents, and recently globally known for the musical parody "Gangnam Style" by the pop singer Psy. Gangnam District government has repeatedly won awards for e-government innovations, including Intelligent Community of the Year by the Intelligent Community Forum (2008).

Gangnam District's e-Democracy project is a form of nonbinding citizens' referendum. Citizens may respond to major policy questions through a questionnaire placed on the district's website or through e-mail (for those who have preregistered on a distribution list); the results are analyzed and reflected in ongoing district policy discussions. Nearly 500 issues were referred to citizens in 2008 (the most recent year of available data). Most remarkable for the supposedly passive citizens of Korea, more than 80,000 respondents participated in the year 2008 alone, roughly 13 percent of residents of the district (including children).

Policy referrals in Gangnam include budgetary questions and project implementations, as well as more general policies. For example, the question of installing closed-circuit TV in alleys to prevent crime was referred to citizens after objections by human rights groups. In the e-Democracy residents' survey, 82 percent of residents supported the safety project. The city moved ahead with the installations, and crime fell by 40 percent in those locations.

Surprising many who hadn't considered the technology carefully, digital cable TV is not a one-way pipe but allows for interactivity in much the same way as the Internet if the users are empowered. (Of course, Internet access can be made available simultaneously through the same wires, but this discussion concerns the cable TV system alone.) The T-Gov (government through television) project of Gangnam District in Seoul allows residents to respond to questionnaires and to complete a variety of typical administrative forms from a TV-top device in the comfort of their home. More than 100,000 of the approximately 200,000 households in the district are now subscribed to T-Gov. It is not a traditional website, nevertheless the information from T-Gov blends seamlessly with the Internet website.

The primary challenge in Gangnam has been related to the unitary form of government in Korea. All local governments operate under a common framework, which makes innovation difficult. The national government prefers a standard approach to innovation, with ideas conforming to central designs. Gangnam managed to innovate and then propose its models as national benchmarks. Not all issues in e-gov are bureaucratic: the Gangnam district council has expressed concern that their authority would be undermined by direct democracy.

FUTURE DIRECTIONS

Technology has become vital to government. Which technology, how, and where—not when or whether—have become the questions. In lesser-developed lands, the challenge may still be to put a telephone on every desk, or a computer with intranet; elsewhere, it may be satisfying the demands of "early adopters" in fields such as latest-generation cell phones and wireless Internet access. Ultimately, integration of all digital communications media would be ideal.

Korea has been a world leader in the "hardware" side of the ICT revolution, in terms of both equipment and wired (or wireless) networks, and has relayed this into e-gov with a strong focus on hardware. The "soft" side, where citizens participate, however, merits further development. Much of this derives from the fact that the term "citizen" is often used interchangeably with "resident" and "inhabitant" in Korea: beyond periodic votes there has been little sense of citizen as a "partner" of, or full-participant ("sailor") in, government. The twin issues of governance and e-governance are receiving increasing attention from scholars in Korea and elsewhere. Websites are viewed by many as a depiction for governments: how receptive are they to input as well as how productive are they in output, and how well do they allow citizens to view the processes of governments?

The mayor of Daegu has asked for ideas in implementing an "e-town-hall meeting." One consideration is a parliamentary-style "Question Time" with questions posed by citizens through a pre-event online petition process. Additionally, the authors are suggesting an online forum much like those described in Gastil and Levine (2005) or Coleman and Blumler (2009) in terms of developing a weekly topic on a city discussion board where citizens can deliberate both on the topic and on other citizens' comments. The history for this concept goes back several decades (see Teledemocracy Action News + Network, n.d.). Ideas for forum topics could originate from city hall and/or from citizen ideas. Expert input could be included, perhaps as part of an introductory posting. Discussions could continue for a period of several weeks (i.e., several, but not many, discussions might run in overlapping periods), after which a general summary of major themes on the topic would be compiled and presented to the mayor's office for further consideration, and reporting back through the e-town hall on the summarization and progress through city hall thereafter. The online discussion forum for the e-town hall would be enhanced through cable TV and/or Internet-broadcast open city town-hall meetings hosted by the mayor, at which citizens could use a variety of ICTs, including Web 2.0 style systems (e.g., Facebook) and cell phones as well as government-hosted discussion boards to provide input and votes.

Apart from top-down e-gov, we are awaiting some of the grassroots-up approaches in what might be more closely identified as e-democracy. Tapscott (2009) points to the UK's E-Petitions and South Korea's ICT-driven "mad-cow beef" protests as examples of citizens framing the questions for government through the use of technology. More problematically, Castells (2009) notes the use of SMS (short messaging on cell phones) as a key tool for political change in the earliest years of the twenty-first century (e.g., Philippines, Ukraine, Thailand, Spain, Ecuador). Although focused on election campaigns, Tapscott's (2009) distinctions between presidential candidate Barack Obama's Web 2.0–style Internet presence and the Meetup.com presence only four years earlier by candidate Howard Dean speak much to the difference between empowering users and merely delving out information.

CONCLUSION

Doing business online has become routine for much of society, who increasingly shop, bank, and socialize through the Internet. However, we reiterate here the caution set out by Nyirenda and Cropf (2010, 26):

> [S]uccessful eGovernance depends on several factors including the political climate, societal values regarding government, technological skill-levels, social attitudes towards eGovernance, and the inspirational basis of the pioneers of eGovernance.

> Essentially, these elements combine with another major concern: the appropriateness of the eGovernance model to the administrative systems values and culture of the country in question.

Some of the factors identified by Nyirenda and Cropf (2010) are beyond the scope of this book. In any case, it is clear that "champions" for the project of governance through the Internet are needed, both within government and beyond (Docter and Dutton 1998).

E-government (e-administration) can therefore be seen as merely a useful stepping-stone toward ICT-driven participatory and deliberative democracy. Whether, and how, that decision making involves digital and Web 2.0–style participation is unclear, but if video conferencing in the business sector and Internet "chats" and Facebook "walls" are any indication, it seems likely that technology will enable and enhance discussions. The television show *American Idol* used telephone counts for decision making, and various telethons have used "tote boards" to indicate progress: these simpler data systems are one type of lower-tech option. The technology exists to do all of this on websites.

E-gov, whatever it is, appears inescapable. As citizens become increasingly "e-"aware, governments will do more online, websites will become more mobile-phone friendly (in their formatting), and citizen discussion boards more prominent. Civil society will become more involved in the decision-making process as the deliberative process becomes more transparent, whether they are invited or not. Castells (2009, 413) observes that there is a "reprogramming of networks" in communication, where the masses, who have been spied upon by government since the beginning, can now spy on government. The question is whether civil society will be invited and made part of the process or will become combative outsiders. Nevertheless, as new forms of technology appear, we run the risk of neglecting the findings from earlier, simpler yet effective designs, such as from Koen (1996). Let us not neglect "what works" in a rush to appear current.

As they move toward greater online presence, it is natural that governments will take careful steps to manage their resources and not make serious missteps: both financial and sociopolitical considerations will be of great concern alongside the technological. Governments will vary in their level of technological acumen as well as in their desire for more inclusive governance. Local heritage may hold that citizen participation in government is less valued, and in these environments, technology might be seen simply as a medium to announce government policies. Instead, technology should be used as a resource to increase the participation of civil society in an inclusive and deliberative decision-making process. Web-based e-gov should be seen as a step forward, such that the values inherent in the governance model are not lost in a trade-off with technology.

KEY POINTS

- *Don't put all your eggs in one basket.* Commitment to developing enhanced e-governance includes financial support for projects that are ultimately unsuccessful. Allowing competition within organizations can allow the best ideas and better deployments to be discovered. It's not waste but investment.

- *All roads lead to . . .* Utilize multiple digital streams to communicate with and direct citizens to the official website: Facebook, instant messaging, and whatever technologies the future may provide. A website is important as a destination, but a website is not the complete online presence—other mediums are important to drive traffic to the official website, and other technologies complement the website.
- *There's more than one way to . . .* Existing technology can often be transformed without losing the initial purpose. A website must allow for data input from non-Web devices. Cable TV and electrical wires both can convey two-way Internet, touch-tone telephones can provide alphanumeric input, and voice-recognition software, while limited, is also available for input into online data systems. There is communication beyond Web forms!
- *Words mean things.* Project titles can be important if they help guide development and expectation of users. Government for Citizens (G4C) instead of Government to Citizens (G2C), or perhaps even Government with Citizens (G+C)?
- *Communication, not just information.* A website must do more than provide information and direct to other information providers. E-governance requires that websites collect public input and display how that input is being processed—promptly. Discussions can be archived and visible to all.
- *Let them eat bread?* The purpose of the Web presence is to enhance service to citizens, not to showcase government technology. The website can make leaders and agencies look good, but if they aren't listening back on the website, the citizens are talking somewhere else. It's far better to be part of the conversation.
- *Make friends, not foes.* Policymakers need to be made aware early that enhanced Web services provide new opportunities for communication with citizens, both outbound (video, text) and inbound (messages, referendums); to make best use of the asset rather than fear it.
- *A winding path, not a superhighway.* Uncertainty is a given. Change will continue, and the best plans of today may appear to be hopeless error next year. Korea's insistence on Active-X (Microsoft Windows) for financial transactions has become an albatross, as Microsoft officially abandoned the technology in 2011 and it does not work with other Web browsers. Information travels fast, but progress is less certain. Be ready to backtrack and leapfrog technologies to try another route.

REFERENCES

Belanger, F., L. Carter, and L. Schaupp. 2005. U-government: A framework for the evolution of e-government. *Electronic Government, an International Journal* 2 (4), 426–445.

Carson, L., and J. Hartz-Karp. 2005. Adapting and combining deliberative designs. In *The deliberative democracy handbook: Strategies for effective civic engagement in the 21st century*, ed. J. Gastil and P. Levine, 120–138. San Francisco, CA: Jossey-Bass.

Castells, M. 2009. *Communication power.* New York: Oxford University Press.

Champ, M. 2001. Overselling IT: The impact of disconfirmed expectations on acceptance. *Canberra Bulletin of Public Administration* 100: 40–41.

Cho, Y., and B. Choi. 2004. E-government to combat corruption: The case of Seoul metropolitan government. *International Journal of Public Administration* 27 (10), 719–735.

Choi, H. 2003. Reforming government with information technology in South Korea. *Asian Journal of Political Science* 11 (1), 40–56.

Choi, Y. 2010. Korea sets global trend on e-government service. *Korea Times*, July 1. www.koreatimes.co.kr/www/news/biz/2010/06/291_66931.html.

Choi, Y., and D. Wright. 2004. Intergovernmental relations (IGR) in Korea and Japan: Phases, patterns, and progress towards decentralization (local autonomy) in a trans-Pacific context. *International Review of Public Administration* 9 (1), 1–22.

Coleman, S., and J. Blumler. 2009. *The Internet and democratic citizenship*. New York: Cambridge University Press.

Docter, S., and W. Dutton. 1998. The first amendment online: Santa Monica's Public Electronic Network (PEN). In *Cyberdemocracy: Technology, cities, and civic networks*, ed. R. Tsagarousianou, D. Tambini, and C. Bryan, 125–150. London: Routledge.

Emmanouilidou, M., and D. Kreps. 2010. A framework for accessible m-government implementation. *Electronic Government, an International Journal* 7 (3), 252–269.

Eun, J. 2009. Collaboration in governance: A study on conflict management in Korean local administration through IAD framework. In *Collaborative governance in the United States and Korea*, ed. Y. Jung, D. Mazmanian, and S. Tang, 19–150. Seoul: Seoul National University Press.

Gastil, J., and P. Levine, eds. 2005. *The deliberative democracy handbook: Strategies for effective civic engagement in the 21st century.* San Francisco, CA: Jossey-Bass.

Heeks, R. 2001. Understanding e-governance for development. *Information Technology in Developing Countries* 11 (3), 13–34. www.iimahd.ernet.in/egov/ifip/dec2001/article3.htm.

Holzer, M., and S. Kim. 2003. *Digital governance in municipalities worldwide (2003): A longitudinal assessment of municipal websites throughout the world.* Newark, NJ: The E-Governance Institute/National Center for Public Productivity (Rutgers University). http://unpan1.un.org/intradoc/groups/public/documents/aspa/unpan012905.pdf.

———. 2006. *Digital governance in municipalities worldwide (2005): A longitudinal assessment of municipal websites throughout the world.* Newark, NJ: National Center for Public Productivity (Rutgers University). http://unpan1.un.org/intradoc/groups/public/documents/aspa/unpan022839.pdf.

———. 2008. *Digital governance in municipalities worldwide (2007): A longitudinal assessment of municipal websites throughout the world.* Newark, NJ: National Center for Public Performance (Rutgers University). http://andromeda.rutgers.edu/~egovinst/Website/PDFs/100%20City%20Survey%202007%20(Full%20Report).pdf.

Im, B. 2003. Strengthening government-citizen connections: A case study of Korea. In *Anti-corruption symposium 2001: The role of on-line procedures in promoting good governance*, 76–88. Seoul: Seoul Metropolitan Government. http://unpan1.un.org/intradoc/groups/public/documents/UN/UNPAN007564.pdf#page=82.

Intelligent Community Forum. 2008. Gangnam district in Seoul, South Korea, named the intelligent community of the year. News release, May 16. www.intelligentcommunity.org/clientuploads/Gov-Tech_Awards_5-16-08.pdf.

Jho, W. 2005. Challenges for e-governance: Protests from civil society on the protection of privacy in e-government in Korea. *International Review of Administrative Sciences* 71 (1), 151–166.

Jung, Y., D. Mazmanian, and S. Tang. 2009. Collaborative governance in the United States and Korea: Cases in negotiated policymaking and service delivery. *International Review of Public Administration* 13, special issue, 1–11.

Koen, B. 1996. Use of internet relay chat (IRC) in distributed consensus forcing. Paper presented at the 1996 Annual Conference of ASEE Gulf Southwest Section, San Antonio, TX. www.me.utexas.edu/~koen/ETH/gsw.pdf.

Kolsaker, A. 2006. Reconceptualising e-government as a tool of governance: The UK case. *Electronic Government, an International Journal* 3 (4), 347–355.

Kolsaker, A., and L. Lee-Kelley. 2006. Citizen-centric e-government: A critique of the UK model. *Electronic Government, an International Journal* 3 (2), 127–138.
Lee, S., X. Tan, and S. Trimi. 2006. M-government, from rhetoric to reality: Learning from leading countries. *Electronic Government, an International Journal* 3 (2), 113–126.
Lee, S., T. Yigitcanlar, J. Han, and Y. Leem. 2008. Ubiquitous urban infrastructure: Infrastructure planning and development in Korea. *Innovation: Management, Policy and Practice* 10 (2–3), 282–292.
Lim, J., and S. Tang. 2008. Urban e-government initiatives and environmental decision performance in Korea. *Journal of Public Administration Research and Theory* 18 (1), 109–138.
Nyirenda, J., and R. Cropf. 2010. The prospects for egovernment and egovernance in sub-Saharan Africa: A case study of Zambia. *International Journal of Electronic Government Research* 6 (1), 23–45.
Oh, Y. 2009. City of 1 million will be launched in July. *Korea Times [Online edition]*, December 11. http://koreatimes.co.kr/www/news/nation/2009/12/117_57123.html.
Osborne, D., and T. Gaebler. 1992. *Reinventing government: How the entrepreneurial spirit is transforming the public sector.* Reading, MA: Addison-Wesley.
Park, H., and M. Park, M. 2009. Types of network governance and network performance: Community development project case. *International Review of Public Administration* 13, special issue, 91–105.
Pascual, P. 2003. E-government. Kuala Lumpur: e-ASEAN Task Force, UNDP-APDIP. www.unapcict.org/ecohub/resources/e-government/at_download/attachment1.
Rethemeyer, R. 2007. Policymaking in the age of internet: Is the Internet tending to make policy networks more or less inclusive? *Journal of Public Administration Research and Theory* 17 (2), 259–284.
Seligman, A. 1992. *The idea of civil society.* New York: Free Press (Macmillan).
Seoul Metropolitan Government. n.d. What is e-government? http://seoulen.seoul.go.kr/government/init/eseoul_init01.html.
Seoul Metropolitan Government. 2009. E-Seoul signs an MOU on e-government collaboration with three cities in Asia and Europe. Press release, December 7. http://e-seoul.go.kr/news/press/1263466_12148.html.
Song, H. 2002. Prospects and limitations of the e-government initiative in Korea. *International Review of Public Administration* 7 (2), 45–53. www.kapa21.0r.kr/data/newsletter_download.php?did=681.
Spirakis, G., C. Spiraki, and K. Nikolopoulos. 2009. The impact of electronic government on democracy: E-democracy through e-participation. *Electronic Government, an International Journal* 7 (1), 75–88.
Tapscott, D. 2009. *Grown up digital: How the net generation is changing your world.* New York: McGraw-Hill.
Teledemocracy Action News + Network. N.d. Project action news. https://fp.auburn.edu/tann/tann2/projects.html.
United Nations. 2010. *United Nations e-government survey.* New York: Department of Social and Economic Affairs. http://unpan1.un.org/intradoc/groups/public/documents/un/unpan038851.pdf.
Welch, E., and S. Pandey. 2007. E-government and bureaucracy: Toward a better understanding of intranet implementation and its effect on red tape. *Journal of Public Administration Research and Theory* 17 (3), 379–404.
Whitmore, A., and N. Choi. 2010. Reducing the perceived risk of e-government implementations: The importance of risk communication. *International Journal of Electronic Government Research* 6 (1), 1–8.
Yildiz, M. 2007. E-government research: Reviewing the literature, limitations, and ways forward. *Government Information Quarterly* 24, 646–665.
Yun, H., and C. Opheim. 2010. Building on success: The diffusion of e-government in the American states. *Electronic Journal of E-Government* 8 (1), 71–82. www.ejeg.com/volume-8/v018-iss1/Yun_and_Ophiem.pdf.

7

Improving Citizen Participation via E-Government

The Why and How

Yueping Zheng and Yuguo Liao

Over the past two decades, researchers have emphasized citizen participation in public administration decision making as a means of collaborating with the public to promote democratic values such as responsiveness and accountability (Franklin and Ebdon 2004; Fung 2006; Irvin and Stansbury 2004; King, Feltey, and Susel 1998; Nelson and Wright 1995; Weeks 2000; Kim and Lee 2012). Irvin and Stansbury (2004) summarized the advantages of citizen participation in government decision making whereby citizens would learn more about the government, gain skills for activist citizenship, and achieve some control over the policy process. They believed that government could also benefit by learning from and informing citizens, building trust and strategic alliances, gaining legitimacy of decisions, avoiding litigation costs, and making better policy and implementation decisions.

The evolution of citizen participation in public administration decision making faces a new phase, as many government agencies have initiated electronic government (e-government) development and have taken advantage of Internet-based applications to facilitate community development and communication with constituents and to provide online application services (Heeks and Bailur 2007; Norris and Moon 2005; West 2004; Kim and Lee 2012). More attention is drawn to government efforts to utilize new technologies to enable greater citizen participation in policy formation and evaluation and to create greater information exchange between citizens and government (Komito 2005; Macintosh and Whyte 2008; Norris 1999; Organisation for Economic Co-operation and Development [OECD] 2001; Kim and Lee 2012).

Although e-government has the potential to improve citizen participation online, the reality is that this online participation still lags. The latest global e-governance report from the E-Government Institute of School of Public Affairs and Administration in Rutgers University–Newark shows that citizen participation online is the lowest when compared to other categories: privacy and security, usability, content, and services. The average score of citizen participation of all the municipalities evaluated is 3.53 out of 20, which is lower than other categories. Both Rutgers and UN reports indicate that a great gap exists worldwide in e-participation development. So, which factors mediate the impact of e-government on citizen participation and which factors influence e-participation need to be clarified. In this chapter, we discuss the importance of citizen participation, the impact of e-government on citizen participation, and the factors affecting e-participation development.

WHAT IS CITIZEN PARTICIPATION?

Citizen participation has been defined differently and "can refer to a range of different actions by different people" (Pateman 1970; Roberts 2004, 318). Roberts (2004) summarized the definitions of citizen participation and found that legal definitions from Cooper in 1984 emphasized the procedural aspects of involvement—the extent to which citizenship was defined in constitutions and statutes that prescribed the qualifications, rights, and obligations within a particular government's jurisdiction. Roberts (2004) also found that citizenship, in other scholars' perspectives, was a substantive ethical and sociological statement, based on which citizen participation included a sense of responsibility and civic devotion to one's commonwealth (Dimock 1990). Combining the viewpoints from these scholars, Roberts (2004) defined citizen participation as the process by which members of a society (those not holding office or administrative positions in government) share power with public officials in making substantive decisions and in taking actions related to the community.

Citizen participation has been narrowly defined as "a process in which individuals take part in decision making in the institutions, programs, and environments that affect them" (Heller et al. 1984, 339; Leung 2009). Zimmerman and Rappaport (1988) also broadly defined citizen participation as involvement in any organized activity in which the individual participates without pay to achieve a common goal, including government-mandated advisory boards, voluntary organizations, mutual-help groups, and community service activities. Glass (1979) argued that the term "citizen participation" was an overgeneralization that often was defined simply as providing citizens with opportunities to take part in governmental decision or planning processes.

As to the forms of citizen participation, Sharp (2012) summarized the most heavily researched forms of local participation: (1) contacting public officials; (2) neighborhood organization involvement and closely linked activities, such as working on community projects and co-production of urban services; (3) attendance at public meetings, and the more elaborate version of this, deliberative democracy; and (4) voting in local elections. These forms reflect the content and aims of citizen participation for citizens to actively participate by expressing themselves, attending public hearings, and directly voting in the government affairs and influencing the policymaking process.

Citizen participation has been used to realize many aims, such as disseminating information to the public, helping citizens to understand the policymaking and government functions better, improving citizen and government relationships, increasing citizen input, enabling citizens to better supervise government, and so on. Glass (1979) discussed the five objectives of citizen participation: information exchange, education, support building, supplemental decision making, and representational input. Glass (1979, 182) explains them as follows:

> Information exchange may be defined as bringing planners and citizens together for the purpose of sharing ideas and concerns. Education, an extension of the information exchange objective, refers to the dissemination of detailed information about a project, about proposed ideas, or about citizen participation itself. Support building would involve such activities as creating a favorable climate for proposed policies and plans or the resolution of conflict among citizen groups or between citizen groups and the government. The decision-making supplement objective refers to efforts that are designed to provide citizens an increased opportunity for input into the planning process. Representative input may be defined as an effort to identify the views of the entire community on particular issues to create the possibility that subsequent plans will reflect community desires.

WHY CITIZEN PARTICIPATION IS NEEDED

The Tradition and Culture of Citizen Participation

Strange (1972) discussed the tradition of citizen participation in the United States. Even before the Revolutionary War, the people placed great emphasis on government. Strange argued that citizen participation and control of government has been a widely accepted objective of U.S. government from its inception. Citizen participation is widely accepted and promoted in the United States, and people believe that it plays an important role in "controlling" government and decentralizing government power. Citizen participation is also an important part of political culture in the United States. From the perspectives of Day (1997) and Irvin and Stansbury (2004), citizen participation seems to hold a sacrosanct role in U.S. political culture. The culture of respecting citizens' rights and limiting government makes citizen participation an important reflection of this culture in political life.

Roots in Democratic Values and Disillusionment with Bureaucracy

Moynihan (2003) (see also Morone 1998) argued that the search for the democratic wish was one of the deep and continuing instincts of American political life, reflected in a yearning for a direct, communal democracy and a fear of public power as a threat to liberty. And participation produces benefits to citizens and offers them the chance to fulfill the "democratic wish" to exert real influence in the government process (Morone 1998; Moynihan 2003). Crow and Stevens (2012) also viewed citizen participation as a vital component of democracy. "The more participation there is in decisions, the more democracy there is" (Verba and Nie 1972; Crow and Stevens 2012). Democracy is a foundational political value in United States. Citizen participation is rooted in democracy and reflects democracy.

The rise of citizen participation also results from citizens' disillusionment with bureaucracy. White (1997) maintained that demands for greater citizen participation in government decision making seemed to rise and fall on waves of dissatisfaction with existing social conditions and, most especially, with a lack of trust in elected representatives. The dissatisfaction and decrease of trust toward government affect the demand for citizen participation. Moynihan (2003) argued that the traditional model of democratic governmental accountability was based on the assumption that elected officials exerted political control of the bureaucracy, designing policy that was implemented by neutral administrators. However, the policy and administration dichotomy has been long demolished (Seidman and Gilmour 1986; Waldo 1947; Moynihan 2003). Recently, the low efficiency, effective, responsibility, and accountability increase the dissatisfaction and distrust of public toward government. In this situation, participation could be a way to supervise the government externally.

Bringing Benefits to Both Government and Citizens

Improving Government Performance

The importance of citizen participation in improving government performance is emphasized by many researchers. For example, "due to lack of citizen engagement in planning, data generation, and decision making, the public sector often fails to succeed in performance improvement" (Holzer and Mullins 2012, 328). Yang (2007, 175) argued:

> Without stakeholder involvement, performance measurement may be guided by bureaucratic interests and the technocratic logic and produce numbers that external stakeholders cannot understand. In turn, when elected officials and citizens are better informed about government performance, they are more likely to participate.

Moynihan (2003) maintained that public input could provide information that helped managers improve public efficiency—either allocative efficiency through better resource allocation choices or managerial efficiency through information that leads to improvement in the processes of public-service provision. Because many public programs require some level of cooperation from citizens, involvement of the public in setting goals is likely to provide more informed goals, to raise acceptance of programs, and even to provide the possibility of citizen-administrative co-production (Thomas 1995; Moynihan 2003). The realization of government performance improvement requires clearly setting goals, efficiently allocating resources, and gaining sufficient public support, all of which cannot be separated from citizen participation.

Providing better services to the public is the goal of government. However, how to provide those services that citizens expect requires efficient planning by government. Citizen participation would reflect their needs and expectations to government and help the services provided by government fit their needs better. Moreover, by involving citizens in policymaking, outcomes can become superior because they are formed by values, experiences, and priorities of the citizenry who will be affected by the policy implementation (Fischer 2005; Roberts 2008; Crow and Stevens 2012). So, with citizen participation playing important roles, services provided and policies made by government would be more citizen oriented.

Also, public agencies are particularly likely to seek public support in times of weakness or environmental instability, to counter negative political or public attitudes toward the public organization or the government as a whole (McNair, Caldwell, and Pollane 1983; Kweit and Kweit 1980; Moynihan 2003). Support from the public would make the policymaking and implementation smoother. The creation of participatory forums may therefore be designed to increase the perception that public organizations are more consultative, thus lending an air of democratic legitimacy to the activities of the organization (Frederickson 1982; Moynihan 2003). Citizen participation would also serve as the external supervision of government, helping government to be more responsible and accountable.

A great discussion of the relationship between citizen participation and performance was provided by Holzer and Mullins (2012). They believed that citizen participation was a critical resource for improving the performance of public organizations and for an agenda:

1. Because citizens have a great deal of evaluative "data" to offer in terms of their experiences and critiques of public-service delivery, agencies need to overcome their reluctance to share power insofar as "information is power." That is, agencies gain only by real-world data and cases that citizens might offer, and power is a barrier to that data sharing. The cases in this chapter are evidence that citizen participation is widespread, works, and contributes to performance improvement.
2. Citizen-based government is, more specifically, a threat to the bureaucracy in terms of rigid hierarchy and specialization of functions. But so what? Intelligent bureaucracies should welcome the participation of citizens, even as untrained observers, because their perspectives offer insights that desk-bound bureaucrats cannot possibly imagine.
3. Even public managers who are open to citizen feedback lack requisite training. This suggests that citizen groups should take the initiative to connect public servants with capacity-building resources such as short courses, but it might also suggest that a citizen group, university, or foundation establish an online certificate program to help improve the capacities of public managers in this regard.
4. Further, beyond the survey research or interviewing skills necessary to obtain valid and reliable citizen feedback, public managers need to master specific sets of skills, such as collaboration with citizen volunteers, negotiation with citizen groups, and conflict-resolution strategies that would foster consensus.
5. Overall, the culture of public management has to change from one that assumes citizens are annoyances to a more progressive and productive concept of citizens as partners. Public bureaucracies are increasingly seeking ways to do more with less. Given that they commonly have far fewer financial resources than they recently controlled, citizen-based government offers substantial and valuable resources—human and informational—that cannot be ignored. Involving citizens is a win-win strategy, an avenue for data- and case-driven analysis, and a partnership that can only help improve agency productivity and performance.

The argument from Holzer and Mullins emphasized the importance of citizen participation in providing valuable opinion and feedback. They also recommended that public managers need to have the capacities to obtain valid and reliable citizen feedback. Also, the culture that respects citizen input is important.

Improving Relationships Between Citizens and Government and Increase Citizen Trust

The advantages of citizen participation in government decision making include that citizens will learn more about the government, will gain skills for activist citizenship, and will gain some control over the policy process (Irvin and Stansbury 2004). The government can also gain from citizen participation. For example, the government can learn from and inform citizens, build trust and strategic alliances, gain legitimacy of decisions, avoid litigation cost, and make better policy and implementation decisions (Irvin and Stansbury 2004). Irvin and Stansbury's argument indicated that citizen participation had the potential to improve relationships between citizens and government and increase citizen trust toward government.

Pateman (1970), Sabatier (1988), Blackburn and Bruce (1995), and Irvin and Stansbury (2004) all emphasized the educational benefits of citizen participation. By participating in the policymaking process, citizens are more likely to understand better the inside running operation and learn more about their governments. With more citizens educated about how government functions, government will be more likely to benefit, since it can get more useful advice and suggestions from the public. White (1997) supported this point and believed that participation has an educative effect on citizens, alerting them to their civic duties and helping them recognize the common good. This educational function of citizen participation would reduce the information asymmetry, which benefits their understanding of government and improves the relationship between citizen and government.

Moreover, Mumford (1991) and Olphert and Damodaran (2007) found that a participatory design process enabled users to contribute their expertise and knowledge, provided an opportunity for learning and skill sharing that benefited both designers and users, and encouraged acceptance and uptake of new systems by giving users a sense of ownership and a good understanding of the system. Although the argument is based on designing a computer-based work system, it can be generalized to other policymaking processes. With citizen participation in the policymaking process, government could not only build better policies but also increase citizens' acceptance and support of the policies, improving relationship between citizens and government. Thomas (1995) emphasized that the impetus for public involvement came from a need to obtain acceptance as a prerequisite to successful implementation. Irvin and Stansbury (2004) also believed that a powerful motivating factor to advocate citizen participation is the prospect of a more cooperative public. More citizen involvement not only can improve the policy quality but also keep the door of communication between government and citizens open and make citizens more cooperative.

Citizen participation also has the potential to increase citizen trust toward government. Wang and Van Wart (2007) argued that participation will lead to trust when it can produce high-quality services that the public wants and enhanced ethical behavior on the part of administration. Participation promotes two-way communication between citizens and government, increasing public input in decision making. Accordingly, government operation is more likely to fit citizens' expectations. Besides, more participation and engagement would improve the quality of the policymaking process and guarantee the fairness and effectiveness of policies. So, citizens' satisfaction with the services provided by the government would likely increase, and citizen trust would follow.

E-GOVERNMENT AND CITIZEN PARTICIPATION

Although citizen participation is needed and can bring benefits to both government and citizens, it is still at a relatively low level. In a survey conducted by the Kaiser Family Foundation and Harvard University, millions of Americans could not answer even basic questions about American politics (*Washington Post* 1996; White 1997). Kleinman, Delborne, and Anderson (2011) argued that, since the 1960s, the level of voter participation in the United States has dropped some 25 percent.

White (1997) listed several reasons for the low citizen participation, for example, citizens lack information, time, and resources to be sufficiently informed on the multitude of complex issues they face. Technology, in White's perspective, would make it possible for the mass of citizens to register their opinions on matters of national public policy and would provide them with a virtually limitless volume of information.

With two decades of development, e-government, by using information and communication technologies, has the potential to promote citizen participation in several ways. It smooths communications between citizens and government, provides new forms and more convenient ways to participate, supplies citizens with information needed, and reduces cost for participation. All of these enable e-government to help government raise its citizen participation.

Smoothing Communications

Barnes and Williams (2012) discussed new digital technologies and their impact on citizen engagement. First, they emphasized the one-way mass communication method for efficiency, such as e-mail distribution groups, which are used to send one e-mail to many people (Barnes and Williams 2012, 171). Technologies enable users to select the people they want to reach in the ways they prefer, thus improving the efficiency and reducing cost of communication.

Technologies also promote two-way interactive communications: "Using interactive cable methodology, a meeting can be conducted and televised, while citizens can provide real-time feedback to opinion polling during the meeting" (Barnes and Williams 2012, 172). With the expansion of municipalities and the deteriorating living conditions of large cities, numerous people have begun to move away from urban areas, which makes it difficult for them to attend public hearings and meetings. Two-way interactive communication technologies enable citizens to watch live video of public meetings and use phone or online methods to give feedback and participate.

Barnes and Williams (2012) also discussed technologies and media that build social, professional, and other interpersonal connections to motivate citizens to express freely: "Facebook, Friendster, My Space, and other social networking competitions provide opportunities for groups (including governments) to create social linkages" (Barnes and Williams 2012). Some networks, such as LinkedIn, also help professional people communicate with one another. Blogs help people to freely express themselves and interact with others. These tools work as a big net that connects people from different groups, careers, and so on, so that they can interact with each other, facilitating relationship building not only among people from different groups but also between citizens and government.

To better attract citizen participation, government needs to know about citizens' concerns more clearly. E-government uses related technologies to smooth communications between citizens and government. By setting up a discussion forum and building its Facebook page and Twitter, government provides convenient ways for citizens to give comments and feedback: "Online surveying software and Web sites have emerged that can allow government to conduct more professional survey research and make more accurate and appropriate conclusions than may have been previously possible" (Barnes and Williams 2012, 174). The data collected would be analyzed to learn citizens' attitudes on policies and issues, and to help government improve its response.

Providing Convenient Methods of Participation

Most traditional forms of citizen participation are limited for citizens, since they need physically to approach the government, make phone calls, or send mail. These methods are high cost, slow, and low efficiency. However, with new technologies, e-government brings new methods for participation, ones that are low cost, fast, and more efficient, thus motivating more participation.

Kakbadase, Kakabadse, and Kouzmin (2003) believed that new information technology has the ability to enhance direct citizen participation in the political process. New interactive media can accommodate dialogue that flows, in a circular fashion, among interested stakeholders and groupings (Kakbadase, Kakabadse, and Kouzmin 2003). In this situation, information technology could enable the building of regular dialogue and feedback, helping citizens and government to interact. They also recalled the argument from London (1994), which emphasized the advantages of citizen feedback when combining with new media technology that had the capacity to enlarge the scope of political dialogue and serve as an educational process that brought issues into focus, allowing them to be further defined.

Information technology also provides new forms of participation. With information technologies, citizens can vote at home or other convenient locales. These methods, which save money and time, motivate more citizens to participate. Many municipalities provide live channels for the public to watch council meetings and public hearings. In the future, coverage of such meetings at the local, state, and national level is likely to expand dramatically, making government deliberations more accessible to the average person (Snider 1994). These technologies also can provide video conferences between citizens and government officials or employees in order to directly discuss issues and find ways to solve problems.

Timney (2011, 86) provided good examples of how technology has changed the ways of citizen participation:

> Technology has expanded the ways that citizens can interact with politicians and administrators. Email makes it easier for organizations to gather support for petitions to Congress while Internet sites like YouTube can spread information—and misinformation—across wide networks. Every member of Congress has an email address, as does even the President of the United States, Queen Elizabeth and Pope Benedict XVI. Speaking out has become much easier and more prevalent, but it may be no more effective in influencing decisions than old-fashioned hand-written letters. Still, electronic communication can give the appearance of a higher level of engagement.

Providing Related Information About the Inside Workings of Government

Research indicates that lack of policy information may contribute to this dearth of citizen involvement, and media reportage patterns may prevent citizens from easily accessing the information necessary for participation (Crow and Stevens 2012). Citizens need to know the background or other related information to have their own understanding or judgment on public issues, which makes meaningful participation become possible. Wang and Van Wart (2007) also emphasized the importance of information in public participation. With the information needed, citizens would likely participate more in the decision-making process of government and engage more. With limited information, it is hard for citizens to know the inside workings of government, not to mention to participate, engage, and supervise.

Cross-sectional data show that better-informed citizens participate more than less-informed ones (Flanagin and Zingale 1994; Zaller 1992, Bimber 2001). For citizens, available information is the precondition for participation or engagement, since they need information to understand the process of decision making and play their roles in it. In the space of five years, between roughly 1995 and 2000, virtually every political candidate, party, interest group, media business, and governmental institution adopted interest-based means of communication and information provision, making readily accessible the largest and most dynamic body of political information ever available to U.S. citizens (Bimber 2001).

Crow and Stevens (2012) believed that media helped determine the level of societal knowledge about environmental issues and the corresponding importance of those issues in the public and policy discourse through an issue-attention cycle. Through reporting on environmental issues, media helps not only to raise awareness about issues but also to define the problems and associated costs of solving those problems (Crow and

Stevens 2012). With e-government, more and more information technologies and new forms of media facilitate information dissemination. Convenient ways to get background information about public issues enable citizens to have their own reasoning and hence participate more.

With official websites where information is posted online, e-government enables citizens to get information conveniently and quickly. The information related pertains to contact information for government staff and administrators, public meeting minutes, budgeting, personnel management, and so on—all provided to enable citizens to have the background to participate. A study from the E-Government Institute of Rutgers University–Newark shows that the municipalities that did well in e-governance provided rich information online, which served as a great base for citizens to discuss government issues and participate. With information in hand, citizens can easily interact with government.

Reducing the Cost of Participation

There are many factors impeding further improvements to citizen participation, one of which is the cost involved for both citizens and government. Since citizen participation is usually volunteerism, the cost is not likely to be compensated. Traditional means of participation absorb time and money. Public involvement also brings costs to government. Irvin and Stansbury (2004) argued that the low end of the per decision cost of citizen-participation groups is arguably more expensive than the decision making of a single agency administrator. Irvin and Stansbury (2004) also remind us that citizen-participation processes require heavy time commitments (Lawrence and Deagen 2001).

To citizens who live far from cities, it might take them several hours, driving or taking a bus, to attend a public hearing or meet with a public administrator to discuss issues. In this situation, incentives for participation would decrease, since participation is time consuming. Participants need to pay their own costs, which blunts their enthusiasm. How to reduce time and other costs becomes an important issue.

Bimber (2001) gathered nationwide surveys that showed that 54 percent (±3.5 percent) of adults in the United States reported having access to the Internet, up from 26 percent in 1996. Bimber also found that of those people, about 52 percent had engaged in one of five explicitly political acts: using the Internet to find out what the government or a particular official is doing, using it to contact a public official or candidate for office, using it to express views about politics or government to others, using it to learn about political issues, or using it just to browse for political information with no specific purpose in mind. Also, about 9 percent of those with access had contacted a public official or candidate using the Internet, and 13 percent had expressed their political view to others. Bimber used the example of the 1998 campaign season to show how the Internet can be used as a great way to entice citizens to participate in political affairs.

The findings from Bimber reflected the impact of information technology on U.S. politics and public participation. Low cost of information and the convenience of the Internet motivate citizens to actively play a role in politics and government affairs.

Bimber treated information technology as pertinent to political engagement strictly because it expanded the volume of political information available to citizens and reduced its cost.

Using advanced information technologies, e-government plays an increasingly important role in reducing the time and costs of participation. When government posts videos of public meetings online or even provides live videos, citizens no longer need to attend meetings themselves, which saves them time and money on travel. Other convenient methods, such as e-mails and online chats, have also been provided for citizens to contact government and give feedback. Online surveys are conducted to collect public opinion. Discussion boards provide citizens with spaces for posting their thoughts and concerns. All of these decrease time and cost spent for citizens to participate.

THE FACILITATORS OF EFFECTIVE E-PARTICIPATION

The previous sections have addressed the potentials of e-participation. This section focuses on how to translate the great potentials of e-participation into realities. We particularly address the following factors in facilitating effective e-participation.

Public and Media Influence

The public constitutes a major source of social pressure to hold administrators accountable (Kuo 2012). Public administrators' perceived public influence directly determines how they view the necessity of e-participation. The greater influence the public exerts, the more likely public administrators are to adopt e-participation.

Media is the primary source from which public administrators acquire public opinions (Moynihan and Pandey 2005). The level of media influence, first of all, largely determines the amount and quality of information that administrators can obtain regarding citizens' expectations and demands related to e-participation. Second, media has the potential to affect the policy process by setting the agenda. If media influence were too weak, citizens would be less likely to take the demands of openness and e-participation seriously, and would not feel motivated to do so (Yang and Pandey 2007).

Role of Public Administrators

Several studies have noticed the influence of public administrators on citizen participation (Almy 1977; Ebdon 2000; Franklin and Ebdon 2005; Marlowe and Portillo 2006; Zhang and Yang 2009). Among them, administrator attitude has been identified as an important predicator (Yang and Callahan 2007; Zhang and Yang 2009). As Moynihan (2003) observes, the preferences of government officials affect the opportunity and nature of participation for all citizens. This observation may also hold true when it comes to e-participation. First, public administrators' positive attitude toward citizen participation facilitates the adoption of multiple e-participation mechanisms. The adoption and maintenance of e-participation mechanisms involves more time and more stakeholders. Public administrators with more positive attitudes about incorporating citizens are more likely to maintain their enthusiasm and commitment and motivate organizational members to implement e-participation mechanisms.

Second, public administrator's attitudes toward empowering citizens could affect whether e-participation mechanisms will have an authentic impact on the actual level of participation. Unless public administrators have a positive attitude toward citizen empowerment, they might merely use various e-participation mechanisms to inform or educate citizens, during which a symbolic process might occur (Berner and Smith 2004; Ebdon 2000; Ebdon and Franklin 2004; Franklin and Ebdon 2005; Miller and Evers 2002; Watson, Juster, and Johnson 1991). For example, e-participation mechanisms may be used only for disseminating information rather than facilitating dialogue and mutual trust.

Political Support

Elected officials assume the responsibility of working as liaisons between the administrators and the public. Political environment is vital in shaping public administrator use of e-participation mechanisms because elected officials will significantly affect the following:

1. The external incentives of administrators to engage citizens. Since the efforts to seek and incorporate citizen inputs through e-participation mechanisms will bring potential disequilibrium into the organizational environment, it is not easy to change the status quo. With citizens entering the policy arena and more citizen voices being sought, the distribution of organizational resources and power, the degree of environmental stability, and the complexity are subject to change. Moreover, to seek citizen inputs and engage citizens in decision making, administrators need to take risks and change their conventional way of working (Yang 2009). This also requires nurturing administrators' motivation for forecasting, creativity, experimentation, and innovations (Crompton 1983). A hostile political environment would hinder the nurturing of e-participation. For public administrators, they would perceive a high cost associated with engaging citizens in a political environment with excessive political distrust. Perceived distrust of elected officials also makes administrators put their job security and stability into priority mode (Rourke 1984; Wolf 1993). Administrators then tend to adhere to established rules and procedures to avoid risks, thus making them less willing to cooperate and compromise (Kelman 2005). As a result, administrators become less likely to appreciate the values of e-participation and incorporating citizen voices.

2. Support from elected officials will also affect the resources that public administrators could deploy. The implementation of e-participation requires additional resources, such as financial and human resources. Elected officials have the power to increase, decrease, or maintain the level of resources they request, which signals legislators' preferences (Wolf 1993; Yang 2009). A supportive and understanding relationship with elected officials will also help administrators obtain resources and policy flexibility more readily (O'Toole and Meier 1999; Rainey and Steinbauer 1999).

AN EMPIRICAL STUDY: E-PARTICIPATION GAP WORLDWIDE

By providing more convenient ways to participate and reducing participation costs, e-government has brought many changes to citizen participation. Governments use newsletters, e-mail, and even Twitter, Facebook, and YouTube to disseminate news and updates. They also use online surveys to collect public opinions. Many governments have adopted various forms of electronic participation (e-participation) applications, including online forums, virtual discussion rooms, electronic juries, and electronic polls (OECD 2003; Kim and Lee 2012). These changes have brought about a new form of citizen participation—e-participation. Macintosh (2004) viewed e-participation as the use of information and communication technologies to broaden and deepen political participation by enabling citizens to connect with one another and with their elected representatives. E-participation refers to the changes brought by e-government to citizen participation, which have the potential to make citizen participation more effective and efficient.

Although the theoretical importance of e-participation has been widely discussed, few studies have been conducted to provide empirical evidence of the development of e-participation. This section specifically focuses on the level of e-participation across countries. In the latest Digital Governance in Municipalities Worldwide 2011–12 report from Rutgers University, Seoul scored highest, with 16.25 out of 20 points, but around 67 municipalities scored lower than 5.00 out of 20, which is very low. Among all the municipalities evaluated, the average score of online citizen participation was 3.53 out of 20. The results indicated that a great gap existed worldwide in e-participation. The pattern also existed at the country level. The UN Public Administration Network conducted a survey in 2010 to find "how governments are including citizens in their decision-making process, how governments are providing information and knowledge, and how governments are consulting citizens to obtain feedback and opinions" (UN E-Government Survey 2010, 85). The data showed that a great gap existed in e-participation worldwide (see Figure 7.1).

According to the UN E-Government Survey 2010, of 191 countries evaluated, the average score was 0.19 out of 1. Thirteen countries scored 0 in the survey, and the mean of the top 10 countries was 0.79, which reflects a great divide at the country level worldwide.

External Determinants of E-Participation at the Country Level

E-participation development at the country level exists in the areas of economy, Internet usage, education, politics, and so on. These factors indirectly affect e-participation by serving as the basis for government to develop e-participation and by influencing the public's needs with respect to participation. Public needs, then, are viewed as pressures to push government to develop e-participation to meet those needs.

Singh, Das, and Joseph (2007) believed that ICT infrastructure limits the proportion of the citizenry that can be served by e-government services. A reasonable level of Internet usage serves as the basis for e-participation development. So, Internet usage is expected to be positively associated with e-participation level. Moreover, a higher level

Figure 7.1 **2010 Worldwide E-Participation**

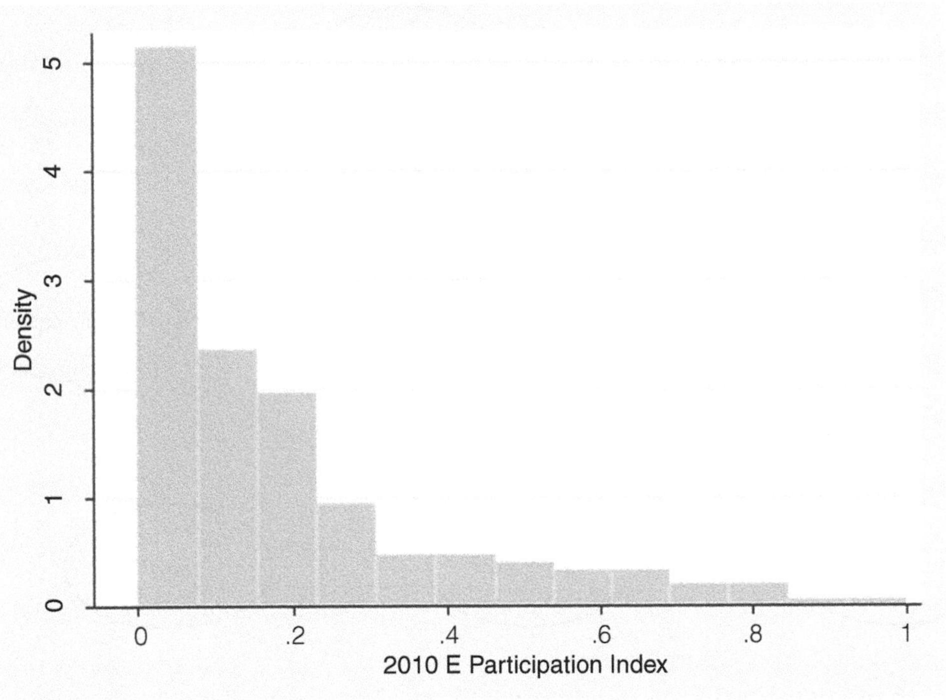

of democracy and freedom are likely to result in the better positioning of e-participation because citizens in those countries or areas with higher levels of democracy and freedom have more desire and are more likely to be motivated by government to participate. Just as Das, DiRienzo, and Burbridge (2009) argued, democratic society is generally more successful in developing e-government, and the same goes for e-participation.

Economy and education play a foundational role in developing e-participation. A better economy is viewed as a sound base for government to develop its e-participation, and citizens living in wealthier areas are more likely to have higher levels of Internet usage. In addition, although the relationship between economy and democracy is controversial, it is believed that countries with stronger economies are more likely to become democratic. By educating citizens with computer usage skills and cultivating citizens with democratic values, education serves as another foundational factor to improve Internet usage and democracy, which in turn improves e-participation. Also, economy and education are expected to have a two-way contribution. The conceptual model is presented in Figure 7.2.

Methods

To test the relations in this model, we use mostly data from many international organizations. For the dependent variable e-participation, we use data from the UN E-Government

Figure 7.2 **Conceptual Model of External Determinants of E-Participation**

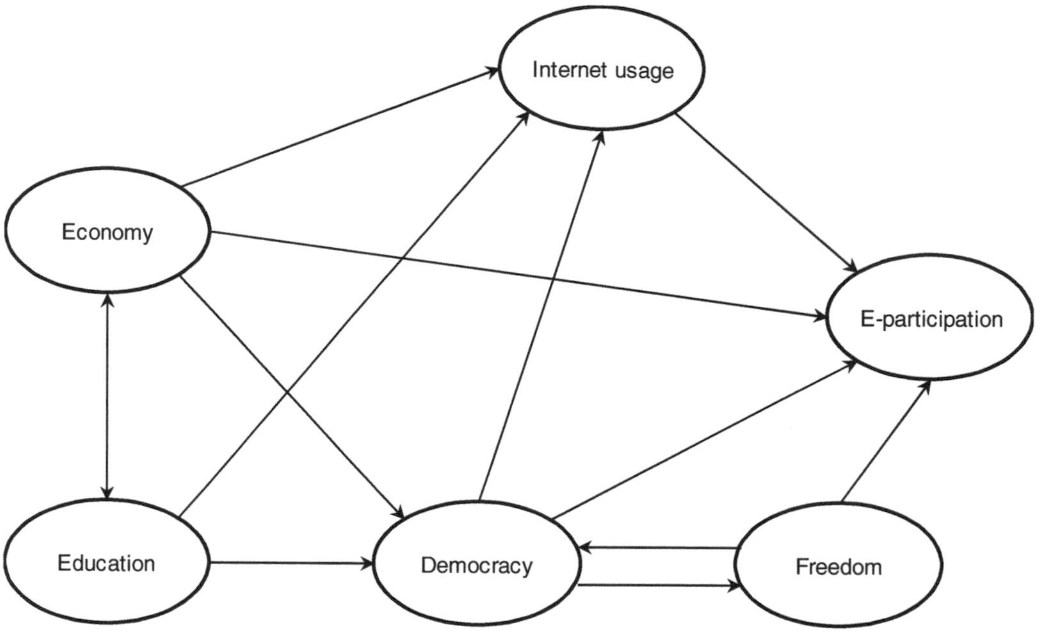

report of 2010, with a sample size of 191. E-participation is a continuous variable and the range of it is between 0 and 1.

For the independent variable education, we use the expected years of education to measure the education level in a country. The expected education life reflects the expected years of schooling. The data are from the UN Development Programme's Human Development Index of 2010, which has a sample size of 173. As to the economy, we use per capita gross national income (GNI) (current $1,000) in a country to measure its economy. The democracy score is from the Democracy Index of 2010 of the Economist Intelligence Unit, which covers 165 independent states and two territories. The Democracy Index is based on five categories: electoral process and pluralism, civil liberties, the functioning of government, political participation, and political culture. We measure the independent variable Internet usage by the percentage of Internet usage, with 2010 data from the International Telecommunications Union. We measure freedom by the Press Freedom Index, which is an annual ranking of countries compiled and published by Reporters without Borders, based on the organization's assessment of countries' press freedom. This variable ranges between 0 and 105. The higher a country's score, the less press freedom it has. The descriptive statistics can be found in Table 7.1.

Results

To estimate the structural model, we obtained maximum likelihood (ML) estimates for the model coefficients with Stata software. The model fit statistics show that the model

Table 7.1

Descriptive Statistics of Variables

Variable	Mean	Standard deviation	Minimum	Maximum
Dependent variable				
E-participation	0.19	0.21	0	1
Independent variable				
Internet usage	33.94	27.76	0.21	95.63
Democracy	5.49	2.23	1.52	9.8
Education	0.62	0.23	0.18	0.99
Economy	1.24	1.35	0.03	6.12
Freedom	30.79	12.68	0	105

Note: The final sample size is 129.

is convincing. The root mean square error of approximation (RMSEA) is 0.05, which is acceptable; Arbuckle (2006) argued that an RMSEA between 0.05 and 0.08 was typically interpreted to represent between a "close" and a "reasonable" model fit. Furthermore, the comparative fit index (CFI) is 0.998 and the Tucker-Lewis index is 0.991, both of which are great, as they are very close to 1. The coefficient of determination (CD) is 0.863, which is also very high. Overall, the model proves strong enough, and most of the hypotheses are supported, as shown in Figure 7.3.

Figure 7.3 **Final Structural Model**

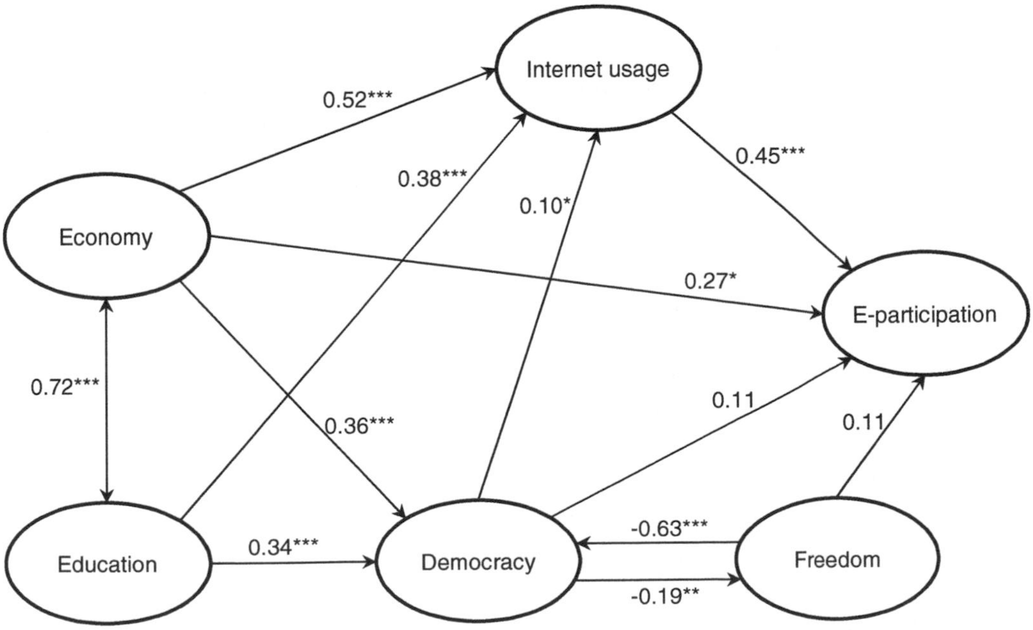

$^{*}p < .1$. $^{**}p < .05$. $^{***}p < .01$.

Table 7.2

Analysis Results of External Determinants of E-Participation

	E-participation	Internet usage	Democracy	Education	Economy
Internet usage	0.45***				
Democracy	0.11	0.1*			
Education	—	0.38***	0.34***		0.72***
Economy	0.27*	0.52***	0.36***	0.72***	
Freedom	0.11		−0.19*		

Note: Model fit statistics: $\chi 2$ (3) = 4.07; root mean square error of approximation (RMSEA) = 0.053; comparative fit index (CFI) = 0.998, Tucker-Lewis index (TLI) = 0.991; standardized root mean square residual (SRMR) = 0.016; Coefficient of determination = 0.863.

*p < .10. **p < .05. ***p < .01.

Findings and Discussion

The study supports the conclusion that the development of e-participation at the country level is affected by its external environment. Countries with better environments (stronger economies, Internet usage, education, democracy, and freedom) are more likely to have higher levels of e-participation (Table 7.2).

Countries with higher levels of Internet usage are more likely to have higher levels of e-participation, as shown in Table 7.2. A higher level of Internet usage provides a great precondition for the development of e-participation and can motivate government to improve its e-participation level.

The study does not support the direct impact of democracy on e-participation, which reflects the relative independence of e-participation from democracy. However, democracy can affect e-participation by influencing Internet usage. The study showed that a higher level of democracy would result in a higher level of Internet usage. In countries with a higher degree of democracy, citizens have more of a desire to express themselves and discuss government affairs. It is also accepted that in such an environment the Internet becomes more important for citizens to communicate and interact. So, it is reasonable that people living in more democratic countries use the Internet more. Since Internet usage can positively influence e-participation level, democracy can affect e-participation indirectly. The results also show that democracy was positively associated with freedom, and higher levels of freedom result in a higher level of democracy. However, it does not find a significant impact of freedom on e-participation.

Also, the results show that higher levels of education lead to higher levels of e-participation, democracy, and Internet usage. Singh, Das, and Joseph (2007) argued that human capital can affect the development of e-government. Countries with better education systems are more likely to have more qualified leaders and employees for government, which becomes more innovative and open-minded to the importance of e-participation. Better education allows more citizens to get information, services, and participate in e-governance.

Education plays an important role in socialization and cultivating citizens to participate. With better education, citizens have more desire and ability to understand the inside workings of government, to supervise government, and to better participate in the policymaking process. In this case, the desire to participate with better services and opportunities is stronger. That desire pushes government to improve e-participation. Also, better education enables more citizens to use the computer and Internet.

It was also found that countries with stronger economies have a higher level of e-participation. Wealthier governments are more likely to providing adequate funding for e-participation. The results also indicated that the stronger economy would lead to more Internet usage. The study supports the idea that a stronger economy leads to more democracy. The results also support the argument that the economy is positively associated with education at the country level and makes a two-way contribution. Countries with more wealth are more likely to spend more money on education, employ better teachers, and provide better facilities. Education can also positively affect the economy by providing more qualified employees, a higher level of technological innovation, more innovative leaders, and so on.

Overall, the study indicates that e-participation at the national level is affected by the external environment. A positive environment (stronger economy, and higher levels of education, democracy, and Internet usage) would result in higher levels of e-participation. The study shows that Internet usage, education, and economy can directly affect e-participation at the national level. Education can also affect e-participation by influencing Internet usage. Further, the economy serves as a foundation for the development of education, democracy, and Internet usage, through which the economy can also affect e-participation indirectly.

SUGGESTIONS AND CONCLUSIONS

Citizen participation has been narrowly defined as "a process in which individuals take part in decision making in the institutions, programs, and environments that affect them" (Heller et al. 1984, 339; Florin and Wandersman, 1990) and broadly defined as involvement in any organized activity in which the individual participates without pay to achieve a common goal, including involvement in government-mandated advisory boards, voluntary organizations, mutual-help groups, and community service activities (Zimmerman and Rappaport 1988). Citizen participation is viewed as a tradition and an important part of political culture in the United States. Rooted in democratic values and disillusionment with bureaucracy, public demand for citizen participation has been increasing for years. It is believed that citizen participation could improve government performance and the relationship between government and citizens by increasing citizen satisfaction and trust. Although citizen participation is important and brings benefits to both government and citizens, the reality is that it is at a relatively low level. In the survey conducted by Kaiser Family Foundation and Harvard University, millions of Americans could not answer even basic questions about U.S. politics (*Washington Post* 1996; White 1997). White (1997) listed several reasons for the low level of citizen participation, including that citizens lack information, time, and the resources to become informed sufficiently about the multitude of complex issues confronting them.

E-government's two decades of development, by using information and communication technologies, is viewed as a potential way to promote citizen participation. E-government plays an important role in smoothing communications between citizens and government, providing new forms and convenient ways for citizens to participate, supplying citizens with information needed to participate, and reducing participation cost. All of these enable e-government to help government raise its citizen participation level.

Both the Global E-Governance Surveys from E-Government Institute of Rutgers University-Newark and the UN E-Government Report indicate that a great gap exists in e-participation at the level of municipalities and countries worldwide. Using data from many international organizations, we found that e-participation at national levels is affected by the external environment. A positive environment would result in higher levels of e-participation. Countries with higher levels of Internet usage and education, and a stronger economy, are more likely to have higher national-level e-participation.

KEY POINTS

For practical concerns, we suggest that effective e-participation be fostered by taking the following steps:

- Start by gaining political support. Political support ensures a public administrator's incentives for the development of e-participation by providing necessary resources.
- E-participation requires effective coordination among different units in government organizations. E-participation is not merely about the digitization of participation mechanisms; it also requires the reorganization and/or reengineering of the administrative process. Government agencies should be integrated in order to facilitate e-participation.
- Make sure that citizens are aware that the e-participation mechanisms are available to them. This requires that government organizations promote the new technologies to citizens and communities through traditional and new media, such as newspapers, television, radio, and social media. By doing this, government organizations can show their commitment to make governmental information transparent and accessible.
- Public administrators should engage citizens primarily through two-way participation mechanisms, such as online discussion boards and e-forums. One-way engagement methods, such as posting information online, may simply educate citizens rather than fostering authentic citizen participation.
- Increase the utility of the information released through e-participation mechanisms. For effective citizen engagement, information released from government organizations should be accurate, understandable, complete, accessible, and low cost. To avoid information overload, citizens should be able to understand the public information to participate meaningfully. It is also extremely important to ensure that public in-

formation and participation mechanisms are accessible through various electronic devices.

- Learn from other government organizations with respect to their successful practices and useful lessons.
- Work with the private or nonprofit sectors to facilitate successful e-participation. In an era of network governance, these sectors can help government organizations with the newest IT technology, share their successful experiences with government officials, provide consulting services to government during the design and implementation of e-participation, and provide outsourcing services to government organizations.
- Government officials should be responsive to the citizen inputs that are solicited through e-participation mechanisms. It is important to establish an institutional framework to enable e-participation to make a difference in administrative decision making. By doing this, citizens will understand the merits of e-participation mechanisms.
- Finally, citizens should have the opportunity to evaluate e-participation. Citizens are entitled to evaluate the process and outcome of their participation. The incorporation of citizen feedback ensures the efficacy of e-participation.

REFERENCES

Almy, T.A. 1977. City managers, public avoidance and revenue sharing. *Public Administration Review* 33 (1), 19–27.

Arbuckle, J. 2006. AMOS 7.0 user's guide. Spring House, PA: AMOS Development.

Barnes, W.S., Jr., and B.N. Williams. 2012. Applying technology to enhance citizen engagement with city and county government. In *The state of citizen participation in America*, ed. H.L. Schachter and K. Yang, 163–194. Charlotte, NC: Information Age Publishing.

Berner, M., and S. Smith. 2004. The state of the states: A review of state requirements for citizen participation in the local government budgeting process. *State and Local Government Review* 36 (2), 140–150.

Bimber, B. 2001. Information and political engagement in America: The search for effects of information technology at the individual level. *Political Research Quarterly* 54 (1), 53–67.

Blackburn, J.W., and W.M. Bruce, eds. 1995. *Mediating environmental conflicts: Theory and practice.* Westport, CT: Quorum.

Crompton, J.L. 1983. Recreation vouchers: A case study in administrative innovation and citizen participation. *Public Administration Review* 43 (6), 537–546.

Crow, D.A., and J.R. Stevens. 2012. Citizen engagement in local environmental policy: Information, mobilization and media. In *The state of citizen participation in America*, ed. H.L. Schachter and K. Yang, 131–162. Charlotte, NC: Information Age Publishing.

Das, J., C. DiRienzo, and J. Burbridge Jr. 2009. Global e-government and the role of trust: A cross country analysis. *International Journal of Electronic Government Research* 5 (1), 1–18.

Day, D. 1997. Citizen participation in the planning process: An essentially contested concept? *Journal of Planning Literature* 11 (3), 421–434.

Dimock, M. 1990. The restorative qualities of citizenship. *Public Administration Review* 50 (1), 21–25.

Ebdon, C. 2000. The relationship between citizen involvement in the budget process and city structure and culture. *Public Productivity and Management Review* 23 (3), 383–393.

Ebdon, C., and A. Franklin. 2004. Searching for a role for citizens in the budget process. *Public Budgeting and Finance* 24 (1), 32–49.

Fischer, F. 2005. *Citizens, experts, and the environment: The politics of local knowledge.* Durham, NC: Duke University Press.

Flanagin, William H., and Nancy Zingale. 1994. *Political behavior of the American electorate.* 8th ed. Washington, DC: Congressional Quarterly.

Florin, P., and A. Wandersman. 1990. An introduction to citizen participation, voluntary organizations, and community development: Insights for empowerment through research. *American Journal of Community Psychology* 18 (1), 41–54.

Franklin, A., and C. Ebdon. 2004. Aligning priorities in local budgeting processes. *Journal of Public Budgeting, Accounting and Financial Management* 16, 210–227.

———. 2005. Are we all touching the same camel? Exploring a model of participation in budgeting. *American Review of Public Administration* 35 (2), 168–185.

Frederickson, H.G. 1982. The recovery of civicism in public administration. *Public Administration Review* 42, 501–508.

Fung, A. 2006. Varieties of participation in complex governance. *Public Administration Review* 66 (S1), 66–75.

Glass, J.J. 1979. Citizen participation in planning: the relationship between objectives and techniques. *Journal of the American Planning Association* 45 (2), 180–189.

Heeks, R., and S. Bailur. 2007. Analyzing e-government research: Perspectives, philosophies, theories, methods, and practice. *Government Information Quarterly* 24 (2), 243–265.

Heller, K., R. Price, S. Reinharz, S. Riger, and A. Wandersman. 1984. *Psychology and community change: Challenges of the future.* 2d ed. Homewood, IL: Dorsey.

Holzer, M., and L.B. Mullins. 2012. Citizen participation and performance: A model for citizen-based government and performance management. In *The state of citizen participation in America*, ed. H.L. Schachter and K. Yang, 325–347. Charlotte, NC: Information Age Publishing.

Irvin, R.A., and J. Stansbury. 2004. Citizen participation in decision making: Is it worth the effort? *Public Administration Review* 64 (1), 55–65.

Kakabadse, A., N.K. Kakabadse, and A. Kouzmin. 2003. Reinventing the democratic governance project through information technology? A growing agenda for debate. *Public Administration Review* 63 (1), 44–60.

Kelman, S. 2005. *Unleashing change: A study of organizational renewal in government.* Washington, DC: Brookings Institution Press.

Kim, S., and J. Lee. 2012. E-participation, transparency, and trust in local government. *Public Administration Review* 72 (6), 819–828.

King, C.S., K.M. Feltey, and B.O.N. Susel. 1998. The question of participation: Toward authentic public participation in public administration. *Public Administration Review* 58 (4), 317–326.

Kleinman, D.L., J.A. Delborne, and A.A. Anderson. 2011. Engaging citizens: The high cost of citizen participation in high technology. *Public Understanding of Science* 20 (2), 221–240.

Komito, L. 2005. E-participation and governance: Widening the net. *Electronic Journal of e-Government* 3 (1), 39–48.

Kuo, N. 2012. Citizen dissatisfaction leads to budget cuts, or not: A case study of a local Taiwanese government. *Australian Journal of Public Administration* 71 (2), 159–166.

Kweit, R.W., and M.G. Kweit. 1980. Bureaucratic decision-making: Impediments to citizen participation. *Polity* 13, 647–666.

Lawrence, R.L., and D.A. Deagen. 2001. Choosing public participation methods for natural resources: A context-specific guide. *Society and Natural Resources* 14 (10), 857–872.

Leung, L. 2009. User-generated content on the Internet: An examination of gratifications, civic engagement and psychological empowerment. *New Media and Society* 11 (8), 1327–1347.

London, S. 1994. Electronic Democracy: A Literature Survey. Paper prepared for the Kettering Foundation, Santa Barbara, CA.

Macintosh, A. 2004. Characterizing e-participation in policy-making. Proceedings from 37th Annual Hawaii International Conference on System Sciences. Big Island, HI: IEEE Computer Society.

Macintosh, A., and A. Whyte. 2008. Towards an evaluation framework for eparticipation. *Transforming Government: People, Process and Policy* 2 (1), 16–30.

Marlowe, J., and S. Portillo. 2006. Citizen engagement in local budgeting: Does diversity pay dividends? *Public Performance and Management Review* 30 (2), 179–201.

McNair, R.H., R. Caldwell, and L. Pollane. 1983. Citizen participants in public bureaucracies: Foul weather friends. *Administration and Society* 14 (4), 507–524.

Miller, G.J., and L. Evers. 2002. Budgeting structures and citizen participation. *Journal of Public Budgeting, Accounting and Financial Management* 14 (2), 233–272.

Morone, J.A. 1998. *The democratic wish.* 2d ed. New Haven, CT: Yale University Press.

Moynihan, D.P. 2003. Normative and instrumental perspectives on public participation: Citizen summits in Washington, DC. *American Review of Public Administration* 33 (2), 164–188.

Moynihan, D.P., and S.K. Pandey. 2005. Testing a model of public sector performance: How does management matter. *Journal of Public Administration Research and Theory* 15 (3), 421–439.

Mumford, E. 1991. Participation in systems design—What can it offer? In *Human factors for informatics usability*, ed. B. Shackel and S. Richardson, 267–290. Cambridge: Cambridge University Press.

Nelson, N., and S. Wright. 1995. *Power and participatory development: Theory and practice.* London: ITDG Publications.

Norris, D.F., and M.J. Moon. 2005. Advancing e-government at the grassroots: Tortoise or hare? *Public Administration Review* 65 (1), 64–75.

Norris, P. 1999. *Critical citizens: Global support for democratic government.* New York: Oxford University Press.

Olphert, W., and L. Damodaran. 2007. Citizen participation and engagement in the design of e-government services: The missing link in effective ICT design and delivery. *Journal of the Association for Information Systems* 8 (9), 27.

Organisation for Economic Co-operation and Development (OECD). 2001. *The hidden threat to e-government: Avoiding large government IT failures.* Policy Brief No. 8. Paris: OECD. www.oecd.org/dataoecd/19/12/1901677.pdf.

———. 2003. Promise and problems of e-democracy, challenges of online citizen engagement. Paris: OECD. www.oecd-ilibrary.org/governance/promise-and-problems-of-e-democracy_9789264019492-en.

O'Toole, L., and K. Meier. 1999. Modeling the impact of public management: Implications of structural context. *Journal of Public Administration Research and Theory* 9 (4), 505–526.

Pateman, C. 1970. *Participation and democratic theory.* Cambridge, MA: Cambridge University Press.

Rainey, H.G., and P. Steinbauer. 1999. Galloping elephants: Developing elements of a theory of effective government organizations. *Journal of Public Administration Research and Theory* 9 (1), 1–32.

Roberts, N. 2004. Public deliberation in an age of direct citizen participation. *American Review of Public Administration* 34 (4), 315–353.

Roberts, N.C. 2008. *The age of direct citizen participation.* Armonk, NY: M.E. Sharpe.

Rourke, F.E. 1984. *Bureaucracy, politics, and public policy.* 3d ed. New York: Little, Brown.

Sabatier, P.A. 1988. An advocacy coalition framework of policy change and the role of policy-oriented learning therein. *Policy Sciences* 21 (2–3), 129–168.

Seidman, H., and R. Gilmour. 1986. *Politics, position, and power.* New York: Little, Brown.

Sharp, E.B. 2012. Citizen participation at the local level. In *The state of citizen participation in America*, ed. H.L. Schachter and K. Yang, 101–129. Charlotte, NC: Information Age Publishing.

Singh, H., A. Das, and D. Joseph. 2007. Country-level determinants of e-government maturity. *Communications of the Association for Information Systems* 20 (1), 632–648.

Snider, J.H. 1994. Democracy on-line: Tomorrow's electronic electorate. *The Futurist* 28(5), 15–19.

Strange, J.H. 1972. The impact of citizen participation on public administration. *Public Administration Review* 32, 457–470.

Thomas, J.C. 1995. *Public participation in public decisions: New skills and strategies for public managers.* San Francisco, CA: Jossey-Bass.

Timney, M.M. 2011. Models of citizen participation: Measuring engagement and collaboration. In *Government is us 2.0*, ed. Cheryl Simrell King, 86–100. Armonk, NY: M.E. Sharpe.

United Nations, Department of Economic and Social Affairs. 2010. *United Nations e-government survey 2010: Leveraging e-government at a time of financial and economic crisis.* Vol. 2. New York: United Nations.

United Nations Development Programme. 2010. *Human Development Report 2010—The Real Wealth of Nations: Pathways to Human Development.* New York: United Nations.

Verba, S., and N.H. Nie. 1972. *Participation in America: Political democracy and social equality.* Chicago: University of Chicago Press.

Waldo, D. 1947. *The administrative state.* New York: Holmes & Meier.

Wang, X., and M. Van Wart. 2007. When public participation in administration leads to trust: An empirical assessment of managers' perceptions. *Public Administration Review* 67 (2), 265–278.

Washington Post. 1996. Survey looks at political insight. *Washington Post*, February 11, 32.

Watson, D.J., R.J. Juster, and G.W. Johnson. 1991. Institutionalized use of citizen surveys in the budgetary and policy-making processes: A small town case study. *Public Administration Review* 51 (3), 232–239.

Weeks, E.C. 2000. The practice of deliberative democracy: Results from four large-scale trials. *Public Administration Review* 60 (4), 360–372.

West, Darrell M. 2004. E-government and the transformation of service delivery and citizen attitudes. *Public Administration Review* 64 (1), 15–27.

White, C.S. 1997. Citizen participation and the Internet: Prospects for civic deliberation in the information age. *Social Studies* 88 (1), 23–28.

Wolf, P. 1993. A case survey of bureaucratic effectiveness in U.S. cabinet agencies: Preliminary results. *Journal of Public Administration Research and Theory* 3, 161–181.

Yang, K. 2007. Making performance measurement relevant: Informing and involving stakeholders in performance measurement. In *International Handbook Of Practice-Based Performance Management*, ed. P. de Lancer Julnes, F.S. Berry, M.P. Aristigueta, and K. Yang, 173–188. Thousand Oaks, CA: Sage Publications.

———. 2009. Examining perceived honest performance reporting by public organizations: bureaucratic politics and organizational practice. *Journal of Public Administration Research and Theory* 19 (1), 81–105.

Yang, K., and K. Callahan. 2007. Citizen involvement efforts and bureaucratic responsiveness: Participatory values, stakeholder pressures, and administrative practicality. *Public Administration Review* 67 (2), 249–264.

Yang, K., and S.K. Pandey. 2007. Public responsiveness of government organizations: Testing a preliminary model. *Public Performance and Management Review* 31 (2), 215–240.

Zaller, J. 1992. *The nature and origins of mass opinion.* Cambridge, MA: Cambridge University Press.

Zhang, Y., and K. Yang. 2009. Citizen participation in the budget process: The effect of city managers. *Journal of Public Budgeting, Accounting and Financial Management* 21 (2), 289–317.

Zimmerman, M.A., and J. Rappaport. 1988. Citizen participation, perceived control, and psychological empowerment. *American Journal of Community Psychology* 16 (5), 725–750.

8

Puzzling Out the Wisdom of E-Crowds in Trustworthy E-Government Practices

From Technological Applications to Networks

Younhee Kim and Seunghwan Myeong

Web-based platforms have been the most influential and preferred vehicle for reshaping relationships between government and citizens. These platforms are considered not only a new face of government (Morgeson and Mithas 2009) but also a counterpart of traditional government structures. The advancement of information communication and technologies (ICTs) has assisted governments in promoting desirable results in disseminating public policies, delivering services, and mobilizing citizen opinion for authentic participation since the early 1990s. In recent years, the consequences of prioritized e-government initiatives have significantly expanded governments' responsibilities in responding to dynamic social changes to interactions. Various stage models that have become fundamental benchmarks for developing successful e-government approaches have been utilized to describe the development of e-government.

Tactical e-government doctrine has focused on website presence to disseminate information and business applications to efficiently deliver public services. While upper levels of e-government stages designate participation, it is insufficient to practice a full-range of public discourse in the policy arenas. In the early period of e-government development, practices seem to be directly inspired by new public management reforms and reinvention of government, associated with efficiency, marketization, and accountability. Later, the value of democracy has become aggressively important for being plugged into political and government spheres, because the impact of interactions between citizens and government has exceeded the initial expectations of the e-government system. Citizens' roles have been redefined to promote deliberative democracy, and their involvement in government has become more organized to obtain direct democracy. As a result, e-democracy has emerged to support these arguments via reciprocal interactions, without the limits of time, space, and other physical conditions.

Emphasizing democratic values enables the e-government paradigm to move forward into an e-governance discourse, but it is not a replacement of e-government practices. Rather, it is part of the continuum in the ongoing e-government system through its embodiment of not only a formation of structures and processes but also expanded key players. Emerging interests in governance require ensuring a confidence level of e-government capacities to incorporate key subjects of governing. The terms "e-government" and "e-governance" are often treated as interchangeable, but clarification of the two notions is needed to improve the quality of an electronic state that is a synonym for a virtual state with long-term development strategies. Discussions on e-governance are given much less importance than in e-government literature, since a distinct layer between e-government and e-governance is quite difficult to identify. Taking governance subjects into electronic regimes, however, is necessary to design a reliable e-government system for the coming decade.

The current e-government patterns have not radically changed, but government has gradually expanded its scope and responsibilities in terms of normative approaches of stage models (Lee 2010; Norris and Reddick 2013). In the early period of e-government development, normative stage approaches provided clear directions to adopt e-government ideas. Since most governments have substantially adopted e-government practices, all components of stage approaches have been implemented, but in different magnitudes. Along this line, an upcoming e-government system should be accountable to citizens and nongovernmental sectors in covering emerging issues of electronic states. There should be a way to ensure citizens' and nongovernmental actors' accountability for their participation and decisions. In lieu of any developments of a new e-government model, this study discusses practical agendas for implementing a trustworthy e-government system that could be a baseline reference for initiating valuable e-government plans on the basis of technological, managerial, and relational dimensions.

DEVELOPMENT OF ELECTRONIC STATES

Affordable ICTs, with respect to infrastructure costs and accessibility, enable governments to keep e-government's promises and verify its potential for improving service operations and enhancing a wide range of interactions with citizens. New possibilities and technological innovations have been seamlessly merged to carry this electronic paradigm to the next level. In fact, after the e-government stage models have been introduced as the first generation of a supplementary government rationale, further ideological progress seems no longer able to move e-government forward to a revolutionary electronic state. The ongoing development of ICTs, however, allows e-government to infuse critical social issues into its base protocol; therefore, an ordinal e-government paradigm has shifted into different archetypes, especially in reaction to the growth of social networking and direct citizen participation. The networking technologies, indeed, promote value-added interactions between citizens and government, as well as between communities and political affiliations (Scavo and Kim 2010).

Garson (2006) applied four theoretical frameworks of information technology and social change to examine the development of technology and e-government, framing the importance of technological and human factors, as well as the level of environmental constraints. Technological determinism assumes that technology itself overpowers to shape government and society, and reinforcement theory proposes that technology is a tool utilized by those who control particular situations. Changes from both technological

Table 8.1

The Development of Electronic Regimes

	First wave: Underdeveloped	Second wave: Developing	Third wave: Developed
Regime	E-government	E-democracy	E-governance
Priority	Website development, business applications	Authentic participation	Partnership
Value	Efficiency, effectiveness	Democracy	Trust
Key player	Governments	Citizens	Governments, nongovernmental partners, community groups
Keyword	Technology infrastructure	Citizens	Networks
Unit	Institution	Individual	Community group
Platform	Web 1.0, content management system (CMS)	Web 2.0	Social media

determinism and reinforcement theory are highly constrained by technological factors, and sociotechnical theory explains that the development of technology is unconstrained by technological factors. Technology is used to assist public managers who plan to lead desirable changes and outcomes in organizational and managerial settings. System theory suggests that changes are unconstrained, but technical factors rather than the humanistic interventions dominate to lead outcomes, which is in contrast to sociotechnical theory. These frameworks are applicable to understanding the impact of technological changes in the early period of e-government development, but they overlook social and political impacts forced by dynamic interactions between government and stakeholders.

As e-government systems have matured over time, their priorities have become broader, to make more sophisticated citizen participation and to simultaneously govern structural and procedural presences. The e-government system is divided into three waves that depend on various conditions (see Table 8.1). These waves cannot be characterized as a paradigm shift; rather, each generational wave has experienced incremental changes, following similar arguments by Norris and Reddick (2013) and West (2004). A noticeable difference across the three waves is a unit of the key actors. The e-government model manages electronic businesses by the institutional approach, whereas e-democracy applies the individual perspective to promote individual empowerment in the government and political processes. The e-governance model practices the communitarian approach to the creation of a collaborative community virtually driven by social networks.

Garson (2006, 18–19) defined e-government as "one aspect of digital government" and e-governance as "a vision of changing the nature of the state." At a glance, e-government focuses information dissemination and convenient service delivery via a Web-based platform, whereas e-democracy prioritizes to promote democratic values through changes in government-citizen interactions. E-governance is contextually inclusive of e-government and e-democracy, so its accomplishments should be "efficient, effective (outcome-driven), politically manageable, and open and democratic (governance-centric)" (Saxena 2005, 505).

E-GOVERNMENT AND TECHNOLOGY INFRASTRUCTURE

International communities have fully employed an e-government platform in different stages, although its capacities have varied across countries and governments since the past decade. Once a physical e-government structure has been presented, online public services and operations have rapidly diversified each year, as has the development of new technologies (United Nations 2008). E-government has been successfully utilized to replace negative images of government in delivering services and building trust in government, in pursuing greater efficiency, in being more accountable, and in empowering citizens in decision-making processes—as early studies proposed these preferred outcomes (Fountain 1999; Layne and Lee 2001; Moon 2002; West 2004).

While e-government stage models used somewhat different metaphors to guide e-government policies, four or five features can be identified as common characteristics of e-government stages. Siau and Long (2005) noted that five stages are divided into two regimes based on a purpose of e-government development. The initial three stages (Web presence, interaction, and transaction) intend to "automate and digitalize the current processes," whereas the last two stages (transformation and e-democracy) expect to transform services and internal operations and reconceptualize citizen participation (Siau and Long 2005, 455). They observed that three distinctive jumps exist between stages in consideration of investment and complexity matters; they are technological, cultural, and political. Although the concept of a cultural jump is not clearly explained, applying these three standards simultaneously is feasible to explain the progress of e-government.

Lee (2010) identified five common keywords of e-government stages after a cross-model comparison with 12 stage models: information, interaction, transaction, integration, and transformation. The first stage is described as the ability of a website to post information, and the next stage, interaction, refers to two-way communication between government and citizens. The transaction stage is related to Web-based self-services that allow citizens to complete entire tasks electronically without assistance from public employees. The next stage, integration, reframes government functions vertically and horizontally. Layne and Lee (2001) found that vertical integration within similar functions is easier than horizontal integration among different functions. As the last stage, transformation expects a radical change in operational processes in order to achieve more efficient government services. The transformation concept seems fairly comparable with integration, but it focuses on service and organizational changes over operational changes (Lee 2010). Besides, only a few models include transformation in their full packages of the stage approaches.

The stages of e-government are interrelated, such that they precondition previous stages, and some functions overlap to some extent. More important, the stage models are not necessarily supposed to be followed sequentially, from one step to another; there was a misunderstanding of the stage models in the early period of e-government development.

E-DEMOCRACY AND CITIZENS

E-democracy refers to any collective action that improves democratic values and the quality of public participation using ICTs (Chadwick 2006; Hacker and van Dijk 2000; Kakabadse, Kakabadse, and Koezmin 2003), which intend to narrow a participatory gap among citizens in policymaking or political processes. ICT-enabled innovations have certainly brought a new level of citizen participation, even though skeptical debates still exist about direct democracy. Substantial objectives to use ICTs for the democratic decision-making process include reaching a wider audience for wide-ranging participation and contribution, supporting participation for the technically skilled citizens, and providing relevant information for the target audience (Macintosh 2008). More informed and educated citizens have taken larger citizen roles in bringing their concerns in government since citizens perceive their roles as more than customers or static voters (Schachter 1997).

It is essential to understand responsibilities of citizens in the e-democracy state. Vigoda (2002) discussed a continuum of citizens' roles along with five types of interactions between government and citizens: citizens are defined as subjects, voters, clients or customers, partners, and owners on the basis of their discretionary practices in decision making. In a coerciveness relation, citizens as subjects are entirely dependent on government decisions, whereas citizens as voters in a delegation zone delegate their chances to be involved in government as representatives. Representative democracy contributes to citizens being away from the core of decision-making processes. The idea behind citizens as customers takes citizens' demands responsively in service delivery but does not consider citizens' social initiatives representatively in a decision-making process.

The last two roles of citizens as partners and owners have extensive citizen involvement in the processes of administrative changes and reforms. A partnership relation intends to promote a certain level of cooperation among all stakeholder groups through strong government commitment to citizens. Although the citizen-owners model as an ideal type of democracy has inherent challenges, given inconsistent participation and lack of citizens' knowledge on government functions, these drawbacks could be diminished with citizen education and information exchange (Schachter 1997). If educated properly and if reliable information is accessible, citizen-owners are willing to view the success of public services in terms of the whole community rather than for individual interests.

As an early study on citizen participation, King, Feltey, and O'Neill Susel (1998) identified three categories of barriers against authentic participation: the nature of life in contemporary society, administrative processes, and techniques of participation. The first set of obstacles is largely driven by busy daily life schedules of ordinary citizens and nonparticipatory attitudes. The second category of barriers is about the lack of opportunities and steps for citizens' input in decision-making processes, given the one-way communication flow from government to citizens. These processes make citizens more frustrated in carrying out meaningful participation. The last issue of limitations noted as the most problematic is administrative barriers, caused by inadequate participatory techniques (e.g., public hearings, citizen advisory councils, citizen panels, public surveys) to access the majority of citizens and deliver representative citizens' voices in government.

To achieve authentic participatory status and processes, electronic platforms are some of the most effective tools for overcoming these barriers.

The e-government development scheme presents e-democracy as the last stage to empower citizens in the political and decision-making processes (Siau and Long 2005). Allowing active or direct citizen participation via an electronic format is somewhat revolutionary, transitioning the development of the e-government state into a different league. The importance of citizen participation is a constant, but there were less systematic approaches to deliver citizens' voices meaningfully to the government. Once e-government is widespread, it is capable of transforming passive citizen reaction to active citizen participation. Thomas (2004) confirmed that greater citizen participation has already become a reality. For the 2008 U.S. presidential election, social networking tools took critical roles for not only distributing information about candidates and policies but also connecting more citizens via the Internet in a real-time stream (Scavo and Kim 2010). The second generation of electronic town-hall formats, such as the 21st Century Town Meeting in the District of Columbia, has been recognized as an effective delivery system for well-represented citizen opinions without a few players dominating in a policy regime. It is a way to stimulate the exchange of thoughts between government and citizens, as well as among citizens themselves.

E-GOVERNANCE AND NETWORKS

Well-developed regimes of e-government and e-democracy have caused issues remaining, with both concepts to be puzzled out through a comprehensive approach of e-governance that could integrate scattered pieces of discussions on electronic states. Unlike e-democracy, which heavily focuses on individual activities, e-governance aims to aggregate the preferences of individuals and groups in a representable, responsible way. E-governance prioritizes networks rather than government agencies and has no clear boundary among government, nonprofit, and private-sector actors (Garson 2006). E-governance would be a parallel term of governance that applies its assumptions to virtual settings. Traditional government tends to be depicted as an entity that controls and regulates organizations and society—an outdated image for representing the contemporary movement of direct democracy and the impact of ICTs. The idea of governance reflects new changes in a networked society, although it is not distinctively separated from other topics, such as new public management and democracy.

Governance refers to "a *new* process of governing; or a *changed* condition of ordered rule; or the *new* method by which society is governed" (Rhodes 2007, 1246). This perspective of governance can be characterized as interdependence between organizations, continuing interactions between network members, gamelike interactions, and a significant degree of autonomy from the state—all of which can be summarized as network governance (Rhodes 2007). In a governance context, the ruling commitment does not belong solely to governments. Rather, private and nongovernmental entities are also involved in the creation of governance, with or without governmental authority (Keohane and Nye 2000).

Unlike other studies that suggested including all participants broadly in governing processes (e.g., Garson 2006; Rhodes 2007; Keohane and Nye 2000), Kaufmann, Kraay, and Mastruzzi (2010) focused on governments and policymakers to explain governance on the basis of governmental processes, capacity of government, and respect for citizens and the state. They developed six governance indicators for describing and evaluating a government's capacity to govern: voice and accountability (degree of citizen participation), political stability and absence of violence (likelihood of instability over violence), government effectiveness (quality of public services), regulatory quality (capacity of rule making and policymaking), rule of law (degree of confidence in the rules of society), and control of corruption (degree of public gain).

Dawes (2009) proposed a dynamic, open socio-technological framework to understand e-governance through the identification of six credential dimensions. The first dimension is the purpose and role of government, which are related to the need for a legal framework and performance assessment, integration, public value of e-governance, accountability, transparency, and stewardship. The second dimension is societal trends, in which demographic trends, multiculturalism, privatization, and institutional changes are critical for controlling e-governance. The third element, changing technologies, offers the means to explore new communities and relationships. The fourth factor is information management, essential for guaranteeing the quality and integrity of information content. Human elements address individuals' identity, autonomy, privacy, trust, and learning. The final dimension is cross-boundary interaction and complexity, which represents multichannel access, system interoperability, multiagent systems, collaboration, and competition. This dynamic system aims to direct future-oriented e-governance research that should extend beyond contemporary priorities of e-government related to achieving efficient service delivery and supporting managerial improvement. One dimension embodies trends, developments, actions, preferences, and choices. In addition, each dimension is independent and mutually influential to other dimensions.

E-governance can be conceptualized by both e-democracy and e-government, even though the distinction between the two notions corresponds to a general understanding of government and governance, by which "government is the institution itself, whereas governance is a broader concept describing forms of governing which are not necessarily in the hands of the formal government" (Saxena 2005, 499). A formality of e-governance should be arranged in both government and nongovernmental organizations. An independent characteristic of e-governance could be found in key players, who are not only government agencies but also networked groups of nongovernmental entities. E-governance tends to target group interactions for greater engagement, whereas e-government and e-democracy pay attention to individual interactions.

TRUSTWORTHY E-GOVERNMENT SYSTEMS

Normative approaches of e-government have proposed that e-government is evolving along with advancement of technology and access to government, thus allowing the government to reach upper stages of e-government practice. There is little doubt that the development of e-government applications has benefited, changing the image and capacity of government (Streib and Willoughby 2010). Most empirical studies, however, have found that the implementation of e-government at the local level across Western countries has mainly remained at lower levels of e-government initiatives, concluding that actual e-government practice has been irregularly developed (e.g., Bekkers and Homburg 2007; Coursey and Norris 2008; Nasi and Frosini 2010). Although some findings are derived from not-so-recent data (e.g., Coursey and Norris [2008], for example, used data from the years 2000, 2002, and 2004), the real progress of e-government is still quite noticeable. Norris and Reddick (2013), in comparing 2004 and 2011 data, also argued that the empirical reality of U.S. local governments does not follow the predictions of normative stage models from information dissemination and service transaction to transformation and e-democracy. Most local e-governments have been locked in one-way activity, and although e-government is considered an effective tool for facilitating citizen participation or e-democracy, there is a lack of evidence confirming this.

Unlike pessimistic analyses of e-government (e.g., Coursey and Norris 2008; Norris and Reddick 2013), recent discussions have posited that e-government in U.S. municipal governments has implemented more than one-way services and interactions (Schlanger 2013). Although not every government has taken full advantage of e-government promises, the practice of contemporary e-government has been devoted to achieving crucial goals of normative e-government approaches without being partial to one or two stages. It is, indeed, a matter of magnitude in practice of e-government stages differently based on a government's strategies and environment. As Siau and Long (2005) asserted, the development of e-government does not necessarily require sequential progresses of whole stages. Depending on demands and costs, e-government strategies should be implemented differently.

A trustworthy e-government system in preparing developing and developed levels of electronic states should articulate balanced conditions in structures, management, and relations within government or in the surrounding environment (see Table 8.2). Although Kraemer and King (2008) asserted that e-government would not transform bureaucratic government—as was predicted by many scholars and practitioners—a holistic e-government system as the latest mechanism of administrative reform may transform traditional government systems and interactions with citizens. Awareness of these dimensions of e-government systems can help governments and communities direct a desirable condition of electronic states and build a new cyber–civil society, synthesizing the emphases of the three electronic regimes.

TECHNOLOGICAL DIMENSION

The technological dimension intends to reorganize infrastructure and operational applications, to facilitate effective service delivery, engagement, and collaboration. As new ICTs have diffused rapidly, a few delivery platforms have led to the implementation of an e-government agenda. In the early period of e-government, Web 1.0 and content management systems were the main tools for conducting online activities. The key relationship of early applications was to transfer information and services from one provider to

Table 8.2

Trustworthy E-Government Systems

Dimension	Priority	Agenda
Technology	• Engineering – Infrastructures – Business applications	• Scaling up to customized-fit structures • Replacing outdated technologies • Minimizing technology vulnerability • Enhancing information security and privacy
Management	• Steering – Processes – Contents – Performance	• Aligning system standards with organizational goals • Supporting cross-agency technological collaborations • Responding and creating demands • Designing feasible performance and reporting reference systems • Applying information stewardship
Relation	• Empowering – Citizens and communities via participation	• Building collaborative networks • Ensuring accountability in government and citizen groups • Cultivating e-ownership culture

many users, which is a bureaucratic and technocratic approach. Web 2.0 was created by a many-to-many interaction that allowed information and discussions to be generated and disseminated directly by governments and citizens. Social media is somehow similar to Web 2.0 but much focuses on building a community rather than creating content that is a primary goal of Web 2.0. Although recent interaction-based websites are often called social networks, authentic social media is not yet ready to offer the technical provision to the e-governance concept.

Given the lack of equal distribution of ICTs, information-poor citizens and communities have limited influences in policymaking and political agenda setting. Thus, developed e-government systems should make ICTs more accessible and affordable to citizens and communities by absorbing their needs, capacities, and usability. Government should consider the situation of the digital divide when developing a practical e-government system. Helbig, Gil-Garcia, and Ferro (2009) identified three aspects of the digital divide: access, multidimensional, and multiperspective. A simple technological dichotomy defines the digital divide as the "haves" and the "have-nots" of material access, influenced by social, organizational, and environmental conditions. The multidimensional approach explains the causing factors of the digital divide by not only access to technology but also socioeconomic status, race, ethnicity, geography, and cultural content. The multiperspective aspect includes the previous two approaches, and also counts the roles of government, values, and beliefs. While the gaps of the digital divide in Internet access have been steadily declining in the United States in terms of gender, ethnicity, age, and community type (see Smith 2009; West 2008), there are still digital gaps to be reduced with respect to material, skills, and usage.

A trustworthy e-government system should strengthen fundamental functions and infrastructures of the stage models by updating technologies and reducing malfunctions of the information society. New digital platforms have emerged as alternatives to computers, such as tablet computers and smartphones. The new mobile platform has changed the patterns of surfing the Internet, transmitting data, communicating with others, and displaying digital content. Cloud computing, which provides shared resources and information over a network, facilitates methods of consolidating hardware and data administration. In a few years, new platforms will be the primary means of accessing the Internet, delivering services, and engaging in government processes; e-government systems should be prepared to incorporate technological innovation. Meanwhile, information security and privacy are very important, given the increased roles of technology and e-government. Since an enormous amount of citizen transactions and data sharing across agencies are conducted online, a new level of concern for the privacy of individual information and the security of technical solutions should be created.

MANAGERIAL DIMENSION

Management issues for trustworthy e-government systems arise in formulating action plans to create demands, respond to various challenges, measure adequate performance, and maintain the long-term commitment of a results-oriented government. Core values of e-government management are significantly grounded in new public management and traditional bureaucracy theory since investment losses of electronic operations and services are relatively expensive and frequent (Heeks 2006). Persson and Goldkuhl (2010) suggested management strategies of e-government to decrease dysfunctional paths of bureaucracy (e.g., less rigid, vertical and horizontal integration), to strengthen bureaucratic values (e.g., legality, predictability, transparency, accountability), to connect the directions of new public management (e.g., performance orientation, accessible service, citizen orientation), and to overcome dysfunctions of new public management (e.g., refocusing impartiality, refocusing equality, exploring e-governance). Managerial directions of a holistic e-government system should work to balance some contradictory issues beyond bureaucratic and new public management approaches.

Management strategies should clarify missions, goals, and objectives of an e-government system for future demands. A set of e-government objectives should be specific in a measurable manner and representative of desirable outcomes. A necessary e-government path is setting appropriate performance measurement and reporting standards that identify gaps and opportunities for committing to quality and accountability. Performance measurement is a pragmatic, information-based management tool for simplifying complex administrative realities into a tangible thing, which allows government to improve productivity and be more accountable. For instance, a performance reference technique provides a common set of outputs to agencies for achieving their targets. However, developing an e-government performance measurement system to evaluate its performance is not an easy task, given the nature of the public sector, which suffers from not only the lack of a public sector counterpart to bottom-line profit projections in the private sector but also the lack of time for collecting performance data that compare the cost and benefits. Under these circumstances, public managers in the United States observed that using performance-based management tools has decreased (Behn 2008), since performance management initiatives do not guarantee performance improvement (Ammons and Rivenbark 2008).

In recent years, e-reporting has become a common way to inform the public on government performance, and it is considered a critical instrument of e-democracy (Lee 2004). Since information-savvy citizens tend to be more dependent on government websites for searching government information, the quality of e-reporting is critical to enhancing democratic accountability. Straightforward actions for quality of e-reporting may be related to integrity, security, reliability, documentation, and maintenance of up-to-date information. In addition to the quality of information, e-reporting management should pay attention to presenting data responsibly and formatting performance information efficiently, so as to be understood by citizens. The managerial aspect for an organic e-government system should be prepared to convert these challenges into a feasible management road map.

RELATIONAL DIMENSION

E-government systems reform dynamic relations among government, citizens, and non-governmental groups. E-government started from simple one-way communication and has progressed to multidirectional social networks. Social networks via networking sites are highly interactive, depend on user-generated content, and feature real-time user control, all driven by social participation (Laudon and Laudon 2013). Individuals are linked through their mutual interests or personal connections and build online communities. The concept of the wisdom of crowds has been increasingly penetrated by technology in both the private and the public sectors. Laudon and Laudon (2013) noted that trust in an organization is built by actively soliciting customers' comments. To a large extent, an active participatory culture has been cultivated through everyday online activities so that individuals have become conscious of owners of a nation. They are neither just users nor customers. In responding to this trend, public employees have redesigned structures and decision-making processes to advocate for participatory culture.

A critical challenge of working with e-democracy and e-governance ideologies is accountability. Input in government and political processes is made not only by government but also by individuals and communities. Citizens and communities "will be responsible for influencing political decisions but will not be held accountable for the results of these decisions" (Reddick 2012, 22). This can result in the lack of consistent policy directions and less bargaining power of public managers, given the separation of responsibility from accountability. As Norris (2007) found, online participation and e-democracy are neither a preferred reason for adopting e-government nor a priority for future implementation for U.S. local governments; most local governments largely focus on information dissemination and service transactions. If there are no systems responsible for sharing the consequences of decisions by external government stakeholders, then it will be hard to implement more democratic participation and adopt better governing ideas.

CONCLUSION

The advent of ICTs has reduced the fears of power becoming centralized in government and has supported an ideology of empowering people and communities. E-government has a tremendous positive impact on trust in government, which results in credible interactions between government and citizens (Tolbert and Mossberger 2006; Welch, Hinnant, and Moon 2005), and it enhances democracy through active citizen participation (Reddick 2012). The quality of e-government has often been evaluated by higher levels of e-government stages. However, the stages of electronic states have made little progress toward enhanced democracy or governance (Dawes 2008; Norris and Reddick 2013). Technology-intensive initiatives have dominated the directions of e-government, although growing e-government research has emphasized both a normative e-government stage framework and a technology-focused framework. Negative consequences and costs of running the higher end of e-government channels have not been clearly addressed yet, and the link between e-government practices and improvement of the overall level of government functions remains doubtful. Fundamental issues may be recurring, regardless of the progress of technology and the levels of government. For example, the adoption of new ICTs is likely to reinforce preexisting power inequalities within government and between government and citizens, since key policy decisions may become more centralized higher up in the organization.

Strategies for reshaping the fundamental characteristics of future-oriented e-government systems should be developed, encompassing the opportunities, challenges, and risks of instrumental and democratic perspectives for government and communities. The proposed sustainable system considers the wide array of concerns in institutional, technical, human, and societal aspects simultaneously to provide a comprehensive perspective of e-government systems. There is no single, separate issue in e-government contexts. An e-government strategy to enhance information security and privacy concerns not only is a technical aspect of ICTs but also concerns managerial and structural issues of government. Without good management and appropriate policies of information security and privacy, a new technological action could be another failure. Management must take the responsibility of designing and implementing a relevant program, whereas legal and regulatory policies should support this initiative with citizen and community awareness. An upcoming e-government system should be prepared to respond to the rapid cycle of changes and mobilization from citizens and communities.

KEY POINTS

E-Government versus E-Governance

The terms "e-government" and "e-governance" are often considered as an exchangeable concept, but clarification between two notions is needed to develop long-term strategies of a desirable electronic state. At a glance, e-government focuses on information dissemination and convenient service delivery via a Web-based platform, whereas e-governance focuses on group interactions for greater engagement in both government and nongovernmental organizations.

Update Technological Infrastructures

The early application of Web 1.0 focused on transferring information and services from one provider to many users, driven by a bureaucratic and technocratic approach that did not intend to foster collaboration. However, Web 2.0 was designed for many-to-many interactions that allow both governments and citizens to generate information and exchange. To support active interactions between citizens and governments, technological infrastructures in the public sector should be updated.

Understand Citizens' Roles

Citizens are empowered to participate in the policymaking processes that accompany the development of e-government. Thus, understanding relevant citizens' roles is critical to implementing public policies via e-government and promoting deliberative democracy via e-democracy. Public managers should redefine roles of citizens that are comparable in given situations.

Three Common Barriers to Citizen Participation

While authentic citizen participation is critical to improving democratic values, there are three common barriers to meaningful citizen participation: busy day-to-day schedules of ordinary citizens and nonparticipatory attitudes, a lack of opportunities and steps for citizens to provide inputs to government, and inadequate participatory techniques accessible to the majority of citizens. The utilization of electronic platforms could be one of the most effective tools for overcoming these barriers.

Overcome the Digital Divide

The digital divide is commonly defined by the "haves" and the "have-nots" of material access, influenced by socioeconomic status, but this dichotomous definition underestimates the multifaceted nature of digital inequalities in accessing information. The scope of the digital divide should be expanded to not only limitations of technological access but also the lack of skills, knowledge, and usage. Information-poor communities and citizens may have limited influence in policymaking processes and political agenda setting. Thus, the broad scope of the digital divide should be taken into account when the government implements e-government policies.

Cultivate an Active Participatory Culture

The wisdom of crowds is increasingly popular in the public sector. Trust in an organization is built by actively soliciting comments of users, so an active participatory culture should be cultivated throughout everyday electronic activities. The government has to accommodate a participatory culture through redesigning structures and decision-making processes.

Incorporate User Comments

Social networks and networking sites produce interactive, user-generated content and real-time user control, driven by social participation. Individuals are linked through their mutual interests or personal connections and build online communities. Public managers should create appropriate ways to incorporate such voluntary comments in policy processes.

ACKNOWLEDGMENT

This work was supported by the National Research Foundation of Korea (NRF) grant funded by the Korean Government (NRF-2012-2012S1A3A2033666).

REFERENCES

Ammons, David N., and William C. Rivenbark. 2008. Factors influencing the use of performance data to improve municipal services: Evidence from the North Carolina benchmarking project. *Public Administration Review* 68 (2), 304–318.

Behn, Robert D. 2008. *What all mayors would like to know about Baltimore's CitiStat performance strategy.* Washington, DC: IBM Center for the Business of Government.

Bekkers, Victor, and Vincent Homburg. 2007. The myths of e-government: Looking beyond the assumptions of a new and better government. *Information Society* 23 (5), 373–382.

Chadwick, A. 2006. *Internet politics: States, citizens, and new communication technologies.* New York: Oxford University Press.

Coursey, David, and Donald F. Norris. 2008. Models of e-government: Are they correct? An Empirical Assessment. *Public Administration Review* 68 (3), 523–536.

Dawes, Sharon S. 2008. Evolution and continuing challenges of e-governance. *Public Administration Review* 68 (6), S86–S102.

———. 2009. Governance in the digital age: A research and action framework for an uncertain future. *Government Information Quarterly* 26 (2), 257–264.

Fountain, Jane. 1999. The virtual state: Toward a theory of federal bureaucracy in the 21st century. In *Democracy.com? Governance in a networked world*, ed. Elaine C. Kamarck and Joseph S. Nye Jr., 133–156. Hollis, NH: Hollis Publishing.

Garson, G. David. 2006. *Public information technology and e-governance: Managing the virtual state.* Sudbury, MA: Jones & Bartlett.

Hacker, Kenneth L., and Jan van Dijk. 2000. What is digital democracy? In *Digital democracy: Issues of theory and practice*, ed. Kenneth L. Hacker and Jan van Dijk, 1–9. Thousand Oaks, CA: Sage.

Heeks, Richard. 2006. *Implementing and managing e-government: An international text.* London: Sage.

Helbig, N., J.R. Gil-Garcia, and E. Ferro. 2009. Understanding the complexity of electronic government: Implications from the digital divide literature. *Government Information Quarterly* 26 (1), 89–97.

Kakabadse, A., N.K. Kakabadse, and A. Kouzmin. 2003. Reinventing the democratic governance project through information technology? A growing agenda for debate. *Public Administration Review* 63 (1), 44–60.

Kaufmann, D., A. Kraay, and A. Mastruzzi. 2010. *The worldwide governance indicators: Methodology and analytical issues.* Policy Research Working Paper No. 5430. New York: Macroeconomics and Growth Team, Development Research Group, World Bank.

Keohane, R.O., and Joseph S. Nye. 2000. Introduction. In *Governance in a globalization world*, ed. Joseph S. Nye and John D. Donahue, 1–44. Washington, DC: Brookings Institution.

King, Cheryl Simrell, Kathryn M. Feltey, and Bridget O'Neill Susel. 1998. The question of participation: Toward authentic public participation. *Public Administration Review* 58 (4), 317–327.

Kraemer, Kenneth, and John Leslie King. 2008. Information technology and administrative reform: Will e-government be different? In *E-government research: Policy and management*, ed. Donald Norris, 1–20. Hershey, PA: IGI Publishing.

Laudon, Kenneth C., and Jane P. Laudon. 2013. *Essentials of management information systems*. 10th ed. Upper Saddle River, NJ: Prentice Hall.

Layne, Karen, and Jungwoo Lee. 2001. Developing fully functional e-government: A four stage model. *Government Information Quarterly* 18 (2), 122–136.

Lee, Jungwoo. 2010. 10 year retrospect on stage models of e-government: A qualitative meta-synthesis. *Government Information Quarterly* 27 (3), 220–230.

Lee, Mordecai. 2004. *E-reporting: Strengthening democratic accountability.* Washington, DC: IBM Center for the Business of Government.

Macintosh, A. 2008. E-democracy and e-participation research in Europe. In *Digital government: E-government research, case studies, and implementation*, ed. H. Chen et al., 85–102. New York: Springer.

Moon, M. Jae. 2002. The evolution of e-government among municipalities: Rhetoric or reality? *Public Administration Review* 62 (4), 424–433.

Morgeson, Forrest V., and Sunil Mithas. 2009. Does e-government measure up to e-business? Comparing end user perceptions of U.S. federal government and e-business web sites. *Public Administration Review* 69 (4), 740–752.

Nasi, Greta, and Francesca Frosini. 2010. Vision and practice of e-government: An empirical study. *Financial Accountability and Management* 26 (1), 85–101.

Norris, Donald F. 2007. Electronic democracy at the American grassroots. *In Current issues and trends in e-government research*, ed. Donald Norris, 163–179. Hershey, PA: CyberTech Publishing.

Norris, Donald F., and Christopher G. Reddick. 2013. Local e-government in the United States: Transformation or incremental change? *Public Administration Review* 73 (1), 165–175.

Persson, Anders, and Göran Goldkuhl. 2010. Government value paradigms: Bureaucracy, new public management, and e-government. *Communications of the Association for Information Systems* 27 (1), 45–62.

Reddick, Christopher G. 2012. *Public administration and information technology.* Burlington, MA: Jones & Bartlett Learning.

Rhodes, R.A.W. 2007. Understanding governance: Ten years on. *Organization Studies* 28 (8), 1243–1264.

Saxena, K.B.C. 2005. Towards excellence in e-governance. *International Journal of Public Sector Management* 18 (6), 498–513.

Scavo, Carmine, and Younhee Kim. 2010. Citizen participation and direct democracy through computer networking: Possibilities and experience. In *Handbook of public information systems*, 3d ed., ed. C.M. Shea and D.G. Garson, 67–88. Boca Raton, FL: CRC Press.

Schachter, Hindy L. 1997. *Reinventing government or reinventing ourselves: The role of citizen owners in making a better government.* Albany: State University of New York Press.

Schlanger, Elliot. 2013. E-gov: Will the real "cyber-optimists" please stand up? *Public Administration Review* 73 (1), 176–177.

Siau, Keng, and Yuan Long. 2005. Synthesizing e-government stage models: A meta-synthesis based on meta-ethnography approach. *Industrial Management and Data Systems* 105 (4), 443–458.

Smith, Aaron. 2009. *The Internet's role in campaign 2008.* Washington, DC: Pew Internet & American Life Project. www.pewinternet.org/~/media//Files/Reports/2009/The_Internets_Role_in_Campaign_2008.pdf.

Streib, Gregory, and Katherine G. Willoughby. 2010. E-government as a public management reform: The experience in the United States. In *Handbook of public information systems*, 3d ed., ed. C.M. Shea and D.G. Garson, 171–185. Boca Raton, FL: CRC Press.

Thomas, John Clayton. 2004. Public involvement in public administration in the information age: Speculations on the effects of technology. In *eTransformation in governance: New directions in government and politics*, ed. Matti Mälkiä, Ari-Veikko Anttiroiko, and Reijo Savolainen, 67–84. Hershey, PA: Idea Group.

Tolbert, Caroline J., and Karen Mossberger. 2006. The effects of e-government on trust and confidence in government. *Public Administration Review* 66 (3), 354–369.

UN Department of Economic and Social Affairs, Division for Public Administration and Development Management. 2008. *United Nations e-government survey 2008: From e-government to connected governance.* New York: United Nations.

Vigoda, Eran. 2002. From responsiveness to collaboration: Governance, citizens, and the next generation of public administration. *Public Administration Review* 62 (5), 527–540.

Welch, Eric W., Charles Hinnant, and M. Jae Moon. 2005. Linking citizen satisfaction with e-government with trust in government. *Journal of Public Administration Research and Theory* 15 (1), 37–58.

West, Darrell M. 2004. E-government and the transformation of service delivery and citizen attitudes. *Public Administration Review* 64 (1), 15–27.

———. 2008. *State and federal electronic government in the United States.* Washington, DC: Brookings Institution. www.brookings.edu/~/media/research/files/reports/2008/8/26%20egovernment%20west/0826_egovernment_west.pdf.

Part III

Applications

9

E-Voting

Domestic and International Successes and Failures

Cecilia G. Manrique and Gabriel G. Manrique

The government's use of technology to make itself accessible to its people and to have citizens feel that they have access to government and can participate in its processes are important goals of the movement toward e-government. There are many areas that these goals cover, all of which are interesting and developing rapidly.

One area of e-government, specifically, is electronic voting, or e-voting: the use of technology to assess the pulse of the electorate through the casting of ballots. This concept has had fitful starts and stops in its development. To replace or to complement the traditional method of voting at polling places, e-voting uses rapidly evolving digital innovations to allow the people to express their will regarding elected officials, initiatives, referenda, and propositions.

In this chapter, the authors demonstrate where electronic voting has made an impact at the local, state, and national levels in the United States; show where e-voting has been or is currently being implemented in other parts of the world; discuss factors why governments choose to adopt e-voting; explore cases of both successes and failures in the implementation of e-voting; examine the reasons for the successes and failures of e-voting; and discuss the issues associated with its implementation.

Through this research, knowledge and understanding of the complexities of e-voting in the United States and the world will hopefully be expanded, which will be helpful to those assessing the merits and challenges of using new ways of bringing government closer to the people. We hope the research will help inform the decision-making process regarding the adoption of e-voting. This work serves only as an early starting point for information gathering and analysis, and we expect there will be more subsequent research in this field as digital technology becomes more closely intertwined with governance and voting.

INTRODUCTION

Fair, free, and honest elections are the most fundamental aspects of a functional democracy. Elections require more than the physical act of casting a ballot in a polling place on Election Day, however; they require that the electorate participates in other aspects of the electoral process, including learning about the candidates and the issues they stand for, registering to vote if required, and actually making it to the polling place to exercise that right.

Political scientists are especially interested in voter participation, and in particular voter turnout, to indicate the strength and viability of a democracy. In a day and age when information technology has increased people's ability to obtain the information they need to make meaningful decisions about their personal, social, and economic lives, there is also a growing notion that the same technology should be used for political decision making.

With the ubiquity of new technology (e.g., smartphones, tablets) that packs more and more power into smaller and smaller devices, and with the increasing use of social media (e.g., Facebook, Twitter, LinkedIn), there is a growing belief that these technological innovations can be used to promote greater civic engagement and a healthier political life. The potential increase in political participation through voting is one of the main factors driving the experiments utilizing newer technology in the electoral process.

In this chapter, we take a look at how technology meets e-government to facilitate electronic voting. In the first section, the chapter presents an overview of where and how e-voting has been adopted in the United States and in other parts of the world. However, there is a growing realization that e-voting will eventually evolve into "i-voting." Originally thought of as straightforward voting using desktop computers connected to the Internet, the notion of i-voting has expanded to allow for the use of newer digital communication devices like smartphones and social media apps paired with these devices. This chapter will attempt to discuss these related developments.

BACKGROUND

In the wake of the controversy surrounding the 2000 U.S. presidential election, there was an increase in attention by political scientists to voter security and voting technology. One legislative response to the 2000 Florida voting problems was the passage of the Help America Vote Act (HAVA) of 2002, which required many states to update their voting technologies and to replace punch card systems with electronic voting machines (EVMs). Much of the literature produced on the subject of voting technologies has focused on how people interact with voting technologies. Subtopics within human interaction with voting technology include technology and voter confidence, in addition to the effectiveness of popular electronic voting systems in the United States.

The two most common e-voting systems are optical scanners and direct-recording electronic (DRE) voting systems, which are most often touchscreen machines that record votes electronically and may or may not produce a paper record of each vote. The paper records of votes provide some assurance of accurate tabulation and provide a means for recounting votes in case of software malfunction. Researchers agree that the use of DREs that include a physical paper record of votes is an effective way to increase both voter confidence and to safeguard against program malfunction (Herrnson et al. 2008)—thus taking care of two qualms, security and transparency, that governments and voters may have about the use of technology for voting.

One broad focus of scholarly research regarding electronic voting in the United States has been the study of residual votes (votes that are considered invalid by voting authorities and not included during the official vote count). Studies such as the Caltech/MIT Voting Technology Project (VTP) and work by Charles Stewart (2009) and Alvarez and Hall (2008) have analyzed the trends and causes of residual votes. In general, these studies have concluded that the changes in voting technology since the 2000 election have resulted in lower rates of residual votes. Alvarez and Hall's study found that in cases when states and counties switched to DRE voting machines, there were lower rates of residual votes than in cases where states or counties switched to optical scan systems (Hall 2009). Hall suggests that this may be due to a disparity in administrative talent. The successful conduct of an election using DRE systems requires a higher level of administrative talent than elections in which optical-scan voting systems are employed (Hall 2009).

Another focus of the field of electronic voting has been the nature and problems associated with human interaction with voting technology. Hall (2009) notes in *Voting Technology and Innovation* that oftentimes the problems that arise with new voting technology are not the fault of some malfunction or irregularity in the technology itself, but instead lie in the technologies' interactions with the human voter, poll worker, or voting administrator. To combat these problems, Herrnson, et.al. suggest education and training for voters, election officials, and poll workers. This education and training can significantly lower the instances of voting irregularities and other problems. The effectiveness of education on voter security and accuracy is in agreement with the findings of Hall's study, which concludes that the successful implementation of DRE systems is largely dependent on the talent of the election administration (Hall 2009, 3).

Some of the most comprehensive research on the topic of voting technology in the United States and abroad has been done by nonprofit organizations such as the Carter Center. The Carter Center has done a number of studies on the elections in Venezuela and the Philippines (2007b) as well as a multiyear study to develop an effective methodology for observing and auditing elections in countries (2007a) that use election voting machines (EVM). Other similar organizations have focused on the United States' voting system and made comparisons with other countries.[1] For example, Rosenberg and Chen (2009) completed a study through the Brennan Center for Justice titled *Expanding Democracy: Voter Registration around the World*, in which 20 jurisdictions, including Canada, Argentina, Great Britain, and Mexico, were studied in terms of their voter registration systems and practices.

In the next section, we attempt to describe the current state of voting technology in the United States and place its state within an international context by providing comparisons with other countries. We synthesize selected scholarship on the subject of voting technology in an attempt to make international comparisons that will show the direction of e-voting in the United States and the world today.

DEFINITIONS

Currently, there is a wide variety of notions when it comes to what constitutes e-voting. Broadly understood, e-voting incorporates any method by which the people who have a right to determine their representatives and determine certain types of government action via referendum or initiative, and then exercise that right through a voting system that uses some type of machine. At the most basic level, punch cards are still considered electronic methods of voting. Despite the advent of smaller, faster, and more powerful machines, many states in the United States and many countries still rely on optical scanners and direct-recording electronic devices for accepting and tallying the votes.

In today's world, where technology has evolved to support a mélange of apps and smart devices linked via the Internet and other wireless technology, there is a need to redefine what constitutes e-voting to accommodate the proliferation of social media and small devices. In other words, "i-voting" rather than "e-voting" may be the more relevant term. Indeed, it is easy to imagine that the voting world is truly in transition as we increase our options for voting, political participation, and counting votes faster.

Such a redefinition from e-voting to i-voting would still include the use of electronic machines—machines that make vote counting easier but do not change the nature of political participation. But in the age of Facebook, Twitter, and other social media, electronic voting encompasses more than just electronic machines: it should incorporate web-based methods using systems including the Internet, wireless technology, e-mail, social interfaces, and a multitude of smart devices, which combined have the potential to change the nature of political participation and the very essence of what is a polling station or polling booth. Whereas traditional e-voting is one in which voting is supervised physically by independent electoral authorities or government representatives like the machines at polling stations, i-voting includes remote electronic voting in which the voting is not physically supervised by government representatives, as the voting is done from any location using any device connected to the Internet. Of course, the absence of physical supervision necessitates sophisticated electronic safeguards to guarantee the integrity of elections.

AN INITIAL LOOK INTO E-VOTING

Preliminary research data indicate that several countries since the 1980s have experimented with e-voting and i-voting to varying degrees. At the most basic local levels, some elections for university councils and student councils in Austria and Germany have used rudimentary e-voting. Some municipalities, states, and provinces have also been experimenting with e-voting. Countries that tried e-voting on a national scale include Estonia, Ireland, and Venezuela. France has used e-voting for party elections and primary elections. Even supranational entities have attempted the use of e-voting, as in the case of European Union parliamentary elections. Thus, there is evidence that e-voting is being adopted, albeit at a slow pace thus far.

Countries like Estonia, which will be discussed more extensively later, have plunged into i-voting, whereas other countries like Ireland have tried e-voting and so far abandoned it. There are numerous countries somewhere in between these two extremes—countries that are surely grappling with the contrasting forces of technology and cultural inertia. While many of the countries experimenting with e-voting are developed countries, there is also some success in implementing e-voting in developing countries such as Brazil and Venezuela.

In the United States, several states still use paper ballots and punch cards for voting. The use of e-voting and i-voting is usually for special populations such as those who are disabled, overseas military personnel and expatriates, the elderly, and those living in remote places. Those involved in the movement toward e-voting include the private companies that stand to gain from the future of the use of such technology, universities that have been in the forefront of the studies of these trends (especially on the part of computer scientists and political scientists), governments, and hackers.

We now look at international and domestic examples of countries and states using or attempting to use i-voting.

INTERNATIONAL EXAMPLES

According to the International Foundation for Electoral Systems (IFES), several states using or testing electronic voting machines are in South America or Asia, see Table 9.1 (Scammell 2013). An important reason for its use in some countries is to help illiterate citizens. The use of fingerprints for identification is an important development for some to ensure integrity, as is the technical limit of allowing no more than five voters to register per electronic device to prevent stuffing of ballots. To help alleviate people's fears that their vote would not count if there were no paper trail, some countries have machines that also produce paper receipts to enable audits.

Estonia

Electronic voting in Estonia began in October 2005 for local elections.[2] Estonia became the first country to have legally binding general elections using the Internet as a means of casting the vote. Estonian election officials later declared it a success. In 2007, Estonia held its first national Internet election, and voting was available from February 26 to 28.

In the 2009 local municipal elections, 9.5 percent of persons with the right to vote exercised their right to vote over the Internet. In the 2011 parliamentary elections held between February 24 and March 2, 96 percent of the electronic votes were cast in Estonia and 4 percent by Estonian citizens residing in 106 foreign countries. Thus, Estonians have been very active in setting international standards when it comes to Internet voting.

Estonia's use of Internet voting is deemed to be the most successful of the international examples thus far. Its success is based on the existence of four major ingredients: a technical framework, a legal framework, a political framework, and a cultural framework.

Clearly, a high level of Internet usage and penetration is necessary for successful i-voting. Furthermore, the existence of laws, rules, and regulations conducive to the

Table 9.1

Countries That Use Some Form of Electronic Voting

Country reported to use electronic voting	Type (if available)
United States	Direct recording electronic system with or without voter-verified paper audit trail
Norway	Internet voting
Canada	Internet voting
Estonia	Internet voting
Switzerland	Internet voting
France	Internet voting
Belgium	Internet voting
Brazil	Internet voting
India	Internet voting
Netherlands	Internet voting—discontinued use of e-voting
Venezuela	Internet voting
Ireland	Internet voting—discontinued use of e-voting
Paraguay	
Germany	Internet voting—discontinued use of e-voting
Australia	
Finland	
Italy	
Kazakhstan	
Philippines	
Romania	
United Kingdom	
Austria	Remote e-voting
Sweden	
Portugal	Polling-place e-voting
Spain	Remote e-voting
Uganda	

Source: Esteve, Goldsmith, and Turner (2012).

use of Internet voting needs to be in place. This requires the installation of a system to authenticate who can vote, to define when voting begins and ends, to carry out security requirements, and to ensure that clear rules are established for when and how ballots will be counted and tabulated. Internet voting is one of three ways Estonians can vote. Aside from the Internet, Estonians can vote early by paper ballot or in person on Election Day. They are also allowed to change their votes electronically as many times as they want to during the voting period. Estonia allows citizens several weeks to vote online, to reduce the impact of technical failures or cyberattacks. To discourage vote buying or voter intimidation, electors may cast their ballot multiple times during the election period, although only the final vote counts. Those who wait until Election Day, however, must vote on paper at a traditional polling station. This ensures that last-minute system crashes cannot disenfranchise voters. It is only the last Internet ballot that counts—unless they used a paper one, which then becomes the ballot of record. The voting is also audited by KPMG Baltics.

The security of the system itself needs to be guaranteed so that people can trust that their vote will be counted. Estonia, like many other countries, has promulgated a Digital

Signatures Act (DSA), which will allow for a person's e-signature to be accepted as authentic for transactions such as banking, purchasing online, and submitting tax returns. Estonia, like a few other countries, has a national identity card that can be used to verify voting eligibility.

The use of Internet voting requires a high level of political will for i-voting to succeed. Support at various levels of government will allow for adoption. In the case of Estonia, support was strong at all levels of government—from the prime minister to the political parties to the public. Voting is also not limited to a day in Estonia but spread over a few days to allow for much greater participation.

A culture that is supportive of Internet voting is also necessary. Because Estonians are used to accessing government services over the Internet, voting through the web is not a difficult process or radical idea. A sophisticated level of e-government services can make broad acceptance of i-voting easier.

The Estonian system of electing public servants into office yielded impressive results. Ballots cast online made up 24 percent of the votes in Estonia's 2011 parliamentary election (up from 5.5 percent in 2007). The Estonian experience sheds hope on those looking for ways to encourage voters to exercise their right to vote, especially those who have never voted or those who find excuses not to exercise that right.

The Estonian study by Alvarez, Hall, and Trechsel (2009) also points out that the replacement effect, the faithfulness effect, the trust effect, and the neutrality effect all come about through Internet voting. It is not unreasonable to suppose that Internet voting will favor the younger voters, who have grown up on the computer and social media. However, it should also be noted that the same younger voters today will become the elderly voters in the future; therefore, the generational divide when it comes to computer use will no longer be an issue in the future. Besides, as long as traditional methods of voting remain in effect, no group ought to be disenfranchised by i-voting. The faithfulness effect indicates that if you i-vote once, you will have a tendency to use it again. It is likely, therefore, that i-voting can mobilize casual voters as well as convert the "never voters."

Likewise, the trust effect could discourage those for whom language is a barrier or for those whose computer literacy is lacking. It is possible that these factors will deter them from using e-voting. But again, like the replacement effect, it could be a short-term issue that will be resolved as the younger, more tech-savvy generation takes its place in the political realm. In addition, technological advancements have made multilingual sites more common.

The same study also showed that gender is not an issue when it comes to i-voting. Men and women tend to use e-voting in the same proportion. Neither does income affect the use of e-voting. Rich and poor tend to use e-voting in the same proportion. It is just as interesting to note that the level of education of voters and their geographic location are not significant factors in determining the use of e-voting. Thus, there appear to be no significant socioeconomic biases associated with voting online. And in the Estonian case the election results were politically neutral in that Internet voting did not favor one party over another. Thus, Internet voting did not seem to be a partisan issue.

What are the lessons that can be learned from the case of i-voting in Estonia? It would seem that Internet voting works well for small, highly centralized countries where politics is not highly partisan and ideologically polarized. It is important that the country has a comprehensive voter registry and that a simplified ballot is used. The experience of Estonia indicates that i-voting can be efficient, cost effective, and hugely convenient compared to the traditional ballot boxes and electronic voting machines more commonly used today.

Ireland

The concept of e-voting was tried and failed in Ireland. Following the 2002 trial, the government tried to introduce a nationwide electronic voting system for the local and European Parliament elections. However, on April 23, 2009, the minister for the environment announced that the electronic voting system was to be scrapped because of costs and the public's dissatisfaction with the system.

On October 6, 2010, the announcement was made that the 7,000 voting machines in existence would no longer be used for voting (McCloy 2010). The total cost of the electronic voting project had reached €54.6 million, including €3 million spent on storing the machines over the previous five years.

Socialist Party representatives said electronic voting should be abandoned because of a lack of transparency and that the new system could be open to "radical manipulation." In contrast, proponents of the system counter that having already spent the money would cause loss of national pride if the system were discontinued. It would seem that electronic voting in Ireland suffered partisanship, which led to it being disposed of anyway (Brennan 2012).

OVERVIEW OF U.S. VOTING: A DECENTRALIZED SYSTEM

The United States comes into electronic voting with several institutional setbacks when compared to Estonia. The United States is a large country composed of 50 individual states that take pride in their ability to determine electoral laws and methods based on a federal form of government. Thus, trying to get all 50 states to agree on a common method of voting is a challenge in itself, beyond the varying levels of capabilities of implementing such a drastic system change. Table 9.2 shows that disparity in voting procedures in the United States.

The administration of U.S. elections is highly decentralized. In a majority of states, elections are run at the county level. Officials at these local levels of government oversee elections for local, state, and national offices. In this sense, the United States does not have genuine "national elections" with regard to administration, but a system of simultaneous elections administered by more than 3,000 county governments throughout the country (Herrnson et al. 2008, 4). The decentralized nature of voting administration in the United States leads to wide variation in the way elections are executed. The technology used, the ballot (including which candidates are placed on the ballot and the design of the ballot

Table 9.2

Voting in U.S. States

State	E-Voting	Type
Alabama	No	Paper ballots or punch cards
Alaska	Yes	DRE w/ VVPAT
Arizona	Yes	DRE w/ VVPAT
Arkansas	Yes	DRE w/o VVPAT
California	Yes	DRE w/ VVPAT
Colorado	Yes	DRE w/o VVPAT
Connecticut	No	Paper ballots or punch cards
Delaware	Yes	DRE w/o VVPAT
District of Columbia	Yes	DRE w/o VVPAT
Florida	Yes	DRE w/o VVPAT
Georgia	Yes	DRE w/o VVPAT
Hawaii	Yes	DRE w/ VVPAT
Idaho	No	Paper ballots or punch cards
Illinois	Yes	DRE w/ VVPAT
Indiana	Yes	DRE w/o VVPAT
Iowa	No	Paper ballots or punch cards
Kansas	Yes	DRE w/o VVPAT
Kentucky	Yes	DRE w/o VVPAT
Louisiana	Yes	DRE w/o VVPAT
Maine	No	Paper ballots or punch cards
Maryland	Yes	DRE w/o VVPAT
Massachusetts	No	Paper ballots or punch cards
Michigan	No	Paper ballots or punch cards
Minnesota	No	Paper ballots or punch cards
Mississippi	Yes	DRE w/o VVPAT
Missouri	Yes	DRE w/ VVPAT
Montana	Yes	DRE w/ VVPAT
Nebraska	No	Paper ballots or punch cards
Nevada	Yes	DRE w/ VVPAT
New Hampshire	No	Paper ballots or punch cards
New Jersey	Yes	DRE w/o VVPAT
New Mexico	No	Paper ballots or punch cards
New York	No	Paper ballots or punch cards
North Carolina	Yes	DRE w/ VVPAT
North Dakota	No	Paper ballots or punch cards
Ohio	Yes	DRE w/ and w/o VVPAT
Oklahoma	No	Paper ballots or punch cards
Oregon	Yes	DRE w/ VVPAT
Pennsylvania	Yes	DRE w/o VVPAT
Rhode Island	No	Paper ballots or punch cards
South Carolina	Yes	DRE w/o VVPAT
South Dakota	No	Paper ballots or punch cards
Tennessee	Yes	DRE w/o VVPAT
Texas	Yes	DRE w/o VVPAT
Utah	Yes	DRE w/ VVPAT
Vermont	No	Paper ballots or punch cards
Virginia	Yes	DRE w/o VVPAT
Washington	Yes	DRE w/o VVPAT
West Virginia	Yes	DRE w/ VVPAT
Wisconsin	Yes	DRE w/ VVPAT
Wyoming	Yes	DRE w/ VVPAT

Source: Individual state websites.

Note: DRE w/ VVPAT = direct recording electronic voting systems that require voter-verified paper audit trails; DRE w/o VVPAT = direct recording electronic voting systems that do not require voter-verified paper audit trails.

itself), and system of voter registration differ significantly among states and counties. As a result, elections in two adjacent counties can potentially have very different voting systems and technology.

One of the main implications of decentralized administration and wide variation in voter technology is that the quality of elections is determined by the talent and organization of local government officials in charge of elections. Hence, if a voter lives in a county with highly organized, prepared, and experienced poll workers, he or she is less likely to encounter problems on Election Day such as long lines, botched registrations, and issues of voter identification verification (Gerken 2009, 14). Such was the case in the most recent presidential election, where long lines caused President Obama to remark in his victory speech: "I want to thank every American who participated in this election, whether you voted for the first time or waited in line for a very long time . . . by the way, we need to change that."[3]

County governments oftentimes have a very limited amount of funds to run important elections using election officials, who on average do not have a college degree, earn less than $50,000 a year, and receive fewer than 20 hours of training (Gerken 2009, 22). More research into the positive effects of a professionalized, better-paid election administration is needed. There is ample evidence that a centralized and well-trained corps of election officials have been successful in other countries.

Use of Partisan Election Officials

The United States is unique among industrialized nations in that it trusts the administration of election to partisan officials, meaning individuals whose political party affiliation is not taken into consideration when allowed to work the polls during elections. Most decisions regarding elections are made either at the state or local level. In Australia, Canada, Costa Rica, Great Britain, and Venezuela, a corps of nonpartisan civil servants are responsible for the administration of elections. Although officials in the United States are subject to federal election regulations, there are only a limited amount of standards and requirements these partisan officials must adhere to (FairVote n.d.).

Because of the partisan nature of election administration—which includes the decisions on adopting various forms of voting technology—several scholars have noted that this can cause administrators to make decisions not based on what would benefit all voters in their jurisdiction in terms of increasing turnout, accessibility, and ease of use, but rather on which technologies would disproportionately help their own party or harm the opposition. In *Voting Technology: The Not-So-Simple Act of Casting a Ballot*, Herrnson and colleagues (2008) described the controversial election in Florida, which involved both parties actively discouraging the use of statewide bipartisan-backed DRE voting machines. Each party instead encouraged voters to send in absentee ballots on the assumption that absentee ballots presented greater advantages to the party. Each party also accused the other of attempting to confuse or manipulate voters. Results aside, the extreme partisanship and the attempt to politicize the voting process more than likely had a negative effect on voter confidence (Herrnson et al. 2008, 6).

Internationally, the voting process and system is less of a political issue. As stated earlier many countries outside the United States employ nonpartisan civil servants to administer and oversee elections. Germany, Canada, and Australia use nonpartisan election administrators. For example, in Venezuela, non-party-affiliated government employees are trained by a national government agency, the National Electoral Council (CNE)(Wilkerson 2012). Coupled with uniform DRE voter machines and a national electronic voter registration system, Venezuela's successful 2006 election led former president Jimmy Carter to hail Venezuela's election system as the best he has seen. Carter claimed, "Of the 92 elections that we've monitored [the Carter Center], I would say that the election process in Venezuela is the best in the world" (Weisbrot 2012, 1).

Voter Registration

The U.S. voting system has a very decentralized voter registration system. Individual voters must register themselves, something relatively unique to the United States among industrialized counties. The rules and regulations concerning when, who, and where citizens can register to vote also varies between and among states and localities. Voter registration is an area of the U.S. voting system that could be vastly improved with technology. The creation of electronic voter records also would cut down on the clerical mistakes that are very common in the U.S. system—a system that is very expensive, labor intensive, and inefficient. In fact, the Brennan Center for Justice concluded in a 2010 study that Arizona and Washington, two state pioneers in Internet voting, implemented both online voter and Department of Motor Vehicles registration at a low cost of $130,000 and $279,000, respectively (Ponoroff 2010).

Modernizing voter registration through coordination among government agencies is a cost-effective way to improve the current voting system in the United States. Internationally, putting fewer burdens on individual citizens for voter registration has resulted in comparatively higher proportions of registered voters. In a 2009 paper by Rosenberg and Chen, the United States ranked relatively low in percentage of registered voters, which they claim is related to the manner of voter registration. When one ranks countries based on "responsibility for voter registration"—where high responsibility means individual citizens must initiate their own registration and low responsibility means the government automatically registers citizens to vote—the United States is ranked among the highest. This is a probable significant cause for the low rate of voter registration in the United States. Rosenberg and Chen conclude that Canada serves as the most plausible model for the United States to follow, given Canada's similar decentralized government coupled with a voter registration process made efficient and cost-effective through the cooperation of government agencies (Rosenberg and Chen 2009, 3).

Voting and Ballot Technology

Voting technology affects the way people vote and can affect the outcomes of elections (Herrnson et al. 2008, 152). This was most drastically demonstrated in the 2000 U.S. presidential election and the use of the controversial butterfly ballots in Florida, a state whose 25 electoral votes decided the outcome of the election. Again in the 2008 book *Voting Technology*, Herrnson and colleagues chronicle the ways in which the type of voting machine affects voting outcomes and the ways in which specific voting technologies disproportionately affect poor, disabled, and less educated citizens. Other studies have likewise shown the different effects voting technology can have on voters (Card and Moretti 2004). Given the power that voting technology has on election outcomes, a uniform national standard of voting technology would effectively level the playing field.

There have indeed been many efforts at moving the United States toward the use of current technology in the process of voting. In the November 2012 elections, many American states allowed voters overseas to receive and/or return their ballots via e-mail (see Table 9.3). Thus, the experimentation—especially with Internet voting—has already been taking place at the state and local levels in the United States. However, wider acceptability has been hindered by various problems and issues, outlined in the following section.

Arizona and New Jersey

Internet voting technology was used in three elections in Arizona: the 2000 Democratic primary, the 2008 general election, and the 2010 general election. One voting system was used for the 2000 Democratic primary. A different voting system was used for the 2008 and 2010 general elections. These were two distinct systems, in two distinct projects, with different sponsors.

Internet voting in Arizona and in many other states is currently only available for Uniform and Overseas Citizens Absentee Voting Act (UOCAVA) voters, who may apply for ballots via mail, fax, and the Internet and may return their ballots by the same means. The average return rate for UOCAVA voters was 28 percent, well below the average return rate of 77 percent.

However, providing an electronic mechanism for UOCAVA voters to access and return their ballot greatly improved their participation and return rate to 68 percent. Native American, African American, and Latino turnouts went up, defying those who claimed that minorities would not use the Internet to cast votes.

Problems experienced while using the voting system on voter personal computers (PCs) during the election included the malfunctioning of antiquated browsers, which led to some users with older browsers not being able to vote, operating system incompatibility, and administrative issues (e.g., loss of the PIN required for accessing the voting system). Despite such issues, the Arizona Democratic primary has been called the first legally binding public election to offer Internet voting.

In the case of New Jersey, the state was allowed to use Internet-based voting after Hurricane Sandy, before the 2012 elections (Government Technology 2013). New Jersey residents affected by the storm could vote by e-mail under the state's overseas voter law, which stated, "To vote electronically, residents will have to print their ballot, mark it, then fax it or scan and e-mail it to their county clerk. They then must mail in the hard copy of the ballot."

Table 9.3

States Allowing Overseas Voters to Vote by Email

State	Ballot application	Receiving blank ballot	Returning completed ballot
Alabama	Not specified	Mail, email, fax, or other secure electronic means approved by Secretary of State	Hand delivery or mail
Alaska	Mail, fax, scanning, or other electronic transmissions	Mail, email, fax	Not specified
Arizona	Mail, fax, and the Internet (secure ballot-upload system)	Not specified	Mail, fax, and the Internet (secure ballot-upload system)
Arkansas	Submit federal postcard application by mail, email, fax	Mail	Mail, fax, and the Internet (secure ballot-upload system)
California	Submit federal postcard application by mail, email, fax	Mail or fax; some counties offer ballots by email or downloadable online versions	Mail; UOCAVA voters may return by fax
Colorado	Mail, fax, email	Mail, email, fax,	May return via fax under emergency ballot procedures; electronic transmission if mail is not available for UOCAVA voters
Connecticut	Mail, fax, email, or other electronic means	Mail or electronic means that have been requested	Mail
Delaware	Submit federal postcard application by mail, fax, email	Mail, email, fax,	If received by mail, must be returned by mail; if received by fax or email, may return by mail, fax, or email
District of Columbia	Mail, email, fax	Mail, email, fax	Mail, email, fax
Florida	Telephone, mail, email, fax, or any other form of written request	Mail, email, fax	Mail or fax
Georgia	Mail, email, fax	Mail, email	Mail
Hawaii	Submit federal postcard application by mail, email, fax	Mail, unless do not receive by mail within 5 days of election then may receive by fax	Mail, unless received by fax then may return by fax
Idaho	Mail, email, fax, or other electronic transmission	Mail, email, fax	Mail, unless emergency then may be returned by email or fax
Illinois	Mail, email, fax	Mail, email, fax, or secure ballot-upload systems	Mail
Indiana	Mail, email, fax; UOCAVA voters: web application or email	Mail or fax; UOCAVA voters: web application or email	Mail, fax, email

Table 9.3 *(continued)*

State	Ballot application	Receiving blank ballot	Returning completed ballot
Iowa	Mail, email, fax	Mail, email, fax	Mail, unless UOCAVA voters are in an "imminent danger pay" area
Kansas	Mail, email, fax or other electronic method authorized by Secretary of State	Mail, email, fax, or other electronic method authorized by Secretary of State	Via the same methods as receiving
Kentucky	Mail, email, fax; email is through web application	Mail, email, fax	Mail
Louisiana	Any means, including mail and fax	Mail, fax	Mail, fax
Maine	Writing (submitted by mail, fax, immediate family or third person), telephone, or electronic means authorized by Secretary of State	Mail, fax; UOCAVA voters may receive through electronic download	Mail; UOCAVA voters may return by email
Maryland	Online through a downloadable version, mail	Mail or downloadable version	Mail
Massachusetts	Mail, email, fax	Mail, email, fax	Mail, email, fax
Michigan	Mail, email, fax	Mail, email, fax	Mail
Minnesota	Mail, email, fax	Mail, email, fax	Mail
Mississippi	Mail or telephone; UOCAVA voters: mail, email, fax	Mail; UOCAVA voters: mail, email, fax	Mail; UOCAVA voters may return by same means as received
Missouri	Mail or fax; UOCAVA voters: mail, email, fax	Mail or fax; UOCAVA voters: mail, email, fax	Mail
Montana	Mail, email, fax, or online electronic absentee system	Mail, email, fax, online system	Mail; unless UOCAVA, then may return by same means as received
Nebraska	In person, mail, email, fax	Mail; UOCAVA voters: receive by any method authorized by Secretary of State	Mail; UOCAVA voters may return by same means as received
Nevada	Mail or fax; UOCAVA voters: mail, email, fax	Mail or fax; UOCAVA voters: mail, email, fax	Mail; UOCAVA voters may return by same means as received
New Hampshire	Submit federal postcard application by mail, email, fax	Mail or electronic transmission	Mail
New Jersey	Mail, email, fax	Mail, email, fax	Same means as received
New Mexico	Mail, email, fax	Mail, email, fax	Same means as received
New York	Mail, email, fax	Mail, email, fax	Mail
North Carolina	Mail, email, fax	Mail, email, fax, Internet	Mail; UOCAVA voters may return by same means as received

North Dakota	Mail, email, fax	Mail, email, fax	Return by same means as received; online ballot-marking system is available
Ohio	Mail, email, fax	Mail, email, fax	Mail
Oklahoma	Mail, email, fax	Mail, email, fax	Mail, email, fax
Oregon	Mail, email, fax	Mail, email, fax	Mail; if serving or discharged within last 30 days may return by fax
Pennsylvania	Mail, email, fax	Mail, email, fax	Mail
Rhode Island	Mail or fax	Mail, fax, or download from secure website	Mail; military and overseas may return by fax
South Carolina	Mail, email, fax	Mail	Mail
South Dakota	Mail, email, fax, or web portal	Mail, email, or web portal	Mail
Tennessee	Mail, email, fax	Mail; UOCAVA voters may receive ballot by email	Mail
Texas	Mail, fax	Mail	Mail
Utah	Mail, email, fax	Mail and Internet, if jurisdiction, offers it	Mail; UOCAVA voters may return by fax or email
Vermont	Mail, telephone, email, fax	Mail, email, fax	Mail
Virginia	Mail, email, fax	Mail; UOCAVA voters may receive ballot by email or fax	Mail
Washington	Mail, email, fax	Mail, email, fax	Mail or electronically if the hard copy is sent before electronic version is received
West Virginia	Mail, email, fax	Mail, email, fax	Mail, email, fax; must return ballot by electronic transmission if received by electronic transmission
Wisconsin	Mail, email, fax; if applied by email, must mail in original signed application	Mail; UOCAVA voters: email or fax	Mail
Wyoming	Mail, phone, email; UOCAVA voters: fax	Mail	Mail

Source: Verified Voting Foundation, Rutgers School of Law and Newark Constitutional Litigation Clinic, and Common Cause Education Fund 2012. Copyright © 2012.

Note: UOCAVA = Uniformed and Overseas Citizens Absentee Voting Act.

What resulted, though, was a bombardment of requests to vote electronically, which slowed the system down to such an extent that it took 15 minutes per person to complete the verification process. Voters were met with busy signals on phone and fax lines as well as full e-mail inboxes, leading to a rejection of incoming requests. At one point, election workers gave personal e-mail addresses to alleviate the situation, while there were voters who simply gave up. Internet voting in New Jersey was too popular, making it less successful than it could have been because the system was not set up for the kind of bombardment it received from the large interest in voting electronically.

Problems and Issues

Included in the negatives of standardization of voting machines is the possibility of widespread fraud and security breaches (which are not exclusive to a standard form of voting technology but would hypothetically affect a greater number of votes if every machine were the same), and issues infringing on state and local freedom to experiment with voting technologies that work for them, thus falling into the pitfalls of a one-size-fits-all solution.

On Friday, October 1, 2010, the District of Columbia's Board of Elections and Ethics learned that the Digital Vote by Mail public examination software had developed an affinity for the maize and blue of the University of Michigan. Professor Alex Halderman and his students successfully hacked the system, thus leading to skepticism toward the Internet voting system's acceptability for use in U.S. elections (Roblimo 2012).

Despite the positive impact of using various Internet methods of voting—which includes the convenience, the instant count feedback, and enfranchisement of those otherwise disenfranchised—there are still several setbacks and negative impacts that must be addressed for a wider acceptability of the method to be obtained. The largest fear of users is security and its concomitant transparency. As the hacking attempt had indicated, much needs to be done with regard to the system's susceptibility to malicious computer software. If a machine fails, it is possible that it can miscount votes with no way to verify the mistake. Because of the dominance of voting machine companies, there is also the fear that Internet voting is susceptible to bribery as well as the lack of quality control. At this stage, this seems to be the major stumbling block to adoption of Internet voting in a much larger scale in the United States.

Findings and Further Research

One of the major findings of this research is that the voting system of the United States is ineffective mainly because of its history of decentralization. The second major finding is that many of the problems with the current voting system and technology deal with the partisan, nonprofessional, and underfunded voting administration. The problem of ineffective election administration is directly related to decentralization. Small county and state governments (that oversee the vast majority of elections in the United States) simply do not have adequate resources to conduct effective and well-executed elections. In addition, most top election officials are closely affiliated with political parties, which have led to numerous cases of deliberate manipulation of election administration procedures to favor their political party. In many cases, the partisan election officials use voting technology to tip the scales in their favor without regard to voter confidence or integrity.

Given the financial limitations of state and local governments, as well as the political gridlock at the national level, attempts at major changes to the United States voting system at the national level are likely to be unsuccessful. This is the reason a reform of the voter registration system becomes a priority, in order to bring about any meaningful change using technology. Nonpartisan organizations such as FairVote, the Brennan Center for Justice, the Carter Center, and the Caltech/MIT Voting Technology Project, as well as other scholarly sources—most notably the work of Michael Alvarez—agree that a reform of voter registration is a cost-effective, realistic, and relatively easy way to improve voter registration and increase turnout. The reforms primarily entail greater communication and coordination between record-keeping government agencies such the Department of Motor Vehicles and voter registration administration. The use of current technology can help facilitate such reform.

However, it is that same decentralization that will allow for the experimentation that might be necessary to bring about the acceptability of Internet voting. Successes in one locality, county, or state can lead to wholesale adoption and should offer enough benefits for the electorate to adopt the technology.

The method of research employed in this chapter has several limitations. By no means is the research on international or U.S. voting technologies and voting systems exhaustive, although an effort was made to choose a variety of sources in both type and source. Attempts were made to include a mix of scholarly sources such as journal articles and popular sources such as newspapers and Internet-based articles. The comparative method employed can also be problematic in that whenever two dissimilar countries are compared, differences in culture, demographics, attitudes, and the like tend to be overlooked. Because of such differences, what may work in one country may not be feasible in another. In the United States particularly, there exists a level of hyperfederalism and an "excess of democracy," which is a long-standing tradition ingrained into its history and culture. This can create roadblocks to any sweeping national reforms regarding voting systems that may try to force states to adhere to a national standard.

One of the largest gaps in the research has to do with the topic of voter security and fraud. The study does not focus so much on reforming voting technology on the national level but more so on pointing out the possibilities for the United States to adopt Internet voting, which some other countries have successfully done. Although it is unlikely that the United States will adopt universal legislation standardizing voting technology, specifically i-voting on the national level, the ability to continue and experiment at the state and local levels should be applauded and encouraged.

Clearly, there are many areas of further research on the topic of what direction e-voting or i-voting is taking in the United States and in other countries of the world. The experiences of various countries will need to be documented, studied, and researched to a greater extent and in greater detail to be able to draw conclusions that may be applicable to various circumstances and instances when countries may want to implement such a method for voting.

Greater analysis in terms of the characteristics of the countries and the states that have adopted Internet voting and those that have not can provide insight into the future direction that Internet voting can go.

Much governmental discussion has been taking place with regard to Internet voting. Members of the academic field including computer and political scientists have chimed in on this topic. Further research on what efforts are being made to either encourage or discourage the use of the Internet in voting needs to be undertaken.

CONCLUSIONS

The source of the majority of problems with voting technology (including voter registration technology) is the decentralized nature of the current voting processes. The largely underfunded, partisan, and nonprofessional election administration in the United States causes the voting process to be manipulated for political outcomes. The United States can learn effective election administration methods from other countries such as Estonia, Venezuela, Britain, Canada, Australia, and Germany. Reform in voter registration technology and organization is the most viable and cost-effective way to improve the current U.S. election system, given the great decentralization and political divisiveness of the present.

Although various studies are of differing conclusions when it comes to whether Internet voting favors the rich or the poor, the right or the left, or the ruling party or the opposition, a bigger question is how online voting affects the choices citizens make regardless of socioeconomic status characteristics. Remote voters have more time to make informed decisions than those herded through busy voting booths, Michael Alvarez and T.E. Hall (2008) note, especially in a political system like that of the United States, where many races run simultaneously.

However, it is important to take seriously the major ingredients that make for a successful attempt at Internet voting. The first one is the technical ingredient. One reason for the success of e-voting in Estonia and in other developed and developing countries is the high Internet penetration. The penetration of Internet usage must improve for e-voting to be successful.

The second ingredient is the legal institution, which may be more difficult to conquer in the United States. There are aspects of the American political system that one cannot do anything about because it is ingrained in the Constitution and the system, such as the federal form of government, which allows each state to determine many aspects of their operations including the method of elections. Other aspects of American politics would be those involved in the complexity of American elections: one-day election periods; complex ballots with a variety of issues to vote on; and the winner-take-all method, which does not allow losers to participate in coalition government, which in turn encourages partnerships.

The beauty of federalism, though, also lies in the ability of states and local governments to experiment with something like the use of Internet voting to adopt changes to the electoral process and allow the voting system to adapt to the technological age.

The bottom line regarding the inability of the United States to adapt Internet voting stems from the lack of cohesive election laws that facilitate online transactions. Clearly there are already-existing advantages to online transactions, as more and more Americans engage in on-line activities including banking, gambling, business transactions such as online purchases, and e-government activities such as tax filing, car registrations, and driver's-license applications. With these online activities available, it begs the question why the ability to vote online is not widespread.

Just as with various aspects of their lives, Americans have a tendency to compartmentalize; therefore, there is a desire to separate the personal from the political, to separate the social media of their personal life from the online voting of their political life. Even if the leaders of the nation were to assert national online voting as the third political ingredient, voters would certainly experience a backlash. Online voting will require a change in culture, which is the fourth ingredient to its adoption. The United States clearly lacks a strong professional election administration culture. Voters will want some assurance that security, integrity, and the transparency of all voting systems can exist in online voting. However, it seems that the nation cannot go back once the use of online voting is introduced. What is needed is to find better alternatives to the security problems posed by hackers and not retreat from them, because voters expect that there will be a day when online voting will be as simple as paying bills or paying taxes.

The move to online voting may not necessarily increase voter turnout, but it provides another method in which voters are able to express their right to vote. Technology can certainly help citizens vote, but it takes more than that to make voters care. Unfortunately, there are no apps in existence for that.

KEY POINTS

Definition of E-Voting

Our definition of what passes for electronic voting (e-voting) varies, but for public policy to be effective and efficient, a consistent and broader definition is necessary. E-voting has tended to be associated primarily with voting machines like optical scanners and direct-recording electronic (DRE) voting systems such as touchscreens. Given the proliferation of digital devices like smartphones and iPads, and the ubiquity of social media on the Internet, e-voting's scope must include these as well and perhaps be renamed to i-voting. This will require more training, resources, and even legal changes.

Adoption of Internet Voting

Adoption of Internet voting should continue to have among its primary aims an increase in political participation and reduction in residual votes (votes considered invalid and therefore not counted). Research shows that these occur with technological adoptions and can therefore improve the democratic process. Public officials must then consider not just the purchase of machines and software but how to make them as user-friendly as possible.

Successful Implementation of E-Voting

At all levels of government, successful implementation of broadly defined e-voting will necessitate significant retraining of both voting administrators and voters. This may become less and less of an issue as larger portions of the population become more adept with digital devices and apps. However, there will still be a portion of the population with less access to digital resources. To ensure the success of the democratic voting process, appropriate training and resources must be devoted to all segments of the voting population. What procedures and regulations are already in place in the local, state, and national levels that can make e-voting and Internet voting viable? What would be the barriers to implementing some of the alternative voting mechanisms described in this chapter?

E-Voting: The Experience of Estonia

While each country is different, we can learn from their successful implementation of Internet voting. In particular, we can learn from the experiences of Estonia by looking at its

- technical framework
- legal framework
- political framework
- cultural framework

In addition, we can ask this question: what has led to the adoption of e-voting by vast segments of Estonia's population?

E-Voting Security Practices

As always, with the adoption of new technology for something as sensitive as voting, the primary concern is security and maintaining the integrity of the process without unduly hindering citizen access. In this regard, policymakers and administrators of the electoral process will need to consider sensitive practices like digital signatures, universal voter identification, and the use of independent auditors.

Considerations for the United States

The United States needs to consider whether the following factors hinder broad adoption of e-voting and what amendments may be necessary:

- The decentralized and fragmented voting systems at the various levels of government need to be assessed.
- At the municipal, county, and state levels of government, a discussion of any necessary changes to laws that will be needed to facilitate the adoption of e-voting and Internet voting will need to take place.
- A discussion will need to occur at every level of government as to which specific resources and personnel will be needed to implement e-voting and Internet voting systems.

Because of its highly sensitive nature and its newness, we can expect many glitches and hindrances to e-voting and i-voting, but the system should be willing to learn from these.

NOTES

1. Another similar organization is FairVote: The Center for Voting and Democracy (www.fairvote.org), a nonprofit organization based in Maryland.

2. Material in this section is based on Alvarez, Hall, and Trechsel (2009).

3. For a transcript of Obama's reelection speech, see "President Obama's acceptance speech (full transcript)," *Washington Post*, November 7, http://articles.washingtonpost.com/2012-11-07/politics/35506456_1_applause-obama-sign-romney-sign.

REFERENCES

Alvarez, R.M., and T.E. Hall. 2008. *Electronic elections: The perils and promises of digital democracy.* Princeton, NJ: Princeton University Press.

Alvarez, R.M., T.E. Hall, and A.H. Trechsel. 2009. Internet voting in comparative perspective: The case of Estonia. *PS: Political Science and Politics* 42 (3), 497–505.

Brennan, M. 2012. €50m voting machines to be turned into "traffic cones or fleeces." *Independent.ie*, November 30. www.independent.ie/irish-news/50m-voting-machines-to-be-turned-into-traffic-cones-or-fleeces-26687597.html.

Card, D., and E. Moretti. 2004. Does voting technology affect election outcomes? Touch screen voting and the 2004 presidential election. *Review of Economics and Statistics* 89 (4), 232–235.

Carter Center. 2007a. *Developing a methodology for observing electronic voting.* Atlanta: Carter Center.

———. 2007b. *Observing the presidential elections in Venezuela: Final report of the technical mission.* Atlanta: Carter Center.

Esteve, J.B.I., B. Goldsmith, and J. Turner. 2012. *International experience with e-voting: Norwegian e-vote project.* Washington, DC: International Foundation for Electoral Studies. www.ifes.org/Content/Publications/News-in-Brief/2012/June/~/media/Files/Publications/Reports/2012/EVote_International_Experience_2012.pdf.

FairVote. N.d. Nonpartisan election officials. http://archive.fairvote.org/index.php?page=70.

Gerken, H. 2009. *The democracy index: Why our election system is failing and how to fix it.* Princeton, NJ: Princeton University Press.

Government Technology. 2013. govtech.com/extra: E-voting in New Jersey. *Government Technology*, 26 (5), 7.

Hall, T.E. 2009. *Voting technology and innovation.* VTP Working Paper No. 86. Caltech/MIT Voting Technology Project. http://vote.caltech.edu/content/voting-technology-and-innovation-0.

Herrnson, P.S., R.G. Niemi, M.J. Hanmer, B.B. Bederson, F.C. Conrad, and M.W. Traugott. 2008. *Voting technology: The not-so-simple act of casting a ballot*. Washington, DC: Brookings Institution Press.

McCloy, J. 2010. Video cure for Internet voting. Ireland voting machines to be traffic cones? *Voting News Daily*, October 8. http://thevotingnews.com/video-cure-for-internet-voting-ireland-voting-machines-to-be-traffic-cones/.

Ponoroff, C. 2010. *Voter registration in the digital age*, ed. W. Weiser. New York: Brennan Center for Justice, New York University, School of Law. www.brennancenter.org/publication/voter-registration-digital-age.

Roblimo. 2012. Prof. J. Alex Halderman tells us why Internet-based voting is a bad idea (video). *Slashdot*, March 12. http://it.slashdot.org/story/12/03/10/2351259/prof-j-alex-halderman-tells-us-why-internet-based-voting-is-a-bad-idea-video.

Rosenberg, J.S., and M. Chen. 2009. *Expanding democracy: Voter registration around the world.* New York: Brennan Center for Justice, New York University, School of Law.

Scammell, R. 2013. Internet voting a success in two European countries. European University Institute, news release, February 12. www.eui.eu/News/2013/02-12-InternetvotingasuccessintwoEuropean-countries.aspx.

Stewart III, C. 2009. *Election Technology and the Voting Experience in 2008.* Midwest Political Science Association. Chicago: Monograph.

Verified Voting Foundation, Rutgers School of Law–Newark Constitutional Litigation Clinic, and Common Cause Education Fund. 2012. *Counting votes 2012: A state by state look at election preparedness* by Pamela Smith, Michelle Mulder, Susannah Goodman, Carlsbad, CA: VVF. www.verifiedvoting.org/resources/internet-voting/.

Weisbrot, M. 2012. Why the US demonizes Venezuela's democracy. *The Guardian*, October 3.

Wilkerson, T. 2012. Venezuelan irony: A tainted election with the world's best vote counting system. *American Diplomacy,* October 17, 1–3.

10

E-Government in U.S. Local Governments

Disparities, Obstacles, and Development Strategies

Hua Xu and Hugo Asencio

The application of information and communication technologies holds enormous potential for the more cost-effective delivery of services to sparsely populated areas. One would expect that the development of e-government would occur more quickly in areas with a large rural population. Nevertheless, these areas face some challenges. Although there is a great amount of empirical literature on e-government based on surveys of state governments, large municipalities, and countries, there is a relative dearth of research focusing on small local governments in more rural areas. This chapter focuses on the development of e-government among small and medium-size local governments. A case study of Alabama county governments is conducted employing the assessment tool developed by the Rutgers University E-Governance Institute to evaluate the websites of Alabama county governments and identify the best e-government practices of local governments. The case study also applies multivariate analysis to identify the environmental (i.e., socioeconomic) and institutional factors that affect the progress of e-government of local governments. In addition, it provides an overview of the political system of Alabama as well as the existing state and federal policies and programs aimed at assisting in the application of information technology at the local government level. Last, it recommends policy and program strategies to facilitate the development of e-government at the local level. This work contributes to the knowledge of e-government development in local governments of the U.S. southern states and the empirical literature of e-government research in general.

THE STATUS OF E-GOVERNMENT IN LOCAL GOVERNMENT

E-government has become widely available in state and local government in the United States and many other countries since the 1990s. According to a recent national survey, more than 90 percent of local governments in the United States have their government documents, such as council agendas and minutes, as well as codes or ordinances, available online (Norris and Reddick 2013). Increasingly, more local governments provide transaction-based services, such as online requests for services and documents and bill payment, through the Internet (Norris and Reddick 2013).

E-government optimists posit that e-government will not only transform the way the government conducts business but also redefine the relationship between government and citizens. However, some recent survey studies indicate that local government's transformation by e-government has been incremental instead of rapid and drastic, as some cyber-optimists predicted; in fact, the development of e-government has been rather gradual over the past decade (Norris and Reddick 2013). One important indicator of this is the adoption and use of Web 2.0 technologies and social media in local governments. Norris and Reddick (2013) found that only about two-thirds of local governments in the United States use social media; of these, 92.4 and 68.8 percent use the social media of Facebook and Twitter, respectively. More important, these social media outlets are used mainly for one-way communication, which does not meet the requirements for e-participation or e-democracy (Norris and Reddick 2013). As Norris and Moon (2005) point out, although the adoption of e-government—defined as the creation of websites—was fairly rapid toward the end of the twentieth century, the transition from transaction-oriented e-government to democracy-oriented e-government has been relatively slow in the United States.

The development of e-government in Alabama is slower than expected, and the disparities in implementation are glaring among local governments. Specifically, the gap between the e-government of the state of Alabama and that of most local governments in the state is evident. The state's official government website was ranked No. 34 among all U.S. states (Holzer et al. 2009) and received national recognition at EGov.com. For reference, other Deep South states—Mississippi and Louisiana, for example—ranked No. 16 and No. 25, respectively (Holzer et al. 2009). Furthermore, a large number of small-scaled governments, including municipalities and counties, seem to lag further behind compared to larger local governments in the state (Xu and Asencio 2012).

Understanding these disparities is one of the main forces driving research in e-government. Researchers are still trying to understand why some local governments are ahead of others when it comes to developing e-government. There are organizational factors (e.g., leadership, organizational capacity), institutional factors, and environmental factors determining the adoption and advances in e-government (Moon 2002; Moon and Bretschneider 2002; Jun and Weare 2010). Some research suggests that the major motivations for local governments to adopt e-government include providing citizens with access to their local government, information, and elected and appointed officials, as well as saving money (Norris and Reddick 2013). Other research has found that lack of both financial resources and technology or Web staff in information technology (IT) departments have been some of the primary barriers to the development of local e-government initiatives (Moon 2002). Other factors, such as staff and citizen resistance to change, privacy concerns, and support of elected officials and top administrators, according to Norris and Reddick (2013), are not among the major barriers.

Another factor to consider is whether citizens—recipients of local government services—have access to the Internet. This is critical for the development of e-government. Research suggests that the use of home computers and the Internet is highly correlated with a number of demographic and geographic factors, such as income, education, age, ethnicity, disability, family size, rural or urban status, metropolitan status, and immigrant status or citizenship (Federal Communications Commission 2010; U.S. Department of Commerce 2011). Demographically, these factors put Alabama at a disadvantage. The population of Alabama is 67 percent non-Hispanic and has a higher-than-average percentage of African Americans—26.2 percent—according to the 2010 U.S. Census.

E-GOVERNMENT AND THE POLITICAL SYSTEM IN ALABAMA

The adoption and use of information technologies in local government are determined by local socioeconomic conditions and indirectly by local political factors. In fact, as our analysis suggests, some economic factors are highly correlated with the development of e-government, measured by the quality and accessibility of websites. The experiences of applying information technologies in the public sector are contrary to what the theory of technological determinism predicts (Garson 2006). On the opposite side of this is the reinforcement theory of technology. According to this theory, the application of technology simply accentuates the existing social and political institutions. A middle theory is the socio-technical perspective, which asserts that system design is critically important but human factors also play an important role in the application and results of information technologies in the public sector (Reddick 2012). Thus, one can hypothesize that the adoption and use of information technologies in the local governments of Alabama are jointly determined by their socioeconomic conditions and political institutions.

The political system may enlarge or mitigate the disparities in e-government or the digital divide. It is important to examine state and local governmental relations in Alabama. The political system in Alabama is unique in several important aspects: According to the state constitution, Alabama is not a home-rule state, and county governments have very limited power in policy and decision making; the only counties that are the exception are Jefferson, Lee, Mobile, Shelby, Madison, Montgomery, and Tuscaloosa. The decision-making power on fiscal affairs, such as new taxes and levies, rests with the state house's Local Legislation Committee. In addition, some county governments do not have the power to decide on local affairs as trivial as mosquito treatment, waste disposal, and land-use zoning. One of the problems of this centralized government system is that policy decision making is not possible when the state house is in recess. The state's current constitutional amendments are aimed at delegating more powers to county governments (Lyman 2012).

There are a total of sixty-seven counties in the state of Alabama. The county government provides a wide variety of public services, such as law enforcement (sheriffs), public school systems, business and building permits, public health, libraries, garbage collection and waste management, elections, emergency management, jail facilities, and courts. Each county elects its legislative body, the County Commission, which is presided over by a chair. In most counties, county administrators are appointed and charged with the daily operations of the county governments. Like other southern states, Alabama is a politically conservative state and has a history of majority voting for Republican presidential candidates (Rogers et al. 2012). Republicans have controlled the state legislature since 2009, and for the past decade, every governor has been Republican. Although Alabama has one of the poorest health records of any state, the state government decided not to join the Health Exchange Program under the Affordable Care Act: the political culture in the state is generally not supportive of an "activist" government, which in turn may constrain the policy interventions for supporting the technological development in local governments.

It is still debatable, however, whether centralized government or state control is conducive to local government technological advances and innovations. Some scholars suggest that a federalist, decentralized system is conducive to technological innovations (Oates 1999). Others suggest that a centralized government is more capable of mobilizing resources to promote priority research and development, and hence fostering innovations. The fact is that the technological advancement in Alabama concentrates in the major industrial cities, which may be conducive to the dissemination of new technologies. For example, Huntsville, a city in northern Alabama, is a conglomerate of the aerospace and military industries. The metropolitan area of the city has a population of more than 400,000, making it one of the largest cities in the state. The National Aeronautics and Space Administration's (NASA) Marshall Space Flight Center is the main employer in the region, among other major companies, including Redstone Arsenal, Cummings Research Park, ADTRAN, Intergraph, and Avocent. In addition, the University of Alabama in Huntsville has a research center for technology and engineering. Nevertheless, the city has undergone some changes, some due to the reduction of federal funding to the aerospace programs.

Alabama's state government started its programmatic e-government initiative as early as 2002 (State of Alabama 2013). The project was contracted to a private company, EGov.com, which works with state agencies, boards, commissions, political subdivisions, local government agencies, and quasi-government agencies. The renewed 2012 contract covers most of the commonly known transactions in e-government, including online transaction processing between the state government and its citizens; interactive voice response (IVR) processing; payment systems (e.g., credit- and debit-card processing, electronic checks, electronic funds transfers, over-the-counter payment processing to include PIN debit transactions, capture reporting of cash and money order payments, lockbox services, payment warehousing, auto-disbursement of funds to the state treasurer); and other services, such as application development, integration with partner's existing systems, security, application hosting and support, and management reporting.

The Alabama eGovernment Initiative aims to improve the following capabilities of the state government (State of Alabama 2013):

- To send requested information or documents electronically to multiple devices;
- To process interactive applications for licenses, filings, permits, registration, renewals, database searches, and other government documents, in order to sell goods and services by interactive applications and to receive documents for filing from

the public, businesses, employees, and local governments that, when a signature is necessary, can be electronically signed by the requesting authority;
- To receive required payments electronically by multiple methods

The services provided by the contractor include the following: customizable applications or applications developed for state agencies that provide electronically delivered services and information (i.e., e-government) to the citizens, businesses, employees, and local governments of Alabama; assisting the state in marketing the state's e-government services in a variety of ways to increase the use of the services it offers, hosting of eGovernment Initiative applications in a reliable and secure environment, and providing customer support to users and agencies (State of Alabama 2013).

In recent years, there were government efforts to make the Internet more accessible to Alabamians. According to the Alliance for Public Technology (2008), since 2008 the following initiatives have been offered: ACCESS Distance Learning, Alabama Research and Education Network, Telecommunications and Technology Assistance Program, and the (federal) Appalachian Regional Commission (APT and CWA 2008). These initiatives are important measures for promoting e-government in the local governments.

THE CASE STUDY OF ALABAMA'S COUNTY GOVERNMENTS

To evaluate the status of e-government in local governments and to identify the challenges and opportunities for developing e-government, a case study of Alabama's local governments was conducted during 2011 and 2012.

Local Government Website and Portal Evaluations

The study first investigated whether each of the county governments had an online website. When the county was found to have a website, the website was evaluated on the five key aspects of e-government, including privacy and/or security, usability, content, services, and citizen participation. This study used the same instrument developed by the Rutgers University E-Governance Institute. First, privacy and security measures refer to whether there are statements on privacy, or if there is a process of authentication on the website, how data are managed, and if the website uses cookies. The second aspect—usability—measures such key attributes of websites as user-friendliness of design, length of homepage, site search capabilities, and the like. The third aspect is content, which measures whether there is access to accurate and current information, such as publications, reports, and multimedia materials. The fourth aspect is service, which measures transactions, such as purchases and registrations with citizens, businesses, and other governments. Citizen participation is the fifth dimension and measures whether there are online civic engagements, policy deliberation, and citizen-based performance measurements in place. Each dimension accounts for 20 points, for a total of 100 possible points.

Table 10.1

Descriptive Statistics for Model 1 (*N* = 67)

	Minimum	Maximum	Mean	Standard deviation
White residents (%)	15.5	95.6	66.501	21.2298
Revenue per capita	3,439	658,466	70,982.63	103,966.934
Economic index	11.0	39.0	23.015	5.5007
Health index	16.0	40.0	32.209	5.6234
Public safety index	1.0	20.0	6.440	3.7885
Education index	11.0	36.0	20.985	4.6693
Population (2010)	3,439	658,466	70,982.63	103,966.934
Population change (2000–10) (%)	−12.3	9.3	1.678	3.5848
Person change younger than 18 (%)	20.3	27.7	23.539	1.5674
Persons 65 and older (%)	8.8	18.8	15.088	2.2008
Female residents (%)	44.5	54.7	51.416	1.6942
Income per capita	21,228	44,658	29,151.34	4,419.477
Home ownership (2005–9)	56.9	85.8	72.961	6.2379
Land area (in square miles)	534.8200	1,596.3500	757.372836	214.8414305
Population density	4.9598	591.8210	89.445460	104.0746270

Table 10.2

Descriptive Statistics for Model 2 (*N* = 67)

	Minimum	Maximum	Mean	Standard deviation
Security and/or privacy	.0000	12.0000	1.540299	3.4879906
Usability	.0000	14.3800	5.141791	4.1739869
Content	.0000	8.8000	2.340299	2.3388718
Service	.0000	6.4400	1.088060	1.4664296
Participation	.0000	6.5500	0.498657	0.9885648
E-government index	.0000	38.3100	10.609104	9.7277863

Data and Data Analysis

The descriptive statistics of the data for the models are presented in Tables 10.1 and 10.2. Evidently, there is great variation in these county-level variables for Model 1, including revenue per capita, population, income per capita, land area, and population density.

Table 10.2 provides the descriptive statistics for the data used in Model 2. It is evident that the e-government of county governments in Alabama largely remains at the early stages of development. The variation among county governments is large. As aforementioned, on the one hand, there is a significant number of county governments without a website. On the other hand, several counties have websites that are fairly developed. The variations are reflected not only in the five variables measuring different dimensions of website but also in the e-government index, which is a weighted mean of the five measures.

Model 1

Regression analysis is used to identify variables, or factors, that are significantly related to the development of e-government in various ways. To identify the factors that explain the development status of e-government in Alabama's county governments, two groups of variables are used in Model 1: fiscal capacity and demographic variables (see below for the model specification). High revenue is related to more financial resources, which in turn facilitate the development of e-government. The size of population and population growth is expected to be positively related to the state of e-government, whereas population density is expected to be negatively related to the state of e-government development. Both ethnicity (white) and percentage of females in local populations are expected to be positively related to the development status of e-government of county government. The percentage of underaged and elderly is hypothesized to be inversely related to the development of e-government:

E-government status = *f* (fiscal capacity, demographic factors, etc.)

Fiscal capacity is measured by two variables, revenue per capita and income per capita. Demographic variables include population size and density, population change between the two censuses, minority population measured by percentage of white residents, percentage of age groups younger than 18 and older than 65 years old, and percentage of female residents. As expected, there is high multicollinearity among some variables, such as population and population density. Multicollinearity occurs when closely related variables are used as predictors in regression analysis.

Model 2

In the second model, index variables are used as explanatory variables to address the potential issue of multicollinearity. The coefficient estimates in the regression analysis are not reliable if multicollinearity exists, although the overall predictability of the model is still valid. The data are extracted from the report *Counties in Crisis: Assessing Quality of Life in Alabama*, published by Alabama State University in 2011. The report employs data from the 2010 U.S. Census to develop the following indices: economic, health, public safety, and education:

E-government status = *f* [environmental factors (resources constraints), institutional, cultural, and organizational factors, etc.]

Specifically, the economic index is composed of four indicators: income per capita, unemployment rate, poverty rate, and average salary. The health index consists of five indicators, including infant mortality rate per 1,000 births, life expectancy, low birth weight in percentage, uninsured population, and obesity in percentage. The public safety index is constructed from the following ten indicators: homicide rate, rape rate, juvenile arrests, adult arrests, robbery, assault, burglary, theft, motor vehicle theft, and law enforcement officers per capita. Last, the education index is based on five indicators, including percentage of population lacking basic literacy skills, high school dropout rates, students per teacher, funding per student, and percentage of persons with a bachelor's degree or higher. Better economic and health conditions measured by economic and health indices are usually associated with higher development of e-government. Further, it is hypothesized that the public safety and education indices, which are regarded as environmental factors, are negatively related to the development of e-government.

FINDINGS FROM THE CASE STUDY

Status of E-Government of Local Governments

The overall developmental status of e-government of Alabama's county governments is rather low. There are a large number of county governments that do not yet have a website. According to some sources, of 67 counties, only 43 have a website (Alabama Department of Finance 2013). Even the evaluation scores of the top-ten counties with a website—Mobile, Jefferson, Houston, Baldwin, Elmore, Shelby, Covington, Geneva, Bibb, and Walker—range from 20 to 38 (see Table 10.3). These counties' scores are lowest on services and citizen participation. It is safe to assume that these counties' e-governments are still in the initial stages of development.

The Black Belt area of Alabama, located in the central and western regions of the state, is famous for its importance during the plantation era and its role in the civil rights movement during the 1950s and 1960s. There is a high concentration of poverty in the Black Belt, with a poverty rate of 33.6 percent in Bullock County, for example. Historically deprived, the region has a high concentration of the state's African American population, accounting for 50 percent of the region's local population. Thirteen out of 18 counties in the Black Belt have more African Americans than whites, compared to the state average

Table 10.3

Rankings of E-Government of Alabama County Governments

Rankings	County	Security and/or privacy	Usability	Content	Service	Citizen participation	E-government index
1	Mobile	12.00	10.63	8.00	4.41	3.27	38.31
2	Jefferson	12.00	11.88	4.00	4.75	1.45	34.08
3	Houston	6.40	9.38	8.80	3.05	1.82	29.45
4	Baldwin	1.60	14.38	8.80	3.73	0.00	28.51
5	Elmore	7.20	10.63	4.00	2.03	1.45	25.31
6	Shelby	10.40	6.88	5.20	1.36	1.09	24.93
7	Covington	10.40	7.50	4.00	1.36	1.09	24.35
8	Geneva	10.40	6.88	4.00	0.68	0.36	22.32
9	Bibb	6.40	10.63	1.60	0.68	1.45	20.76
10	Walker	6.40	7.50	3.20	2.71	0.73	20.54

Table 10.4

Racial Composition and Websites of County Governments in the Black Belt

County	Black (%)	White (%)	Website?
Macon	82.6	15.5	No
Greene	81.5	17.4	No
Sumter	75.0	24.2	No
Lowndes	73.5	25.3	No
Wilcox	72.5	26.8	No
Bullock	70.2	23.0	Yes
Dallas	69.4	29.1	Yes
Perry	68.7	30.3	Yes
Hale	59.0	39.8	No
Montgomery	54.7	39.5	Yes
Marengo	51.7	46.4	No
Barbour	46.9	48.0	No
Butler	43.4	54.4	No
Choctaw	43.4	55.8	No
Russell	41.8	53.7	Yes
Pickens	41.6	56.3	No
Pike	36.6	58.2	No
Crenshaw	23.4	72.6	Yes

of 26 percent. Whereas statewide about one-third of all counties (23 of 67) do not have a website, 12 of these 23 counties (more than half) in the Black Belt are without a website (see Table 10.4). Obviously, the counties in the Black Belt are overrepresented in the counties without a website in our study.

Correlates of Local E-Government Development

Results from the regression analysis of Model 1 suggest that only percentage of white population is significant in predicting the development of e-government in Alabama's county governments. Although other coefficient estimates are not significant, the directions of other variables are consistent with the hypotheses. For instance, the development of e-government is negatively associated with the two age groups (younger than age 18 and older than age 65) and positively related to revenue per capita.

As expected, the results of regression analysis of Model 2 suggest that the state of e-government is negatively, but not significantly, associated with the public safety and education indices, thus suggesting that a low level of public safety and education attainment is negatively associated with underdeveloped e-governments. In contrast, the state of e-government development is positively associated with economic and health factors. In particular, the coefficient estimate is significant at the .05 level, thus reaffirming the findings from Model 1. In other words, the development of e-government is related to economic conditions in a similar way, as it is related to the fiscal capacity of local governments.

In summary, this analysis suggests that there are indeed large disparities in the e-government of local Alabaman governments. The preliminary cause-effect analysis further suggests that the main obstacles to e-government are some socioeconomic factors, in addition to the lack of human and financial resources to support the development of e-government. Certain demographic variables such as the elderly and underage population are unfavorable conditions, whereas some other socioeconomic variables, such as revenue and income per capita, are positively related to the development of e-government, as they are indicators of fiscal resources needed for supporting the development of e-government. The political system in state and local governments can affect the local e-government in two ways: on the one hand, a powerful centralized government allows the state government to intervene in e-government development through intergovernmental aid programs and transfers; on the other hand, it is arguable that a centralized government is unfavorable to local innovations, as it may stifle the initiatives of local governments. Apparently, in the case of Alabama, the current political system has not significantly alleviated the disparities of e-government. The ongoing administrative reforms in the state, including the amendments to the state constitution and other initiatives, may be able to readjust the state-local relationship and thereby help create a more conducive environment for e-government development.

STRATEGIES TO ADVANCE E-GOVERNMENT IN LOCAL GOVERNMENTS

In a federalist system, local governments, vested with more power than the national government, are positioned to be more innovative. Nevertheless, small and medium-size local governments are disadvantaged in developing e-government in several key aspects as compared to the state government and large local governments. As found in the case study, one of the major constraints is lack of financial resources to fund e-government initiatives. The second disadvantage is lack of IT personnel. The third is the information on IT services known to the local government and local residents. Fourth, cost-effectiveness is a problem in providing e-government services for some local governments. Large cities tend to have the advantage of economies of scale. Strategies designed to guide and assist e-government development must consider these factors. Last, the development of e-government should consider special local needs. As indicated in the case study, certain demographic groups cannot access government services online. The development of e-government should make alternative service delivery mechanisms available to these groups so they are not left behind.

Solutions to e-government development should also take into consideration various modes of telecommunications available to local residents. Internet can be accessed through dial-up, DSL, broadband, satellite, mobile and smart phones, and local WiFi connections, each of which is different in terms of costs and accessibility. Different groups and localities may experience some advantages in using these communication tools but disadvantages in others. The design of development strategies should fit the local conditions and meet local preferences. Generally, there are five strategies: government interventions, market solutions, collaborative programs among local governments, public-private partnerships, and the role of professional and nonprofit organizations. These strategies are the means to overcome some of the common administrative, financial, and personnel barriers to the development of e-government in local governments.

Intergovernmental Programs and Government Intervention

In U.S. history, the federal government has played an integral role in funding public infrastructure. The information highway has been one of the federal government's priorities. In the twenty-first century, access to the Internet has become more important for citizens' work and living. Ensuring equal access to the Internet will be a very important role of the federal government. In 1996, the federal government created the E-Rate program through the federal Telecommunications Act, which provides discounted rates on Internet services for schools and libraries. However, the legislation did not address funding for Internet services in local governments.

As part of its stimulus plan, the federal government invested $7.2 billion in broadband initiatives in state and local governments in 2009 (National Telecommunications and Information Administration 2013) through the National Broadband Plan. The state of Alabama alone received more than $4 million in grants for studying broadband access by local governments (National Telecommunication and Information Administration 2013). Even after the phaseout of most federal stimulus funding, some state governments, such as that of California, have been active in capitalizing the opportunities offered by the stimulus plan (California Department of Technology 2013). It is important for resource-constrained local governments to take advantage of these intergovernmental assistance programs and funding opportunities in their e-government initiatives.

The state government can play a leading role in developing e-government at the local government level. In the case of Alabama, the state government has been able to leverage its size and the scale of some services, such as revenue collection, to contract with an IT consulting firm in order to acquire needed services. The state government can share experiences with local governments and, in some cases, consolidate some services provided by its local governments to get those local government services online. This is particularly important in light of the fact that most local governments are disadvantaged by their size and scale, information, and experiences in transitioning to e-government. In addition, intergovernmental assistance will be necessary in some areas. The federal and state government can further fund programs and invest in the information highway infrastructure. The funding to train IT personnel can be especially helpful. Some pilot projects and programs can be used to demonstrate benefits and potential problems, and to test the feasibility of some new programs for IT development in local governments.

Market Solutions

While there are obvious advantages of government interventions in promoting e-government, there are also inherent limitations. Government interventions can result in a monopoly of broadband services and may displace private service providers. Ensuring the competitiveness of the telecommunication market is key to having access to low prices for telecommunication services. The Federal Telecommunications Commission plays an important role in regulating the market, but direct provision of telecommunication services, including Internet, by government can be problematic.

It will be helpful for state governments to identify potential vendors for e-government contracts. Making the information of experienced and reliable IT consulting firms available to local governments will be very helpful to small local governments, since they tend to lack access to such information. In the case of Alabama's state government, EGov.com appears to be an option for the state's local governments. Additional vendors can be identified, and a nationwide directory or database for such information could be extremely valuable (NIC Inc. 2012).

Collaborative Programs Among Local Governments

Regional and interlocal cooperative programs can bring significant benefits to the development of local governments' e-government. Small governments are disadvantaged in bargaining with vendors of IT equipment or service providers. In some areas of Alabama, school districts purchased or rented laptops and computers as a group to bargain for a bulk discount. Like many school districts, local governments can collectively procure such services. In fact, the local governments in some states have been using this practice. Another strategy related to this sort of collaborative programs is shared service agreements. Small local governments can share server hosting and other services with larger governments for reduced rates. In turn, large local governments can enjoy the benefit of less financial burden from the reduction of overhead costs. Some other shared services that can be established through contracting among governments can be customer service and training: it may be too costly for local governments to hire their own full-time personnel to answer phone calls from public users of the local government's online services. The consolidated provision of such services can result in significant savings in maintaining the online government services.

Public-Private Partnerships

In 2013, the *Wall Street Journal* reported on the digital divide in K–12 education in Alabama. Students used free Internet access at local fast-food restaurants to do their homework because of a lack of Internet at home for low-income households in rural areas. The article further reported that McDonald's has 12,000 WiFi-equipped locations, whereas Starbucks has 7,000 nationwide (Troianovski 2013). E-literacy has become an important component for student learning. Local businesses can potentially partner with local communities and governments to make these sorts of services more accessible not only to students but also to local residents. In addition, local governments, including school districts, can work with telecommunication service providers, such as cell phone companies and cable companies, to forge partnerships to explore these possibilities. In fact, some local governments in Alabama have already started to work along these lines.

Role of Professional and Nonprofit Organizations

Organizations such as the International City/County Management Association (ICMA), the Alabama County Commissions Association (ACCA), and the Alabama League of Municipalities (ALM) can play a role in disseminating best practices and providing training for e-government use. The best e-government practices from other state and local governments and other research can be learned across local governments. Likewise, IT professional organizations can make conscious efforts to communicate the opportunities to local governments. Free open-source programs are another resource local governments can tap into.

Institutions of higher education can play an important role, as well. Academic programs and courses can be designed in such a way that students with IT skills volunteer to create and manage websites for local governments and communities that are in need of such services. Examples include the service-learning and policy research projects required for master's students in public administration and affairs. In addition, universities can organize training and conferences that bring together academics and practitioners from local governments to provide the best practices in developing e-government.

KEY POINTS

Intergovernmental Programs and Government Intervention

The state government should play a leading role in developing e-government in local governments, sharing experiences with local governments and, in some cases, consolidating some services provided by its local governments to get those services online. The federal and state governments can fund programs, especially for training IT personnel and invest in the information highway infrastructure.

Market Solutions

State governments need to identify potential vendors for e-government contracts. Providing information on experienced and reliable IT consulting firms will be very helpful to local governments, as they tend to lack access to such information.

Collaborative Programs among Local Governments

Small local governments can share server hosting and other services with larger governments to get reduced rates. Other shared services that can be established through contracting among governments include customer service and training.

Public-Private Partnerships

Local businesses can potentially partner with local communities and governments to make services more accessible not only to students but also to local residents. In addition, local governments, including school districts, can work with telecommunication service providers, such as cell phone companies and cable companies, to forge partnerships to explore these possibilities.

Role of Professional and Nonprofit Organizations

Organizations such as the International City/County Management Association (ICMA), the Alabama County Commissions Association (ACCA), and the Alabama League of Municipalities (ALM) can play a role in disseminating best practices and providing training for e-government use. Institutions of higher education can play an important role, as well. Academic programs and courses can be designed in such a way that students with IT skills volunteer to create and manage websites for local governments and communities that are in need of such services.

REFERENCES

Alabama Department of Finance. 2013. Alabama county web sites. http://info.alabama.gov/directory_county.aspx.

Alabama State University. 2011. *Counties in crisis: Assessing quality of life in Alabama.* Montgomery: Center for Leadership and Public Policy, Alabama State University.

Alliance for Public Technology (APT) and Communications Workers of America (CWA). 2008. *State broadband initiatives: A summary of state programs designed to stimulate broadband deployment and adoption.* Washington, DC: APT. www.speedmatters.org/page/-/SPEEDMATTERS/Publications/CWA_APT_StateBroadbandInitiatives.pdf?nocdn=1.

California Department of Technology. 2013. Broadband and Digital Literacy Office. www.cio.ca.gov/broadband/.

Dawes, S.S. 2008. The evolution and continuing challenges of e-governance. *Public Administration Review* 68 (S1, December), S82–S106.

Federal Communications Commission. 2010. *Connecting America: The National Broadband Plan.* http://download.broadband.gov/plan/national-broadband-plan.pdf.

Garson, G.D. 2006. *Public information technology and e-governance: Managing the virtual state.* Sudbury, MA: Jones & Bartlett.

Holzer, M., A. Manoharan, R. Shick, and G. Stowers. 2009. *U.S. States e-governance report (2008): An assessment of state websites.* Newark, NJ: E-Governance Institute, Rutgers University, Campus at Newark.

Jun, K.-N., and C. Weare. 2010. Institutional motivations in the adoption of innovations: The case of e-government. *Journal of Public Administration Research and Theory* 21 (3), 495–519. doi: 10.1093/jopart/muq020.

Millard, J. 2010. Government 1.5—Is the bottle half full or half empty? *European Journal of ePractice* 9 (March), 35–48.

Lyman, B. 2012. Could counties get new powers? Modest home rule proposals up for consideration. *Montgomery Advertiser*, December 9, 1A, 1C.

Moon, M.J. 2002. The evolution of e-government among municipalities: Rhetoric or reality? *Public Administration Review* 62 (4): 424–433.

Moon, M.J., and S. Bretschneider. 2002. Does the perception of red tape constrain IT innovativeness in organizations? Unexpected results from simultaneous equation model and implications. *Journal of Public Administration Research and Theory* 12 (2), 273–291.

National Telecommunications and Information Administration. 2013. State broadband initiative. BroadbandUSA. www2.ntia.doc.gov/SBDD.

NIC Inc. 2012. Alabama.gov wins silver award for 8th Annual Davey Awards. eGov.com, Press release, November 5. www.egov.com/Media/PR/Pages/ViewRelease.aspx?PR_ID=20121105005152.
Norris, D.F., and J. Moon. 2005. Advancing e-government at the grassroots: Tortoise or hare? *Public Administration Review* 65 (1), 64–75.
Norris, D.F., and C. Reddick. 2013. Local e-government in the United States: Transformation or incremental change? *Public Administration Review* 73 (1), 165–177.
Oates, W. 1999. An essay on fiscal federalism. *Journal of Economic Literature* 37 (3), 1120–1149.
Reddick, C. 2012. *Public administration and information technology.* Burlington, MA: Jones & Barlett.
Rogers, W.W., R.D. Ward, L.R. Atkins, and W. Flynt. 2010. *Alabama: The history of a deep south state.* Tuscaloosa: University of Alabama Press.
State of Alabama. 2013. eGovernment initiative. www.alabama.gov/portal/secondary.jsp?id=eGovernmentInitiative.
Troianovski, A. 2013. For the internet-deprived, McDonald's is study hall. *Wall Street Journal*, January 29, A1, A12.
U.S. Department of Commerce. 2011. *Exploring the digital nation: Computer and internet use at home.* Washington, DC: U.S. Department of Commerce, November. www.ntia.doc.gov/files/ntia/publications/exploring_the_digital_nation_computer_and_internet_use_at_home_11092011.pdf.
Xu, H., and H. Asencio. 2012. E-government in local government in the era of Web 2.0: Experience of Alabama municipalities. In *Citizen 2.0: Public and governmental interaction through Web 2.0 technologies*, ed. Kathryn Kloby and Maria J. D'Agostino, 114–128. Hershey, PA: IGI Global.

11

Relevant Issues of Accountability and Transparency in IT Shared Services

Gautam Nayer

Among e-government theorists, accountability and transparency issues are at the forefront of critical relevance concerning delivery of services and citizen participation. Shared information technology (IT) services employed by federal and municipal governments are considered crucial in the continual development of e-government and a pertinent tool for governments to create citizen participation in the process. The objective of this chapter is to examine the impact of e-government on the lifestyles of citizens and shared IT services in Australia, the United Kingdom, and the United States. Additionally, issues of accountability and transparency in the context of shared services and e-government are evaluated. Each country—Australia, the United Kingdom, and the United States—has been analyzed, and their issues, problems, and solutions are discussed in the chapter.

The delivery of services and its effects on e-government are the main structure of this chapter. Shared services in the IT sector are one of many functions of governments that have come under increased scrutiny in the past few years because of the nature of shared services and their impact on average citizens. Shared services can encompass all variations of community services shared between either several departments of a city or municipality or between cities and/or municipalities. Examples include driver's-license renewal, online provision of citizen feedback, garbage collection, emergency medical services, and police services.

If we ask the average taxpayer what he or she expects from the government, the likely answer is to involve public resources utilized in a responsible and transparent manner, in order to provide valuable services. These concepts represent two pillars around which public management disciplines have concentrated their research in the past 20 years. In the following subsections, brief definitions of the notions of accountability and performance in the public sector are discussed, along with their linkages to e-government.

What do average citizens *need* from their government? Citizens usually desire accountable and transparent methods to provide and keep track of the usage and distribution of public services. The reasons for the consideration and eventual implementation of IT as a shared service among governments vary widely. The most common reason for governments to consider implementing shared services could paradoxically be the most aggravating: saving taxpayers money. Other reasons include effective and efficient delivery of services, increasing citizen participation by creating shared services and implementing a feedback policy, improving performance of services already in place, or updating services to provide better quality. Inevitably, this new approach to delivery of services can most arguably be thought of as a customer-driven approach rather than a citizen-oriented one.

As increasing numbers of cities and states are pressured either to raise taxes or to curtail services, the need for shared services among various counties and districts becomes exponentially attractive. Shared services encompass all types of municipal and public services, which also includes information technology. As the systems and needs of governments become more complex and diverse, it will be essential for services to be provided with the highest level of efficiency, effectiveness, and performance. This chapter examines attempts to create, implement, and manage e-government services in Australia, the United Kingdom, and the United States.

The chapter is divided into several sections, each essential to the topic of accountability and transparency in e-government. The first section is a brief introduction to the topic of e-government. The next considers theories such as new public management and reinventing government, accountability, transparency, and the purpose and necessity of shared services. These concepts are addressed and resolved in accordance to their importance in regard to accountability and transparency.

The third section involves the three countries and their struggles, issues, resolutions, problems, and solutions to accountability and transparency issues in e-government. Finally, the conclusion addresses and revisits the issues of accountability and transparency in the three nations with emphasis on IT shared services. Before the conclusion, a section is devoted to future research suggestions and trends.

NEW PUBLIC MANAGEMENT

An alternative approach to governments' management of public services has been proposed since the mid-1980s, when new public management (NPM) first came into vogue (Hood 1989). NPM is a broad and complex term used to describe the wave of public-sector reforms that have occurred throughout the world since the 1980s. The primary hypothesis in the NPM-reform wave is that increased market orientation in the public sector will lead to greater cost-efficiency for governments, without having negative side effects such as a deteriorated quality or level of public services (Pollitt 1993).

New public management has its roots in the 1968 Minnowbrook Conference. Prominent theorists such as Christopher Hood (1989) and Christopher Pollitt (1993) have written that NPM fosters a stronger managerial role of government, a concept that allows governments to provide a higher level of quality and efficiency in public services, a focus on public accountability, and core public-service values (Hood 1995). NPM is oriented toward optimum outcomes through amplified effective management of municipal budgets. Its doctrines tend to be opposed to egalitarian ideals of managing without managers, judicial doctrines of rigidly rule-bound administration, and doctrines of self-government by public-service professionals (Hood 1995).

New public management applies marketlike mechanisms to the public sector and encourages the usage of privatization and outsourcing of municipal functions (Pollitt 1993). These theories promote free-market competition to organizations of the public sector, emphasizing economic and leadership principles. NPM addresses beneficiaries of public services much like customers (another parallel with the private sector) and conversely citizens as shareholders (Pollitt 1993).

NPM has had more than one type of definition, depending on which author's view is examined (Lynn 1996). Pollitt (1993) wrote about the managerialism aspect of NPM, which involves (1) continuous increases in efficiency, (2) the use of "ever-more-sophisticated" technologies, (3) a labor force disciplined to productivity, (4) clear implementation of the professional management role, and (5) managers being given the right to manage.

Throughout the history of the public sector, there have been cycles examining the need and rediscovering a focus on productivity, performance, and control (Walsh 1995). Another definition of NPM focuses on the idea of indirect control rather than direct authority (Walsh 1995). Strategically, the bureaucracy attains its objectives through creating processes of management that involve appropriate incentives and value commitments. The emphasis is on the need for managers to be appropriately motivated and believe in the correct method of achieving the right goals (Walsh 1995). Accordingly, indirect control in NPM has several principles: (1) continual improvements in quality, (2) emphasis on devolution and delegation, (3) appropriate information systems, (4) emphasis on contract and markets, (5) measurement of performance, and (6) increased emphasis on audits and inspection (Walsh 1995).

REINVENTING GOVERNMENT

In the 1980s and early 1990s, the NPM model shifted paradigms and experienced new outgrowth in its theories, known as the reinventing government model, proposed by David Osborne and Ted Gaebler (1992). The model advocated the usage of private-sector innovation techniques, which most notably allowed greater flexibility for managers. Osborne and Gaebler believed that a business customer-oriented model would work more effectively and efficiently for citizens than the traditional government model. Citizens were to be referred to as clients or customers, and their input was to be actively sought.

Osborne and Gaebler (1992) argued that government services often fail to meet the needs of their customers, because funding for services comes not from customers but from elected representatives, such as legislatures and city councils. As governments throughout the world become increasingly complex and diverse, the needs and preferences of customers are no longer homogeneous, yet governments still provide standardized services. Often, a one-size-fits-all approach is not efficient.

Osborne and Gaebler (1992) wrote that governments must make a greater effort to perceive the needs of customers and give them a choice of producers. To learn the needs and preferences of its customers, the government should give them a voice through methods such as surveys, customer contact, and customer interviews. To respond to the needs of citizens as customers, however, it is not sufficient to know about their needs—it is also necessary to offer customers a choice of providers by putting resources in their hands through vouchers and cash grants.

This "customer-driven system" approach has many advantages:

1. Accountability: It makes service providers accountable to their customers: if customers will choose their providers, providers will meet customers' needs.
2. Apolitical: It can minimize political influence from choosing the service providers. When a public agency selects providers, politicians may interfere with the decision. In this case, the providers with the largest constituencies will be selected, regardless of the quality of the service they can provide.
3. Innovation and competition: It stimulates more innovation. Competition will make providers pursue the most efficient way of providing service, so they will invest in innovation.
4. Choice: It allows customers to choose the service they want.
5. Demand, supply, and parity: This approach wastes less, as the quality and quantity of service are determined when supply meets what consumers want rather than when supply meets what legislatures or city councils want.
6. Consumer loyalty and commitment: Consumers commit themselves to the service—for instance, families of students are more committed to education in their respective schools.
7. Equity: It provides the growth of opportunity for greater fairness.

For example, if a government funds institutions rather than individuals, institutions that are targeted at the poor will deteriorate and the poor will be stigmatized. On the other hand, institutions not limited to the poor will promote inequality, as the most intensive users of the service are the affluent. In contrast, through this approach, governments can equalize the funding for each individual and eradicate the stigma of the poor (Osborne and Gaebler 1992).

There are several limitations to this approach. First, it cannot be applied to the regulatory sector, because in this case the primary customers are not individuals but the community as a whole. This approach, therefore, is best applied to service delivery. The other drawback is that it cannot be applied when the market is monopolized and when competition for a service would result in inefficiency—as is the case with garbage collection routes, for example.

Osborne and Gaebler (1992) note that in addition to putting resources in their customers' hands, governments must also restructure their existing bureaucracies. Since the traditional public systems are designed for administrators and service providers, it is somewhat unrealistic to expect public managers to serve customers. The bureaucracy, instead, should be transformed from the old system to a new system that is both user-friendly and transparent. Customers should not be faced with a confusing maze of fragmented programs, conflicting eligibility requirements, and multiple forms to fill out and wait to be processed. Instead, customers should be able to choose options without having to sort through the complex web of bureaucracy.

The reinventing government model promotes the usage of private-sector innovation, resources, and organizational ideas to improve the public sector. This model was advocated by Vice President Al Gore in the 1990s and adopted by the Clinton administration and has had broad appeal in the United States and other countries, especially in Europe. Critics of the model argue that it emphasizes people as customers rather than as citizens, as well as that customers are placed as an end-product user of government rather than part of the policymaking process. This model focuses on the citizen as a unit of the economy rather than democracy.

Some public administration theorists define new public management as a combination of disaggregation (splitting large bureaucracies into smaller, more fragmented ones), competition (between different public agencies and between public agencies and private firms), and incentivization (Dunleavy, Margetts, Bastow, and Tinkler 2006). Defined in this way, NPM was the dominant intellectual force in public management outside the United States from the early 1980s to the early 2000s.

ACCOUNTABILITY

Accountability is directly related to the average citizen's perceptions of trust with his or her government (Pollitt 2003). Average citizens consider themselves a majority shareholder in a democratically elected government, and by right they demand effective services that benefit them. Governments must be aware of the services provided and maintain accountability if citizens question the reasons or methods by which such services are provided and later improved upon.

Accountability relates most directly to the NPM reform movement. As previously mentioned, new public management and the reinventing government movements have tended to focus on accountability as a key variable toward increasing citizen trust in government by making services directly accountable to the citizen. Increasing citizen trust in government is hypothesized to increase citizen participation in a democracy and to alleviate potential mistrust. Accountability is related not just to the idea of trust with citizens but also to a higher degree of responsibility to which the government must obligate itself.

TRANSPARENCY

Transparency in e-government is defined as the usage of IT to allow for public-sector decisions and actions to become more open to public scrutiny (Kirkham and Chapman 2010). Furthermore, transparency could be also thought of as simply providing basic information about government up to enabling public control over civil servants. There are two readily identifiable types of benefits with regard to transparency in e-government: process benefits and governance benefits. Fox (2007) defines process benefits as those that reduce costs for transparency efforts, such as access to better and more effective data for citizens and policymakers. Governance benefits refer to greater transparency—leading to increased public scrutiny—and allow corruption by public servants to become obvious, thus leading to citizen empowerment (Fox 2007).

Transparency in IT is particularly helpful for citizens in poor and developing nations. Transparency can assist in saving money, improving the equality of treatment among all citizens, and creating better citizen participation and feedback for future policy decisions (Hale 2008).

WHAT ARE SHARED SERVICES?

During the early 1980s, shared services were an organizational and management tool first used by the private sector and later adopted by the public sector a decade later. In the business sector, shared services work as distinct units within individual organizations that then unite to provide services to a group of organizations (Spoeher, Burger, and Barrett 2007). By the mid-1990s, shared services began to be used in the public sector as well.

Public-sector shared services can be thought of as an extension of the reinventing government movement, given the shared-service emphasis in a community-oriented government, less wastefulness, and an entrepreneurial approach to public management. Shared services in the public sector occur when two or more county or municipal governments join together to provide a service for all the residents within their jurisdiction (Vazquez-Cortes 2008). Within the context of the public sector, there are usually two types of services. Corporate services, also known as back-office services, are generally administrative and transactional (Spoeher, Burger, and Barrett 2007). Administrative services provide services to the community in the forms of human resources, information and communications technology (ICT) (which includes e-government and IT services), finance and legal services, and estate management. Finally, transactional type services include payroll, council tax administration, housing benefits administration, and planning and environmental inquiries, among others (Spoeher, Burger, and Barrett 2007).

The need for shared services in various countries and across dissimilar forms of government differs widely. Shared services were originally created to provide better and more efficient services, but in recent years there has been a movement toward cost-saving measures as an expedient rationale to implement shared services in communities (Vazquez-Cortes 2008).

PURPOSE OF SHARED SERVICES

While controlling or reducing spiraling costs may be the primary motivation for most governments to engage in shared-service delivery, it cannot and must not be the only reason. Depending on the circumstances of each government, there can be compelling circumstances for sharing services (Sinclair 2005), including increased efficiencies from economies of scale (the combined service provision may be less costly than separate activities), a higher level of service (or more services) for the same resources, or greater expertise and professionalism for service delivery.

Australia

In Australia, a number of cities and states such as Queensland, New South Wales, and Western Australia have implemented shared services in their jurisdictions (Spoeher, Burger, and Barrett 2007). Shared services in these jurisdictions are both administrative and transactional. Payroll, leave entitlements, and IT services are examples of services that were jointly shared between departments or were outsourced (Spoeher, Burger, and Barrett 2007).

In 2008, Sir Peter Gershon produced a report detailing Australia's use of ICT among the varied government departments (Gershon 2008). Gershon focused on the efficiency and effectiveness of the Australian government usage of ICT with a specific focus on whether the government was maximizing its investments in ICT. Using the benefits and value realized from ICT and the measurement of benefits, the report offered future recommendations for improvements. It also focused on improvements suggested for measuring and improving efficiency of the current ICT operations (2008).

An evidence-based approach to the methodology was initiated (Gershon 2008). Solicitations and submissions were invited from ICT-involved agencies, industry leaders, and key stakeholders within the Australian government. Meetings and video conferencing were used to gather additional data. The Australian Bureau of Statistics 2002–03 Government Technology Survey was also analyzed to compare and identify findings.

In 2009, the Australian Government's Department of Finance and Deregulation distributed excellence in e-governance awards to several Australian municipal departments that had created or offered e-governance tools and programs (Australian Government, Department of Finance and Deregulation 2010). Among the winners was the Child Support Agency (CSA) in the Department of Human Services. The CSA had developed an online program known as the Child Support Estimator v2 initiative that allowed for separated and separating couples to estimate the amount of child support they would pay or receive under the law. Initially, the program had been rolled out in July 2008, but citizen and staff feedback showed that the program needed improvement, as it was hard to use, provided insufficient contextual help, and did not assist parents in planning for their finances based on potential changes in incomes (Australian Government, Department of Finance and Deregulation 2010).

Solutions and Recommendations in Australia

Results from these shared-service experiences have been mixed. In 2007, researchers concluded that although shared services do have benefits and merits, the experiences in Australia show that the services are simply not in the best interest of the public and need improvement (Spoeher, Burger, and Barrett 2007). Furthermore, the researchers concluded that the shared-service initiatives conversely deteriorated the quality and quantity of public services. Other problems with shared-service initiatives, including union resistance and the actual cost-benefit savings analysis, showed that the savings were not as much as had been projected (Spoeher, Burger, and Barrett 2007).

In some of the cities examined, shared services were being cited in name only, utilized as a basis to slash jobs. This encouraged a downward slide in employee morale, which meant less satisfied workers and ultimately a lower quality of service delivered. It was recommended that municipalities be cautious in their approach to implementing shared services and that once implemented, follow-up studies be conducted routinely (Spoeher, Burger, and Barrett 2007).

Several months after its initial launch, the Child Support Agency relaunched the online tool of the Child Support Estimator. This time their efforts were met with a higher degree of success. The improved version of the estimator received a 30 percent increase in Web traffic on the CSA website (Australian Government, Department of Finance and Deregulation 2010). Citizens also complimented the CSA on their improved website. The Estimator v2 became easier and faster to use than the original version, providing greater transparency about how child support is calculated through the simple step-by-step process and assistance. The Estimator v2 met all the needs of separated parents to understand their child-support obligations and the process of calculating child-support payments under the new website. Feedback from citizens, stakeholders, and staff assisted in the successful deployment of the redeveloped website.

The improved Estimator v2 has an eight-step process for calculating child support, improving the accountability and transparency of calculations, reducing confusion, and meeting a commitment to stakeholders to modify the estimation process (Australian Government, Department of Finance and Deregulation 2010). The CSA believes that the estimator's speed and ease of use of the service has assisted citizens' maneuverability through the child-support calculation process while using the estimator as a common reference point. This allowed citizens to understand and manage their options. The CSA was successful in reaching other goals: to reinvigorate the citizen and community information process, specifically with regard to allowing them to be well informed, motivated, and engaged (Australian Government, Department of Finance and Deregulation 2010). In this regard, the CSA conducted follow-up surveys that showed a high satisfaction level with the improved service level of the v2.

United Kingdom

In the United Kingdom, IT shared services have been used for almost 20 years, with mixed successes. In a survey conducted by the law firm Browne Jacobson consisting of 178 public-sector managers, adult social care and children's services were the most positive benefits of shared services (Community Care 2008). Two-thirds of the managers felt that shared services allowed for better response time and flexibility, as well as effective delivery of shared services. Back-office functions, such as IT services, were among the most common type of shared services (Community Care 2008). Among social-care managers, however, only 11 percent felt that shared services could be used to curtail costs in their organization's budget (2008). The majority of the managers believed that shared services allowed for improved relationships with their clients and brought about a more personalized approach to government. In addition, accountability and transparency were likely to increase as a result of the shared-service approach.

IT service websites are considered intermediaries for service provision for citizens, and in terms of their designs they have found strong success among researchers. The content and style of government websites and management have also been shown to be successful among citizens (Griffin and Halpin 2005). Page (2004) stressed the importance for governments to determine what the public desires and to focus on quantifiable results. Other researchers have argued that there are numerous accountability challenges that result from newly created interagency collaboration brought about through IT services (Page 2004; Ryan and Walsh 2004).

Solutions and Recommendations in the United Kingdom

Problems in the United Kingdom's experiment with shared services relate to unions having a fear of a loss of jobs or demotions. Some of these fears are well founded, as reports have found that most shared-service endeavors involve simply firing personnel to cut costs (Spoeher, Burger, and Barrett 2007). However, although shared services may not work in every instance or department, they have worked in some departments: IT shared services not only are cost effective but also become an improvement on the service being provided, such as 911 emergency shared-service phone calls (Bolton 2008).

E-government public evaluation and scrutiny meetings have attracted very little citizen participation. Without adequate feedback, council members reported feeling disappointed with the lack of citizen participation (Griffin and Halpin 2005). However, one council member suggested that efforts be made to provide the public with comparative information for evaluation purposes. Without providing the public with adequate benchmarks, it would be difficult to compare the success and progress of different departments. Without this feedback, it would be impossible to judge how accountable and transparent IT services can be.

The United Kingdom has moved through digitization changes, defined as electronic channels of communication and information systems that become the central feature of administrative and business processes (Lips, Taylor, and Organ 2009). Examples of such digitization changes are new forms of automated processes in which no human intervention is needed in an administrative operation, such as electronic monitoring of customers (e.g., patients in a medical facility such as a hospital or clinic). Another example is increasing transparency and enabling of citizens to track and monitor the processing of their service applications (Lips, Taylor, and Organ 2009).

United States

In the United States, IT shared services have undergone a fresh resurgence. In the field of law enforcement, IT services among police departments are being shared jointly, for example, in the towns of Wrentham, Norfolk, Plainville, Franklin, and North Attleborough in Massachusetts. These departments have banded together to create a wireless data-sharing network (Bolton 2008). Their efforts are to improve police services in the communities. This type of shared-service technology idea came about because criminals often move through various jurisdictions and municipalities, allowing them to bypass a warrant for their arrest or record of prior transgressions given a lack of a common link between departments. In Massachusetts, state and local law enforcement departments have already begun work on an information exchange network among police departments, known as the Statewide Information Sharing System, or SWISS (Bolton 2008).

Several other police departments have begun to recognize the need and usefulness of technology and have even created specific technology specialists. These technology specialists have become creative in their approach to using technology that is both germane and innovative. At the police department in Franklin, Massachusetts, for example, the usage of podcasts and YouTube broadcasts has been successful in communicating effectively with police officers regarding announcements or public-service messages (Bolton 2008). Committees in other cities and towns have been created to explore other possibilities to share services using IT management (Bolton 2008).

In New York, IT shared services have been implemented since 2005 when the Shared Municipal Services Initiative (SMSI) was created, which allocates money through state grants to create and manage projects for communities. In New York, there are two types of shared-service agreements between local governments, joint agreements and service agreements (Vazquez-Cortes 2008). In joint agreements, local governments pool their resources and share in the provision of services. Service agreements are those in which one local municipality contracts to provide a service for another (2008). Both types of agreements can be advantageous to local governments, because they can trim costs and continue the uninterrupted flow of services to their constituents.

In the field of IT shared services, the New York Department of State has made a substantial effort to involve all municipalities in exploring possibilities for collaboration by creating a website that lists information regarding the grant processes as well as a database with shared-service publications (Vazquez-Cortes 2008). There are also examples of intermunicipal agreements, case studies of shared projects, and a listing of all the grant awards. Information online includes links to other useful websites as well as the committed and dedicated involvement of major research universities and colleges, such as the Government Law Center of Albany Law School (2008). All these efforts culminated in the creation of additional resources, allowing for greater communication among municipalities interested in creating effective shared services.

In the state of New York, employing IT in shared services has proved useful in saving money while maintaining effectiveness. Estimated savings from all shared-service projects is hypothesized to be more than $245 million for the years 2007 to 2012 (Vazquez-Cortes 2008).

Shared services have been aggressively pushed throughout the state of Michigan. The Southeast Michigan Council of Governments (SEMCOG) is a strong supporter of consolidated and joint services and has created a computer database with examples of success stories throughout the state (Davis 2005). SEMCOG recognizes the concerns and nervousness among public officials when entering into agreements, and it has published pamphlets to aid local officials' transitions. SEMCOG has also brought to light programs and administrators with awards since 1998 and has uploaded a series of reports in conjunction with the Metropolitan Affairs Council to assist communities with the creation of intergovernmental services online (Davis 2005).

In Minnesota, there have been efforts made to craft effective IT shared services throughout the state. There have also been examples to establish and manage IT shared services. Starting in 2001, the city of Anoka entered into a license agreement with Anoka County for direct access to the county's TAXSYS computer system to provide better information for residents (City of Anoka 2001). The Anoka Police Department, with the assistance of the state Joint Law Enforcement Council, has established a countywide computer system for law enforcement departments for more effective policing. In addition, like other counties, the Anoka Police Department uses a countywide shared 911 emergency system for central communications, thus reducing costs overall for each individual municipality (City of Anoka 2001).

In 2006, in an effort to become more accountable and transparent, the state of Texas began to post detailed records of the expenses of the government's office online (Kirkham and Chapman 2010). The Texas Controller's Office had been under extensive pressure from the public to create more transparency; thus, a separate website was developed and over the following several years was continuously redeveloped as new updates and improvements became possible. The website approached the issue of transparency from a multilevel perspective and aimed for accountability at every level of state government.

Solutions and Recommendations in the United States

A continuing problem for government officials while striving to consolidate and regionalize services is appeasing the police and fire unions. These two unions fought hard against the sharing of services because of fear that their members would lose their jobs with the introduction of shared services (Bolton 2008; Davis 2005). Retired or injured fire and police officers manned the emergency 911 services as an alternative job once their career circumstances had changed (Bolton 2008). Even though the communities had no plans to cut jobs from either the police or firefighters, their unions wanted some type of monetary assurance or settlement fee if the plans were implemented (Bolton 2008).

Expertise and effective management is another problem when examining the creation of IT shared services in communities. Unions could be considered another barrier to solving the shared-service dilemma. The most serious difficulty lies in the form of adequate amounts of funding. As the economic recession occurred, state and county budgets tightened across the United States. Services became curtailed, cut back, or eliminated entirely in many jurisdictions. State and local governments entered into heated debates for the raising of property taxes, but so far they have been unsuccessful in their efforts. However, as the current economic woes draw out, taxpayers may be forced to either pay more for services by a rise in their taxes or will be coerced to accept changes or cuts in their services, perhaps affecting the quality of service.

Effective communication among interested municipalities also allows for the monitoring of contracts awarded to various localities (Sinclair 2005). Fortunately, educational institutions such as Albany Law School have been instrumental in providing research opportunities when awarding grants. Also, these institutions work with municipalities in creating effective case studies of shared-service agreements and consolidated mergers. These case studies not only are efficient in categorizing why such agreements occur but also analyze and examine why certain services succeed while others fail (Vazquez-Cortes 2008). A partnership network among colleges and universities has been established. Issue-specific research developed with the aid of universities provides technical assistance for the creation of program metrics to effectively analyze and assess cooperative and shared-service efforts (Vazquez-Cortes 2008). Regional training conferences are held on college and university campuses and involve local and municipal government officials to bring together ideas, share notes, and improve shared services (Benjamin and John 2008).

In Texas, since 2006, the state Comptroller's Office redesigned and improved the accessibility and usability of its website (Kirkham and Chapman 2010). Increased levels and details of transparency have prodded government officials to realize that citizens monitor officials' spending habits. At election time, citizens can make their vote heard. Government officials are therefore encouraged to increase their efficiency and eliminate waste. The perception of government transparency can only positively affect the level of citizen trust and satisfaction.

FUTURE RESEARCH DIRECTIONS

Local officials should not try to implement shared services without first considering the input of members of the local community (Benjamin and John 2008). There are a plethora of justifiable reasons community members would not be interested in establishing shared services in their city or town. Ideally, city officials would not be able to provide satisfactory services or improve existing services without taking into account community perspectives.

Research through surveys and reports listed several key concerns when shared-service programs are being considered. Among them are the following:

1. A concern over loss of control over services and a reduced level of responsiveness by service providers
2. Fear over the potential loss of municipal identity if services are provided by workers wearing the uniforms or driving the vehicles of a different municipal entity, such as county workers driving a county truck and taking care of town streets
3. Fear that efficiency will lead to uniformity of service levels, with service levels dropping to a common level instead of rising
4. Fear that larger communities will be favored over smaller ones

5. Concern over the loss of jobs and the loss of a personal level of service that might be provided by a fellow resident of the community
6. Suspicions that costs will increase later as employee bargaining units utilize salary and work rule differences to increase wages and benefits to the level offered by the highest paying community (Benjamin and John 2008)

CONCLUSION

The purpose of this chapter is to "break" the window and allow for more accountability and transparency in the definitions, theories, solutions, issues, and problems of e-government among three nations. Australia, the United Kingdom, and the United States have all contributed heavily to the advancement of e-government, but much improvement remains. The development of myriad systems of information and communication technology (ICT) between municipal governments and their subdepartments has been a seismic shift since the late 1990s. Moreover, most e-governance operations focus on usability and are not necessarily correlated with accountability and transparency. Additionally, most types of e-government services are concerned with efficiency and effectiveness, again not the best measurement of accountability and transparency.

Some cities and towns examined had created municipal and local government feedback channels such as roundtable discussions and open forums for citizens to comment, praise, or criticize IT services. However, these approaches could be considered rudimentary to effectively creating feedback, as effective feedback was not always possible. In some cases, citizens either did not have knowledge of the process or simply did not turn up, leading to no feedback. In others, citizens possibly may have known but didn't seem to care. One interpretation could be that if there were no complaints, citizens could be considered satisfied with the level of service.

However, simply because feedback doesn't materialize doesn't necessarily allow government officials and researchers to believe that service levels are satisfactory or even close to being acceptable. One of the key ingredients in e-governance is the ability for citizens to collectively like, dislike, or influence the service level process. The other ingredient to a successful redevelopment and continuous improvement in e-governance service levels is the ability of government and municipal officials, policymakers, and researchers to hear the whispers, rants, praises, and criticisms of the public.

Feedback channels cannot operate in a vacuum. Government officials and policymakers, as well as researchers of e-governance, should be more involved with the process and structure of accountability and transparency in service deployment. Government officials have the ability to create more channels of conversation, allowing for better and more effective feedback from the public. However, it is essential to involve researchers and other policymakers and stakeholders in the process. With the availability of information online currently, all participants in the e-governance improvement process should be able to create better feedback channels. It should start with effective communication and build on this process.

When governments consider implementing shared services in their communities and neighborhoods, officials would be wise to evaluate all types of services prior to voting to change or modify services provided. As research has demonstrated, the most vital reason for implementing shared-service programs should not be about cost savings, but the reasons should be more intrinsically related to improvements in service delivery and quality (Spoeher, Burger, and Barrett 2007).

While important, cost savings should not be the primary motivation when entering into IT shared-service agreements. The principal reason should be an interest in providing the most efficient and effective service to the citizen. Secondary reasons are those of accountability and transparency with a clear focus on service delivery and expectancy. It is worth cautioning government officials that implementing shared services can be a costly and time-consuming effort and should not be entered into with haste.

A performance measurement approach should be applied following the implementation of IT shared services. One method of accomplishing this would be collaborations with colleges and universities for the development of a common benchmark and comparison system while analyzing the services in various communities. If appropriate, unions and other workers who are fearful of a loss of jobs should be reassured that they would not lose their job; efforts should also be undertaken to compensate workers adequately or provide alternative employment for any jobs being severed. It is paramount to ensure that these efforts will improve the citizens' welfare and interest while preventing employees from creating mischief with the implementation of shared services. Ideally, transparency should be linked to government accountability and integrity to citizens. Therefore, governments should strive to be as transparent as possible and provide effective measures to constantly improve their accountability.

KEY POINTS

There are several methods through which IT shared services can be successfully implemented:

- Designate a person or office to serve as a clearinghouse of local information and facilitator of new agreements.
- Generate public participation and involvement in developing and carrying out an agenda for shared services.
- Work with local government employees who will be directly affected by service-sharing agreements.
- Commit to specific action items as soon as possible.
- The shared service provided must be equal or better than the existing service.
- Financial benefits must be demonstrable and meaningful.
- The arrangement must be seen as mutually beneficial and not a "bailout" for one jurisdiction.
- The parties to the agreement must have an opportunity to back out of the agreement with appropriate notice.
- The discussions leading up to the agreement should involve employee representation.

REFERENCES

Australian Government, Department of Finance and Deregulation. 2010. *Excellence in e-government award: 2009 finalist case studies.* Parkes, ACT: Department of Finance, Australian Government. www.finance.gov.au/files/2012/04/2009Excellenceine-GovernmentpublicationFinal.pdf.

Benjamin, G., and R. John. 2008. Shared services. New York State Commission on Local Government Efficiency and Competitiveness. www.nyslocalgov.org/pdf/Shared_Service_brief.pdf.

Bolton, M.M. 2008. Shared services getting a fresh look. *Boston Globe*, October 30. www.boston.com/news/local/articles/2008/10/30/shared_services_getting_a_fresh_look/.

City of Anoka (MN). 2001. Chapter 5: Partnership-shared services. In *City of Anoka community plan.* www.ci.anoka.mn.us (accessed May 14, 2013).

Community Care. 2008. Shared services back but few bosses see cost benefits. *Community Care.* Reed Elsevier, Inc. 1722.

Davis, T. 2005. Shared services and the economies of scale they provide local governments. In *Urban and regional planning economic development handbook.* University of Michigan, Taubman College of Architecture and Urban Planning. www.umich.edu/~econdev/jointservice/.

Dunleavy, P., Margetts, H., Bastow, S. and Tinkler, J. 2006. New public management is dead: Long live digital era governance. *Journal of Public Administration Research and Theory* 16 (3), 467–494.

Fox, J. 2007. The uncertain relationship between transparency and accountability. *Development in Practice* 17 (4–5), 663–671.

Gershon, Peter. 2008. Review of the Australian Government's Use of Information and Communication Technology. www.finance.gov.au/files/2012/04/Review-of-the-Australian-Governments-Use-of-Information-and-Communication-Technology.pdf.

Griffin, D., and E. Halpin. 2005. An exploratory evaluation of UK local e-government from an accountability perspective. *Electronic Journal of e-Government* 3 (1), 13–28.

Hale, N.T. 2008. Transparency, accountability and global governance. *Global Governance* 14, 73–94.

Hood, C. 1989. Public administration and public policy: Intellectual challenges for the 1990s. *Australian Journal of Public Administration* 48, 346–358.

———. 1995. Contemporary public management: A new global paradigm? *Public Policy and Administration* 10 (2), 104–117. Reprinted in *The modern policy process: A reader*, ed. Michael Hill, 404–417. London: Prentice Hall.

Kirkham, L., and G. Chapman. 2010. Government transparency: Trends in Texas. *Texas Business Review* (April). http://ic2.utexas.edu/pubs/government-transparency-trends-in-texas/.

Lips, A.M., A.J. Taylor, and J. Organ. 2009. Managing citizen identity information in e-government service relationships in the UK. *Public Management Review* 11 (16), 833–856.

Lynn, L., Jr. 1996. The new public management as an international phenomenon: A skeptical view. Paper presented at the Conference on the New Public Management in International Perspective, St. Gallen, Switzerland, July.

Osborne, D., and T. Gaebler. 1992. *Reinventing government: How the entrepreneurial spirit is transforming the public sector.* Reading, MA: Addison-Wesley.

Page, S. 2004. Measuring accountability for results in interagency collaboratives. *Public Administration Review* 64 (5), 591–606.

Pollitt, C. 1993. *Managerialism and the public service: The Anglo-American experience.* Oxford, UK: Blackwell.

———. 2003. *The essential public manager.* Berkshire, UK: Open University Press.

Ryan, C., and P. Walsh. 2004. Collaboration of public sector agencies: reporting and accountability challenges. *International Journal of Public Sector Management* 17 (7), 621–631.

Sinclair, T. 2005. *Broome County shared services summit: Final report.* Binghamton, NY. www.gobroomecounty.com/files/planning/_pdf/BCSharedServicesFinalReport.pdf.

Spoeher, J., A. Burger, and S. Barrett. 2007. *The shared services experience, report 2: Lessons from Australia.* Adelaide: Australian Institute for Social Research, University of Adelaide. www.european-services-strategy.org.uk/outsourcing-library/shared-services/shared-services-in-australia/psa-shared-services-australia.pdf.

Vazquez-Cortes, A.L. 2008. *Local government shared services: Progress report, 2005–2007.* Albany: New York State, Department of State.

Walsh, K. 1995. *Public services and market mechanisms: Competition, contracting and the new public management.* London: Macmillan.

About the Editor and Contributors

Hugo Asencio is an assistant professor in the Department of Public Administration and Public Policy at California State University, Dominguez Hills. He holds a PhD in public administration and public policy from Auburn University. Dr. Asencio serves on the Board of Directors of Lunches for Learning and is serving a three-year term (2014–17) on the Chapter Council of the American Society for Public Administration Southern California Chapter. His research focuses on public-sector ethics, management, human resource management, nonprofit management, social media use, and e-government. His publications include *Cases on Strategic Social Media Utilization in the Nonprofit Sector* (coedited with Rui Sun), articles on scholarly journals, and chapters of multi-authored books. He teaches graduate courses on public-sector management, ethics, human resource management, and nonprofit management.

Robert J. Dickey is currently an assistant professor in the Department of Public Administration at Keimyung University in Daegu, South Korea. He holds an MPA from California State University, Long Beach, and a JD from Thomas Jefferson School of Law. His principal areas of research include local leadership and civil society, particularly public reform that incorporates the participation of nongovernmental organizations and the private sector. He has worked in Korea since 1994, where he is highly involved in various teacher and researcher organizations, and has worked on projects in Vietnam. He also teaches and conducts research in the field of English-language learning, particularly as it relates to learning language while also learning in the social sciences.

Matthias Finger holds a PhD in political science and a PhD in adult education from the University of Geneva. He has been an assistant professor at Syracuse University (New York), an associate professor at Columbia University (New York), and a full professor of management of public enterprises at the Swiss Federal Institute of Public Administration. Since 2002, he has held the Swiss Post Chair in Management of Network Industries at the École Polytechnique Fédérale in Lausanne, Switzerland. Since 2010 he has also been a part-time professor at the European University Institute in Florence, Italy, where he directs the Florence School of Regulation's Transport Area. Professor Finger is known internationally for his expertise in the liberalization, re-regulation, and governance of infrastructures in the transport (railways, air transport), energy (electricity), and communications (postal services and telecommunications) sectors. He is the co–editor in chief of the journal *Competition and Regulation in Network Industries.*

Marc K. Fudge is an assistant professor in the Department of Public Administration at California State University, San Bernardino, where he teaches public budgeting and finance, public financial management, and program evaluation. His work appears in *Public Administration Review, American Review of Public Administration, Journal of International Business and Economics,* and *International Journal of e-Governance and Networks.* Professor Fudge is Associate Director of the E-Governance Institute and the managing editor of the *Journal of Public Management and Social Policy.*

Thomas J. Greitens is an associate professor of public administration and director of the Master of Public Administration program at Central Michigan University. His research focuses on the challenges of implementing public management ideals in government, from performance-driven metrics to privatization mandates, e-government transformations, and effective citizen engagement. His work has appeared in *Public Administration Review*, *Administration & Society*, and *Public Performance and Management Review*, and in several books on e-government and citizen participation.

M. Ernita Joaquin is an assistant professor of public administration and policy at San Francisco State University. Her papers on bureaucratic politics, performance assessment, local government privatization, and citizen engagement have been published in *Public Administration Review, Administration & Society, American Review of Public Administration, Public Performance and Management Review,* and *International Review of Administrative Sciences.* She is currently studying adaptive behaviors in state budgeting and nonprofit management.

Jonathan B. Justice is an associate professor in the School of Public Policy and Administration at the University of Delaware. His areas of specialization include public budgeting and finance, accountability and decision making, and local economic development. He has published articles examining the meaning and methods of fiscal transparency and the ethics of government debt; has collaborated with Chris Skelcher and Catherine Durose on a seminar series "Beyond the State: Third Party Government in Comparative Perspective"; and has coedited, with Helisse Levine and Eric Scorsone, *Handbook of Local Government Fiscal Health.* He has also worked for the City of New York as a capital program administrator, and for nonprofit organizations in the New York metropolitan area as an economic development program manager.

Younhee Kim is an associate professor of public administration in the Department of Political Science at East Carolina University. Her research focuses on public and performance management; public entrepreneurship; and information technology management, including electronic government. She has published widely in the fields of public administration and public management.

Mordecai Lee is a professor of governmental affairs at the University of Wisconsin–Milwaukee, where he teaches public administration and nonprofit management. His research interests focus on public relations in government and the nonprofit sector. He is author of *Promoting the War Effort: Robert Horton and Federal Propaganda, 1938–1946* (2012) and *Congress vs. the Bureaucracy: Muzzling Agency Public Relations* (2011). He edited *Government Public Relations: A Reader* (2008) and coedited *The Practice of Government Public Relations* (2012). He received a PhD in public administration from Syracuse University. Before joining the academy, Lee was a guest scholar at the Brookings Institution, legislative assistant to a congressman, elected to three terms in the Wisconsin legislature's state assembly and two terms in the state senate, and executive director of a faith-based nonprofit involved in social justice advocacy.

Yuguo Liao is an assistant professor at the University of Missouri, St. Louis. He received his PhD from the School of Public Affairs and Administration at Rutgers University. His main research interests are citizen participation in local budgeting, organizational theory and behavior, research methods, and government performance improvement.

Aroon Manoharan is an assistant professor of public administration in the Department of Political Science at Kent State University. His research focuses on e-governance, performance measurement and reporting, strategic planning, and organization theory. His work has been published in *American Review of Public Administration*, *State and Local Government Review*, *Public Administration Quarterly*, *International Journal of Public Administration*, *International Journal of Organization Theory and Behavior*, and *International Public Management Review*. He holds a PhD from the School of Public Affairs and Administration, Rutgers University–Newark and an MPA from Kansas State University.

Cecilia G. Manrique is professor and chair of the Political Science/Public Administration Department at the University of Wisconsin–La Crosse. She received her doctorate in political science from the University of Notre Dame. She has published in the fields of immigration (*The Multicultural or Immigrant Faculty in American Society*) and incorporation of technology in the political science classroom (*The Houghton Mifflin Guide to the Internet for Political Science*). She has been a member of the American Political Science Association (APSA) since 1988, was president of APSA's Computers and Multimedia Section (now Information Technology and Politics), and has been treasurer since 1995. She is also treasurer of the Wisconsin Political Science Association. In 2012 she completed a second three-year term as president of the International Leadership Council of the Golden Key International Honour Society.

Gabriel G. Manrique is chairman and professor of the Department of Economics at Winona State University. He teaches in the areas of macroeconomics and international economics. He is also the globalization specialist for Fastenal Company, a multinational industrial corporation. His areas of interest include the comparative analysis of economies, government procedures particularly as they relate to businesses, and the economic and political environments for foreign investments.

John G. McNutt is professor of public policy and administration at the University of Delaware. He is a specialist in the application of high technology to political and social engagement. His work focuses on the role of technology in lobbying, e-government and e-democracy, political campaigning and deliberation, and organizing and other forms of political participation. He has conducted research on professional associations, child advocacy groups, consumer and environmental protection groups, social action organizations, and legislative bodies. His most recent work looks at Web 2.0 political change technology and e-government and fiscal transparency. Dr. McNutt has coedited or coauthored four books and many journal articles, book chapters, and other publications. He regularly presents at national and international conferences. He sits on several editorial boards and was a grant reviewer (1999–2003) for the U.S. Department of Commerce's Technology Opportunities Program.

Seunghwan Myeong is professor in the Department of Public Administration at Inha University in Korea. His research focuses on electronic government and governance, government organization innovation, social networks, information technology management, IT project strategy, and the digital divide. He has served as consultant and published widely in the fields of e-government and public administration.

Gautam Nayer is an assistant professor in the Administration of Justice Department at the Barbara Jordan–Mickey Leland School of Public Affairs at Texas Southern University. He has been published in *Journal of Public Management and Social Policy*, *International Journal of Arts and Commerce*, and *European Journal of Social Sciences*. His research interests include prisoner reentry programs, DWI courts, and e-governance issues in municipal and local governments.

SeJeong Park (DPA, public management, University of Georgia) is a full professor of public administration and dean of the Graduate School of Public Policy at Keimyung University in Daegu, Korea. Past president of the Korean Association of Governmental Studies, he has a strong interest in local leadership, having served on the (Daegu) mayor's special committee for city administrative reform. He has also done extensive consulting work in dealing with local governments, government corporations, and business organizations. Dr. Park is the author of *Intelligent Organization* and *Public Administration in the Age of Globalization.*

Edward S. Smith Jr. earned his Ph.D. in urban affairs and public policy from the School of Public Policy and Administration at the University of Delaware in 2014. His dissertation focused on the state-level determinants of the federal EB-5 Immigrant Investor Program.

Hua Xu is an assistant professor in the Department of Political Science and Public Administration, Auburn University at Montgomery. His research focuses on public finance and budgeting, e-government and public-sector technology, public performance management, quantitative research methods, and comparative public administration. His work has been published in *Public Administration Review*, *Journal of Public Budgeting, Accounting, and Financial Management*, *Journal of Public Affairs Education*, *Public Administration Quarterly*, and *State Tax Notes*, as well as in several books.

Yueping Zheng received his MPA from the School of Public Affairs at Arizona State University. Currently, he is a PhD candidate at the School of Public Affairs and Administration, Rutgers University–Newark. His research interests are e-government, performance management, and citizen participation. His recent research involves e-government and citizen participation together, trying to explain the factors that affect citizen participation online.

Index

Italic page references indicate tables and figures.

Milton Keynes UK
Ingram Content Group UK Ltd.
UKHW020821141024
449569UK00008B/511

9 780765 646569